MW01061704

THE ECOLOGY OF THE
AUTOMOBILE

THE ECOLOGY OF THE AUTOMOBILE

Peter Freund and George Martin

BLACK ROSE BOOKS

Montréal/New York
London

BLACK ROSE BOOKS No. W201
Hardcover ISBN 1-895431-83-2
Paperback ISBN 1-895431-82-4

Library of Congress No. 93-72748

Canadian Cataloguing in Publication Data

Freund, Peter E.S.
The ecology of the automobile

Includes bibliographical references and index.
ISBN: 1-895431-83-2 (bound) –
ISBN: 1-895431-82-4 (pbk.)

1. Automobiles—Environmental aspects.
2. Automobiles—Social aspects. 3. Automobile industry
and trade. I. Martin, George T. II. Title

HE5613.F73 1993   388.3'42   C93-090490-7

Cover design: Nat Klym

BLACK ROSE BOOKS
C.P. 1258
Succ. Place du Parc
Montréal, Québec
H2W 2R3 Canada

BLACK ROSE BOOKS
340 Nagel Drive
Cheektowaga, New York
14225 USA

Mailing Address

Printed in Canada

A publication of the Institute of Policy Alternatives of Montréal
(IPAM)

TABLE OF CONTENTS

To Doris Gale,
for many gifts through the years

Preface

This book is a sociological and critical analysis of the ecology of the automobile. We believe that it is extremely timely. The social problems engendered by auto-centred transport systems are reaching a critical point. Virtually every day there is something in the mass media about air pollution, traffic congestion, vehicle safety, or energy waste, which head the list of auto-related problems. Because of the influence of the auto-industrial complex on public policy, efforts to reduce auto-dependence and to expand alternatives to the auto are often marginalized. However, two irreversible secular trends—the environmental and energy crises in all their manifestations—are working against continued auto hegemony in transport.

The book grew out of exchanges between two colleagues and friends as we walked and hiked extensively across some of the world's great cities—Amsterdam, Beijing, Berlin, Budapest, Chicago, Hong Kong, London, Los Angeles, New York, Paris, Prague, San Francisco, and Toronto. When we first conceived this project and began to articulate our experiences and to draw together empirical materials, we had little sense of how deeply the ecological and political economic dimensions of transport affected social life.

We bring more than a common sociological and critical focus to our subject. We also share ecological concerns and progressive political goals. But we do offer different perspectives. Our differences with regard to our specializations are complementary. Freund's micro and theoretical concerns are balanced by Martin's more macro and empirical ones. Freund's substantive interests in the body and in health and illness complement Martin's interests in social policy and urban issues. However, our differences with regard to experiences with and opinions of the auto itself are somewhat divergent. Freund does not drive; Martin does. The resultant tension served creative ends because it challenged both of us to question our respective positions.

While the authors are from the United States and much of the material is based on the U.S., substantial attention is given to comparative and global issues. There is a chapter on the dispersion of the auto into the Third World and there is considerable material on other mature industrialized nations, notably Canada, Britain, Germany, and the Netherlands. We have conducted field research in Britain and Germany, including the former East Germany. It has to be noted that because data collection lags behind political change some national units referred to in the book are now obsolete, including the U.S.S.R., Czechoslovakia, East and West Germany.

There are a number of people who deserve acknowledgement for help rendered in the process of writing this book. However, because we did not always heed their worthy advice, we alone bear full responsibility for the final text. Miriam Fisher and Joanna Foley were generous in their editorial assistance, trenchant commentary, and personal support. Jack Hammond provided leads on useful information. Laura Kramer, who chaired our department while we wrote the book, was as usual, very supportive. George Haikalis was a source of inspiration and information. A number of academic institutions provided facilities that were helpful in collecting bibliographic data and in preparing the manuscript: The University of California, Berkeley; The University of Hertfordshire, Hatfield, England; Montclair State, Upper Montclair, New Jersey; and Sonoma State, Rohnert Park, California.

This book is intended for a broad, interdisciplinary, academic, scientific, and popular audience, which includes students, graduate and undergraduate, as well as specialists in the areas of urban studies, public policy, social problems, and technology. Beyond this academic audience, the book is relevant to the applied fields of urban planning, human ecology, architecture, and environmental design. A significant readership is the people around the world who are actively confronting the issues of automobility, ecology, and social justice that we raise in this book. This segment of our audience includes activists of all stripes, whatever labels may be used by them, including environmentalists, ecosocialists, feminists, progressives, and others.

We believe that the problems engendered by auto-centred transport are serious ones and should be resolved by reducing our dependence on autos. Autos will remain one important mode of transport but we must offer desirable alternatives to them, in the context of fully diversified transport systems.

The Parameters of Auto-Centred Transport Systems

The story of the everyday transport of people in the twentieth century is about the automobile. Considering the widespread impact of the auto in contemporary societies it is surprising how little attention its social and political dimensions receive—even from ecologically oriented thinkers. Transport does figure in the analyses done in human ecology, urban political economy, and locational theory, but none of these can reasonably lay claim to a comprehensive understanding of how transport relates to society.[1] Only a few scholars have taken on the task of formulating a sociology of transport: The field "is as much underdeveloped as it is of great potential importance, both for sociology and also for physical and transport planning."[2] Our work here addresses a sociology of transport but our perspective is more general. We are concerned with the broader connections between social organization and the natural and built environments, between social relations and ecological arrangements. Auto-centred transport is a compelling vehicle for such a broad socio-ecological analysis.

A thorough analysis of the connections between automobility and society is timely. The central role that auto production and consumption have played in twentieth century economic growth, through the organization of production known as Fordism, is ending. Major auto markets are saturated and the costs of auto-centred transport are becoming prohibitive. Auto-centred transport is a technological system with major impacts on public policy, land use, cultural patterns, social relations, community, natural resources, environmental quality, and options for the spatial mobility of individuals. Auto-centred transport is one expression of how society subsidizes a system of individualized consumption that is highly energy and resource intensive and is not viable on a global or a long-term scale. This individualized mode of consumption has an affinity with, though it is not determined by, the political economy of advanced capitalism.

In this century the auto, powered by gasoline-fuelled internal combustion engines, has become the dominant means of transport

1

for people in mature industrialized countries. In fact, in many areas of these countries, including parts of the United States, it is the only viable means of mobility. In such areas, not to own a car or not to have a driver's license means that one is effectively transport disenfranchised. An auto-centred transport system is one in which the car is the dominant or only means of conveyance used for everyday activities such as going to work, to shop, and to appointments.

There are three major motorized vehicles in addition to the auto—the bus, truck, and motorcycle. Much transport data lump the three types of conveyance together. Of the three, the auto is the most pervasive; it is for that reason that one can speak of an auto-centred transport system. In sheer numbers, the auto is overwhelmingly dominant among motor vehicles. In the United States in 1991, autos represented 74.4 percent of all motor vehicle registrations and 70.6 percent of all vehicle miles of travel; thus autos and auto travel outnumbered the combined total of trucks, buses, and motorcycles by about two-and-one-half to one. Worldwide, in 1990, 76.3 percent of all registered motor vehicles were passenger cars. Additionally, although trucks and buses contribute a disproportionate share of the air pollutants that emanate from motor vehicles, autos still contribute more. For example, in the United States in 1990, passenger cars contributed 31 percent of carbon monoxide pollution from all sources, while trucks contributed 19 percent and buses only a negligible amount.[3]

Heavy trucks do cause a greatly disproportionate share of highway degradation. The Federal Highway Administration reports that heavy trucks cause more than 95 percent of highway deterioration in the United States. Despite this fact, heavy trucks pay only 29 percent of the nation's highway bill.[4] While the specific problems of heavy truck traffic are not addressed here, it is increasingly apparent that stricter regulations and higher user fees are the order of the day.

Despite the fact that trucks contribute a disproportionate share of the problems of our transport system, the number of autos justify referring to that system as an auto-centred one. Furthermore, many of the issues raised by auto-centred transport also apply to trucks. For example, as is the case with autos, the socioenvironmental costs of truck use are subsidized by the public.

The auto not only prevails in everyday transport, it and its supporting infrastructures dominate the landscapes of contemporary cities. Urbanism and the auto both came of age in the twentieth century and the forms that urban development have taken in this century reflect the functional needs of auto transport. Until the end of the nineteenth century the car was unknown and those who planned cities had no idea of the role it would come to play in the twentieth century. One noted example is Chicago. Harold Mayer and Richard Wade wrote in their comprehensive history of that city: "Perhaps the best symbol of the new dominance of the automobile in the metropolis is the fact that the spot that the Burnham Plan had marked for the civic heart of Chicago is now the site of the most elaborate expressway interchange in the city."[5]

In a motorized society the car is a primary means of personal autonomy. To get one's driving license is to come of age; to have it taken away because of old age or impairment can be interpreted as a loss in social standing. It is in precisely such carless situations that one can view auto transport in another light—from the other side of the windshield, so to speak. Such a perspective can be quite enlightening. The cultural symbolism of the car—as an icon of freedom, power, and individuality—has produced a blind spot in our ability to critically assess auto-centred transport. The blindspot is cultivated by the very experience of driving; it is noted even in advertisements for autos. One 1993 car ad in the U.S. described the driving experience: "Illogical as it may seem, the simple act of motoring down the boulevard, exhaust burbling, that's what Viper ownership is all about. Only behind the wheel does it all make perfect sense."[6] The ideology of individual car ownership is deeply ingrained in industrial culture and shared by the general public as well as by transport planners, by the politics of the left as well as of the right. In Britain, for example, analysis reveals that both Tory and Labour governments have consistently underestimated the negative effects of automobility and have failed to take measures to counteract these effects.[7]

The auto as a particular form of transport technology is not only the basis for a physical world constructed for its uses (woven into the tapestry of everyday life), it is also embedded as a cultural artifact in our personal experiences and our belief systems. It is seen as an inevitable and desirable feature of life. It is this ubiquitousness and routine nature of automobility that is the basis for our neglect of it as a topic for critical analysis. The sources of the neglect of auto-generated problems lie in their diffuseness and ordinariness. A major oil spill poses a great threat to a local ecosystem—a threat that is highly concentrated and visible. Also, while major oil spills are all too common today to be called unusual, they are nevertheless dramatic events. Thus they get great public attention and remedial measures follow quickly. Additionally, oil companies must pay for damages. Autos, on the other hand, for which much of the oil is destined, receive little critical notice even though their polluting threat to environments is also great. A major oil spill involves one event that is considered extraordinary, and it claims the lead in news reports. Automotive emissions (of the same product) involve millions of events that are considered quite ordinary.

Auto-centred transport then—even its deleterious features—become taken-for-granted aspects of our lives. Thus, while dramatic multiple crashes command some brief notice, television and other media trivialize or overlook the habitual and routine harm associated with auto use. Public discourse, including that of experts, treats auto accidents primarily as a matter of individual culpability. To question the pervasiveness of auto use is, at worst, to be labelled a Luddite, an eccentric, or even an enemy of freedom. At best, one is likely to be dismissed as a critic of the necessary, the inevitable, or the trivial.

Certainly the infrastructure of a system based on transport by individual passenger car is a reality and has the characteristics of an unchangeable fact of life. Nonetheless, such a reality is a human product; it *is* a socially constructed reality. This fact is overlooked by those who readily recognize the socially constructed nature of other societal arrangements and who can easily envision alternatives, for example, in the organization of work and of the family. The auto-centred transport system, while problematic in terms of the objective problems that it creates—environmental pollution, traffic congestion, and injuries and fatalities—is a system that is not fundamentally questioned.

It is this taken-for-granted assumption that privately owned and utilized cars are inherently desirable and efficient which may account for the blind spot in the vision of North American and European transport and urban planners, most of whom of course are themselves auto-dependent. It has been said that most transport planners see the world from a windscreen (or windshield) perspective—from the point of view of drivers who rarely use mass transit, who seldom cycle or walk. Thus, based on their experience and common sense, both of which partake of auto culture, planners develop mistaken assumptions about the motivations and transport needs of others. In a survey conducted in German cities, while three-quarters of the respondents expressed a desire that bus and rail transport be

given more priority, local transport planners and politicians had estimated that only one-third of those queried would have this
response.[8] Similar results have been found in surveys of Australians.[9]

The windscreen perspective is not only shared by individual
professionals but pervades the institutions for which they work.
Transport planning agencies demonstrate a general institutional bias
towards auto transport. For example, the California state transportation agency focuses almost exclusively on trying to facilitate auto
traffic flow and devotes less than one percent of its personnel to mass
transit concerns.[10] This institutional blind spot prevents a realistic
scrutiny of the full ecological, social and economic consequences of
auto-centred transport and the forces that shape and limit the
development of alternative transport modalities.

The task of a realistically critical perspective is to deconstruct existing material arrangements and their accompanying ideologies—to
analyze them as products of particular political, economic and social
contexts. This is especially needed in order to examine those aspects
of material existence and accompanying forms of ideology and consciousness that are harmful. While many of the negative consequences of the resource and energy intensive nature of the auto have been
generally acknowledged, the full range of social, spatial, and political
effects of auto-centred transport *systems*, as well as viable alternatives
to them, have yet to be adequately analyzed.

Auto-centred transport systems illustrate the social and spatial
consequences of the proliferation of a single commodity. The bottom
line is that too many autos are being used for too many activities for
our own social good. Nevertheless, the potential exists for creating
more environmentally benign and economically efficient transport
systems. The auto is here to stay and its advantages in terms of individual convenience are indisputable. It will remain part of (perhaps
even the most important part of) *diversified* transport systems. Our
task is not to eliminate but to reduce our auto-dependence and to
move away from auto-centred transport systems toward systems that
feature a greater variety of modalities. In order to develop the full
potential of diversified transport systems, individual preferences and
social needs must somehow be reconciled.

The widespread use of the private auto and its hegemony over
other forms of transport manifest in a concrete form the major structural contradiction that haunts capitalist society, a contradiction first
outlined by Karl Marx.[11] Marx's form of the contradiction existed in
the realm of production; essentially it was a contradiction between

what is rational activity for individual capitalist firms (in their pursuit of profit) and what is rational for the economy and society as a whole. Auto hegemony represents a similar contradiction in the realm of consumption. Millions of individual drivers pursuing their rational self-interest in using autos for journeys to work, to shop, and to play create problems of exaggerated energy consumption, traffic congestion, and environmental degradation on the collective level—the level of the society and the economy.

The seriousness of this contradiction has been noted even by those who produce autos, for example, in the following comment by an executive of a German auto company: "The apparent contradiction between the car as a symbol of individual mobility and its questionable environmental compatibility confronts the industry with one of the greatest challenges it has ever had to face."[12] While millions of individuals consuming in a similar fashion manifest the problems of automobility, no single individual is responsible for and cannot eliminate the social and economic problems created by auto-dependence. Indeed, the overwhelming majority of individual drivers probably do not give the issue any attention.

The Marxist emphasis on production in its critique of capitalism has led to a neglect—even trivialization—of patterns of consumption. Yet it is a particular mode of auto consumption that has contributed to our present ecological problems. The use of large amounts of energy and resources and the ruin of health and environment are issues that are dramatically raised by the consumption of the auto as the primary or sole means of everyday transport. Since Marx, analysts of capitalism have continued to underplay the role of commodity consumption in the private sphere except as expressions of and responses to alienation. Even the contemporary Green Parties, with their environmental politics ("eco-Marxism"), have focused on the destructive conditions of modern production. They have paid little attention to the ecological consequences of patterns of consumption that capitalism not only fosters but upon which it creates a physical and psychic dependence. However, there is at least implicit in environmental politics a criticism of global auto production and the detrimental modes in which its commodities are consumed. Our task is to begin to formulate a thorough critical analysis of transport that addresses the social organization of both production *and* consumption, and does so for the former centrally planned economies of Eastern Europe and the Soviet Union as well as for market countries.

It is the nature of individualist ideology, so prevalent in the United States, to portray the individual as an autonomous actor who stands apart from an alien and diffuse society. Unfortunately, however much auto travel maximizes individual autonomy, its excesses eventually result in a wide range of ecological and social dysfunctions. On a personal level consider the vastly increased number of auto drivers, who acting rationally as individuals clog highways so that their average speed is *decreasing*. Auto traffic in central London streets moves more slowly today than horse-drawn carriages did in the mid-nineteenth century. Technological gains have not resolved this contradiction. Despite the development of faster autos and the profusion of limited-access roadways, the average time of the journey to work has remained about the same in the U.S. since World War II.[13] For urban areas with auto-centred transport systems, the average travel time to work has actually increased. Rush-hour auto speeds in major cities are low and are decreasing because of increased congestion. Today's average speed is about 7 mph in London, 12 mph in Tokyo, and 17 mph in Paris. Even in Southern California's auto-friendly freeway environment, the average daily auto speed is just 33 mph.[14] Traffic congestion results in high costs in economic inefficiency (wasted time and energy) and in societal problems (more air pollution as cars idle more).

Auto travel promotes a subtle form of false consciousness about the relationship of the individual to society; as E.P. Thompson noted, driving fosters "the illusion of self-motivated freedom" and "disempowers people from confronting the determinism of the larger social process."[15] On a practical level, individuals have become wedded to auto use and its advantages, including travel flexibility and convenience. Auto use has become habitual. Now that modern societies have transport systems which are based on the auto, it is difficult or impossible for individuals—on their own—to contemplate alternatives. In this way, practical and ideological factors are woven together in a way that impede full consciousness of the effects of auto-centred transport and the possibilities for changing it.

A significant part of the ideology of auto transport is that it maximizes individual choice, and to some extent it does. However, while it has been widely hailed as the quintessentially democratic means of transport, the auto actually is not usable by, or available to, large sectors of populations, even in the most auto-saturated societies. In this sense one may speak of groups in society that are transport-disadvantaged, including many poor persons. It is in this way that auto use has political outcomes. In addition, dependence on the auto more generally reduces individual choice for those who prefer another form of transport at some time.

The overuse and misuse of the auto also highlight international policy issues. For example, the export of auto-centred transport systems from the North to the South is increasingly being recognized as a multifaceted problem for the South. More generally, auto-dependence serves as a useful handle for analyzing a number of long-standing concerns of social theory, including individualized patterns of consumption *vis-à-vis* social needs. Finally, the auto is a useful material instrument through which to analyze the complex relationships among technology, individual consumption, social space, and social life.

While its overuse and misuse create problems, it is also readily apparent that the auto is a source of pleasure and unprecedented mobility for many people. It is important to recognize that the auto, like all technologies, is not inherently good or bad; however, once utilized, technologies do have ecological and social consequences. For instance, the consequences of the use of nuclear power for generating energy have been a major focus in ecological debates. Transport has not received as much attention as have other technologies despite its widespread social impact. In fact, automobility may be the prime exemple of the problems of the misuse of technology that can contribute to ecological degradation.

Auto transport has been widely hailed since its inception at the turn of the century. As a technology auto transport offers unparalleled advantages of privacy and flexibility (of course, autos need not be used privately and their movements are actually controlled in a fashion). The downside of auto transport has been recognized only relatively recently. It took a threshold level of auto saturation and auto-produced environmental damage to bring the negative features of auto-centred transport to public awareness. As well as its generally acclaimed advantages, use of the auto invariably leads to specific social-ecological consequences. For instance, the use of the auto by sole individuals for everyday transport is inevitably energy and resource intensive and has negative environmental consequences. Technological fixes such as catalytic converters mitigate but do not eliminate such problems. Perhaps in some techno-utopia one can envision solar-powered autos made from materials that do not need replacement. Even then, such problems as congestion would remain. Private teleportation systems might be the ultimate answer!

What André Gorz has called the social ideology of the private motor car exemplifies an unlimited faith in absolute mobility, speed, technology, and the ability of every human being to move through space in his or her own hermetically sealed module, thus transcending time, space and the "messiness" of nature.[16] Such an ideology results in the auto being seen as an isolated consumer commodity whose effects are limited to the user. In fact, in countries where the auto is the central form of transport it is not simply an isolated commodity but part of a system of motorization. This system of technology-in-use includes supplies of metals, chemicals, fuels, roads, signals, repair sites, fuel distribution sites, traffic police, courts, insurance, scrap dealers, and various car lobbies and associations. Thus, to consider the auto and its socioenvironmental costs means to examine the whole auto-centred transport system.

Because various transport modes comprise an interrelated transport system, transport is intimately connected to other spheres of daily life. Unfortunately, most urban planning schools teach transport, housing, and energy issues in separate curricula. In the division of labour among policy makers and public agencies the separations are similar. However, our ability to think clearly about transport depends on not making it a singular issue. Transport must be considered in a holistic and ecological fashion. Transport is not unrelated to the general fragmentation of social life, to the ghettoization of space and to the erosion of the seamless niche of life that sustains the social ecology of a community.

Americans, especially, spend an increasing proportion of their time by themselves, alone in their autos. According to "Journey to Work" studies by the U.S. Census Bureau, in 1985, 86.7 percent of all workers traveled to their jobs by private vehicle; 72.6 percent drove alone (up from 64.4 percent in 1980) and 14.0 percent car pooled. Of the remaining journeys to work, 5.2 percent were by public transit, 4.0 percent were on foot, and 1.2 percent were by other means. Some 3 percent of all workers worked at home.

Auto commuting is a structural condition of modern social life that has potentially serious consequences, not only for our physical environments and our psyches but for the quality of our social life as well. For example, a survey by Norway's Ministry of Transport concluded:

> The traffic situation is marked by competition. Many are strongly concerned with getting there first, and

> take chances in overtaking others. The ruthlessness
> that often characterizes the traffic setting is seldom ob-
> servable where people meet without the immunizing
> armour that the car represents.[17]

Anti-social behavior is in part the product of our ability to separate or to distance ourselves from others. The separations and splits in various social discourses about work, play, shelter, transport and the quality of life are products of our division of labor and have ideological consequences. They inhibit us from seeing the connections between the quality of transport and the quality of our community life, our health, our level of empowerment, and our relationship with nature.

Like other costly aspects of contemporary production the environmental and health costs of individualized transport are increasingly externalized; that is, they are shifted from the producer or user to the public sphere. What appears as a "pay-as-you-go" system of transport is thus in many ways a socialized one. The benefits are individualized for those who can afford them while the costs, such as pollution, are socialized—shared by all, regardless of whether or not they can afford them. For example, it was estimated that drivers in Ontario in 1992 paid just 41 percent of the full costs of that province's auto bill. The remaining 59 percent was paid by all tax payers, whether or not they drove, in the form of expenses for accident victims, traffic law enforcement, and others costs.[18] In the U.S., it has been estimated that 70 percent of all state and local law enforcement activities are devoted to traffic management duties.[19] Furthermore, this system, which is problematic for developed countries, has become a model for economic development. There its inappropriateness is amplified and its social costs are borne by a heavily indebted and underdeveloped public sector.

The ascendance of the private passenger auto as a dominant mode of transport, along with the fact that this mode is held to be part of a global model for economic development, represents a major triumph of twentieth century capitalist production. This global victory not only lies in making a particular commodity a necessity for many people but in shaping beliefs and discourses about transport as well. While the ascendance of the auto as the principal or sole means of everyday transport has traditionally been represented as unmitigated progress for democracy as well as for individual convenience, it is increasingly apparent that this triumph carries large—and increasing—social costs. While the auto is here to stay and its advantages need to be *fully* utilized, society has reached the point at which serious thought is being given to controlling auto diffusion, reducing auto-dependence, and diversifying transport systems.

The auto's appeal partially lies in its deep embeddedness in our cultural and psychosocial experiences as an icon of individual mastery over technology, of individual freedom, of power and speed, of social status, and of sexuality. Individualist and consumerist ideologies mystify the problems engendered by auto hegemony, including environmental degradation; transport disenfranchisement of populations, even in the fully industrialized world; intense resource and energy use; bodily mayhem and more subtle health problems; and distortions in the fabric of social life, particularly the losses of public space and street life. A phenomenology of automobility reveals landscapes which promote a sense of sameness and placelessness, as well as a confusion of image and reality, the essence of the postmodern visual sensibility. The very social organization of space that auto-centred transport fosters helps to further auto-dependence and to mask any sense of realistic alternatives to automobility.

In Part One the focus is on the objective problems of auto-centred transport. We begin by highlighting the energy-resource intensive nature of auto-centred transport systems, their environmental and health effects, their resulting social inequalities, as well as the implications of the global extension of such systems into the former Second World and into the Third World. In Part Two, we analyze the ideological assumptions shared by auto drivers and transport planners alike, as well as the subjective dimensions of automobility and the relationship between automobility and the socioecological landscape. To conclude, in Part Three we examine the political context of transport policy and present ideas and projects for modifying auto-centred transport in the short run. We end by analyzing the structural properties of auto-centred transport systems, as well as possible alternatives.

NOTES

1. See: Glenn Yago, "The Sociology of Transport," *Annual Review of Sociology*, 9 (1983):171-190.
2. E. de Boer, "Transport Sociology," in Enne de Boer, ed., *Transport Sociology: Social Aspects of Transport Planning* (Oxford: Pergamon Press, 1986), p. 7.
3. Motor Vehicle Manufacturers Association, *Facts & Figures '92*, Detroit, 1992, pp. 25, 38, 84.
4. Carolyn S. Konheim and Brian Ketcham, "Toward a More Balanced Distribution of Transportation Funds" (Brooklyn NY: Konheim & Ketcham, 1991), p. 12.
5. Harold M. Mayer and Richard C. Wade, *Chicago: Growth of a Metropolis* (Chicago: University of Chicago Press, 1969), p. 442.
6. Matt De Lorenzo, "Viper Brings Wide Grins," *San Francisco Chronicle*, February, 1993, Supplement.
7. Carmen Hass-Klau, *The Pedestrian and City Traffic* (London: Belhaven Press, 1990); Women and Transport Forum, "Women on the Move: How Public is Public Transport?" in Cheris Kramarae, ed., *Technology and Women's Voices: Keeping in Touch* (New York: Routledge and Kegan Paul, 1988), pp. 116-134.
8. Manfred Peitschmann, "Eine Stadt Macht Mobil," *GEO Wissen: Verkehr-Mobilitat* 2 (1991):31-41.
9. Werner Brog, "Verhalten beginnt im Kopf: Public awareness des offentlichen Personenverkehrs," in Tom Koenigs and Roland Schaeffer, eds., *Forschritt vom Auto* (Munchen: Raben Verlag, 1991), pp. 291-306.
10. Advisory Commission on Cost Control in State Government, "Getting the Most Out of California's Transportation Tax Dollar," Sacramento, Joint Publications, 1990.
11. Karl Marx, *Capital*, ed. Frederick Engels, trans. Samuel Moore and Edward Aveling, Volume I: A Critical Analysis of Capitalist Production (New York: International Publishers, 1967).
12. Ferdinand Protzman, "The Greening of the Auto Makers," *The New York Times*, September 16, 1991, p. D1.
13. Yago, *op.cit.*
14. Judy Wajcman, *Feminism Confronts Technology* (University Park: The Pennsylvania State University Press, 1991), p. 127.
15. E.P. Thompson, "Last Dispatches from the Border Country," *The Nation*, March 5, 1988, p. 311.
16. André Gorz, *Ecology as Politics* (Montréal: Black Rose Books, 1980).
17. Hakon Stang, *Materialized Ideology: On Liberal and Marxist Power Analysis, Westerness and the Car* (Oslo: University of Oslo, Trends in Western Civilization Program No. 12, 1977), p. 19.
18. Neale MacMillan, "Index on Cars," *Canadian Forum*, April, 1993, p. 48.
19. Charles L. Wright, *Fast Wheels, Slow Traffic: Urban Transport Choices* (Philadelphia: Temple University Press, 1992), p. 91.

PART ONE

**Auto-Centred Transport
as a Social Problem**

CHAPTER 1

The Consumption Intensity of Auto-Centred Transport

The current forms and uses of auto technology substantially contribute to the growing problems of worldwide resource depletion. Increasing overuse of the auto, as well as its particular internal combustion engine form, play notable parts in the worldwide energy crisis. In this chapter, the auto's role *vis-à-vis* energy is described and analyzed as having three salient aspects: (1) growth in auto fleets and auto densities; (2) energy and resource intensity of auto-centred transport; (3) the inefficiency of individualized energy and resource intensive consumption.

The Worldwide Auto Fleet

Prior to 1915 the car was rare—a luxury item. Since then it has become a worldwide mass-produced commodity. Despite its universality in the contemporary world, the auto's use is geographically concentrated. Auto densities and auto fleets for various parts of the world are shown in Table 1. The data show the enormous differences that exist between areas of the world in car densities and fleets, especially between the nations of the North and those of the South (or the Third World). Both auto density and fleet size are highest by far in the United States; it has more cars and fewer persons per car than any other nation. Despite the relocation of some auto production to the Third World and the increased auto consumption there, developed societies still produce and consume the overwhelming proportion of all motor vehicles. In 1990-1991, North America, Western Europe, Japan and Oceania had only 15 percent of the world's population but consumed 78 percent, and produced 85 percent, of its motor vehicles.

It is important to note that car densities and fleets have been increasing in all places of the world. Worldwide the population per car declined from twenty-nine in 1960 to twelve in 1990, a decrease of nearly 60 percent. Thus, car production is considerably outstripping population growth. The sheer number of autos in the world grew by over 300 percent between 1960 and 1990, while world population

Table 1
World Auto Densities and Fleets, 1990

Area	People per Car	Car Fleet (millions)
Africa, (except South Africa)	113.0	5.4
South Africa	12.0	3.4
Asia, (except Japan)	125.7	22.8
Japan	3.5	34.9
Americas, (except Canada, U.S.)	14.6	30.0
Canada	2.1	12.6
United States	1.7	143.6
Western Europe	2.5	144.9
Eastern Europe*	11.3	37.7
Oceania	2.3	9.4
World	12.0	444.9

*Bulgaria, Hungary, Poland, and the former nations of Czechoslovakia, East Germany, U.S.S.R., and Yugoslavia.

Adapted from: *Motor Vehicle Manufacturers Association, "Facts & Figures '92," 1992, Detroit, Michigan, pp. 38-41.*

grew by about 100 percent. By 2010 the number of autos is expected to reach 1.1 billion, as their number is rising about two-and-a-half times as fast as the world's population. This rapid increase in autos is overwhelming technological improvements in fuel efficiency. In the United States between 1970 and 1990, fuel consumption per auto declined 34 percent but total auto fuel consumption increased by 7 percent. The reason for this apparent anomaly is that, while average miles traveled per auto rose only 2.8 percent between 1970 and 1990, the overall number of autos rose by 60.9 percent.[1]

In the United States and other auto-saturated nations the multi-car household has increasingly become the norm. The dispersal of places in which daily activities occur is one of the transformations of social space that accompanies auto hegemony. This dispersal requires families to set up elaborate transport schedules for shuttling children to school, commuting to work, shopping, and other activities. Such complex transport needs make multiple car ownership a necessity for many families. As a result, the number of vehicles per household has increased dramatically. According to U.S. Department of Transportation data, in 1990 nearly 60 percent of households had two or more vehicles, compared to only about 10 percent in 1960. The auto is the second most expensive commodity (after homes) that Americans purchase and a large percentage of the population makes monthly car payments throughout their adult lives. In 1990 in the United States, transport (dominated by auto expenses) accounted for 18.1 percent of all consumer spending. Only housing, at 31.3 percent, accounted for more consumer expenditure.

According to the Census Bureau's "American Housing Survey for the United States in 1987," the multi-car household is associated with suburban living. Therefore, car ownership in the United States is correlated with place of residence. If we look at the extremes, high vehicle use (owning three or more vehicles) tends to be concentrated in the suburbs, the West, and among home owners. Low vehicle use (owning no car, truck, or van) is higher among residents of central cities and the Northeast, and among renters. Home ownership and suburban residence are associated with each other, while the West is a region that is more sparsely settled and more recently developed. Both of these factors contribute to higher car use.

Energy and Resource Depletion

Auto fleets require vast amounts of nonrenewable energy. The internal combustion engine, even in its most technologically sophisticated form, is not very efficient in converting oil into usable energy. The auto is considerably more energy intensive than other modes of transportation. The single-occupant auto uses 1,860 calories per passenger mile, about twice that used by rail transit (885) or bus transit (920). [Nonmotorized locomotion modes do not require nonrenewable energy and are health conducive—bicycling uses 35 calories per mile; walking, 100.]

Transport, and auto transport in particular, consume inordinate amounts of energy as compared to stationary (domestic and commercial) consumption. In 1985 the transport sector consumed 63 percent of all oil used in the United States, 44 percent of oil used in Western Europe, 35 percent of oil used in Japan, and 49 percent of oil used in Third World countries.[2] According to data from the Federal Highway Administration and the Environmental Protection Agency, in 1991 the auto consumed over one-tenth of all the energy used in the United States for all purposes.

Generally, cars are too big, transport too few people, and use too much fuel to operate engines that are overly powerful for the tasks they perform. Thus, most autos are as appropriate for transport needs, to use Wolfgang Sachs' hyperbole, as a "chainsaw is for cutting butter."[3] This excess embodies social meanings regarding power and speed. These meanings resonate in particular with the dominant masculine ethos in our culture—bigger, faster, and more powerful are better.

The addition of amenities such as air conditioners to autos has been increasing and they add to energy use. Air conditioners encourage auto use, create the illusion of a pollution-free car interior, use gasoline and emit chlorofluorocarbons when they are discarded. Not only air conditioning but automatic transmissions and power steering as well require considerable energy, all of which is derived from gasoline. Furthermore, other optional accessories, including power brakes and automatic windows, add to vehicle weight and reduce fuel economy. Each additional 100 pounds added to an auto decreases fuel economy by 1 percent.[4]

In addition to their high uses of petroleum, autos require vast amounts of other natural resources. Car production uses considerable quantities of copper, steel and light metals such as aluminum. In 1990 in the United States, the motor vehicle industry consumed the following shares of the total national consumption of assorted materials: steel—13 percent; aluminum—16 percent; lead—69 percent; iron—36 percent; platinum—36 percent; and rubber (natural and synthetic)—58 percent.[5] Many of these resources are limited and at the current rate of consumption are not expected to last more than a century. An additional problem is that our ability to recycle these materials is limited since they are fused together and not easily separable. Newer U.S. cars are using less steel and more plastic. While some plastic is at least potentially recyclable, it is difficult to separate it from other materials in cars.

The waste of resources in autos is readily apparent in our landscapes that are so visually polluted with scrapped vehicles, which have created a whole new refuse disposal problem. In some neighbourhoods of New York City abandoned derelict autos remain on the streets for months because the fiscally strapped city lacks the money to collect and dispose of them expeditiously. In 1989, New York City's auto hulk count was a staggering 140,000. In the United States as a whole 11 million cars are junked annually. While some material is recycled, two million tons of unusable, often contaminated waste remains.[6]

It should be noted that some advances are being made in recycling autos. In Landshut, Germany, the BMW disassembly plant dismantles twenty-five cars a day. About 80 percent of the parts are reused. This recycling effort is being undertaken, over the opposition of the German Industry Federation. At the end of 1993, the German parliament is expected to have passed legislation requiring manufacturers to take back and recycle their products at the end of their use.[7]

The problems involved in recycling autos demonstrate that the production and consumption of energy are not merely economic but have natural or organic dimensions as well. In their natural aspect, at the front end of the process is production, which depends on subtractions of energy and resources from the ecosphere; at the other end of the process—through consumption—wastes are added to the environment. Thus, our vision of technology-in-use is a circular one; technology is viewed as a system with outputs and inputs that are part of the same process. There are two general lessons to be drawn logically: (1) natural resources, whether fuel or space, are finite; (2) synthetics cannot be wholly recycled or contained after their use.

Auto fleets not only consume large quantities of nonrenewable energy and other natural resources, they also require vast amounts of land. Including the necessary approaches, each mile of roadway requires about 25 acres of land. (A railway uses about one-sixth as much land as a roadway and yet is capable of transporting some 67 percent more passengers.) Autos are extremely wasteful of land, not only because roadways and other supporting infrastructures require so much space but also because autos carry so few people. As Mike Hamer has noted, "there are alleys in Venice, barely 12 feet wide, that regularly carry more people (on foot) than the average motorway."[8]

Up to 10 percent of the arable land in the United States is taken up by the auto infrastructure. During the heyday of interstate highway construction in the 1960s, it has been estimated that 50,000 people each year were displaced from their homes by roadway construction in the United States.[9] About half of all urban space in the U.S. is now devoted to auto-centred transport. In Los Angeles, two-thirds of land space is devoted to auto use. Much of this space is inefficiently used. As sections of social space become more homogeneous in the functions they provide (only residential or commercial, for example), the duplication of auto space (parking lots at the various locales) increases. It is estimated that in Los Angeles the average car uses up to eight parking spaces daily—each located at different activities. In suburban New Jersey, developers are now required to build 3,000 square feet of parking space for every 1,000 square feet of commercial office space. Although the consumption of space by the auto infrastructure may be extreme in the United States, other nations exhibit a similar pattern. For example, in the former West Germany about five percent of land is taken up by streets; if one adds parking areas and other auto-dedicated space the figure rises to eleven percent.[10]

In the United States arable land is not yet scarce but in other countries it is. For many Third World countries the land intensive character of auto-centred transport is not currently feasible, as noted by Lester Brown:

> An automobile-centred transportation system is land-intensive. Parking a subcompact requires a ten-by-twenty-foot plot of land; a parking lot to accommodate 200 vehicles requires an acre. In addition to the need for several parking spots for each automobile, land is required for streets, roads, and highways. In some densely populated countries there is not enough land to support a fleet of automobiles. In China, for example, which has only one-tenth of a hectare (about one quarter of an acre) of cropland per person, there is no room for cars. China, which exports a million barrels of oil a day, has virtually no private automobiles. Other areas unable to develop a full-fledged auto-centred transportation system because of land shortages include Bangladesh, Egypt, and the island of Java.[11]

In addition to adding to land shortages, auto-centred transport poses other problems for Third World nations. For example, for the many Third World countries that must import oil the cost of this resource increases the foreign debt.

Despite the space that is made available to accommodate cars in the United States, it has not kept up with the rate at which car fleets are increasing. In 1970 there were 61 yards of road per vehicle; by 1986, it was down to 39.[12] The consequence is rather obvious—greater traffic congestion. Unfortunately, building more roads does not solve the problem but generally increases traffic, thus necessitating building more roads. This counterintuitive process has been called the black hole theory of highway construction, which operates in the following five progressive steps:

1. Highway congestion
2. Added capacity, through highway construction
3. Urban sprawl grows, creating new auto-dependent spaces
4. Number of auto trips and their length rise
5. Renewed highway congestion

The real beneficiaries of highway spending are usually not motorists but construction firms and the auto industry in general. The black hole theory of congestion finds scientific support in Braess's paradox, a statistical and probability theory that holds that adding an additional street to a congested area can actually slow traffic down.[13] Based on the work of Dietrich Braess at the Institute for Numerical and Applied Mathematics in Munster, Germany, the traffic paradox is that, in the case of congested networks, the addition of a street increases congestion at least half the time. The reason is because drivers (including new drivers attracted by the new street) prefer the alternative, clogging it and its feeder streets, causing even more congestion. Another term for this problem is the auto sprawl syndrome, in which cars make urban sprawl possible and by so doing make suburbanites auto-dependent. Urban sprawl is defined spatially by single-use (i.e., residential or commercial) and low-density land use patterns.

The Inefficiency of Individualized Consumption

The post-World War II sprawl phase of suburbanization was an important factor in the increase in the total number of cars in daily use. While technological innovations can make cars less resource intensive and more environmentally friendly, there are limits to improvements in these areas. One can envision smaller and more fuel-efficient cars, yet the space dedicated to auto use will not change much as long as cars are primarily used by one individual and the number of autos continues to increase.

The ecological feasibility of a worldwide auto-centred transport system is based on two premises: (1) that the availability of resources to build and maintain individualized transport does not have limits; (2) that the environmental and other consequences of such a system can be corrected through technological fixes, and done so at a manageable cost. While such devices as the catalytic converter reduce some emissions they do not prevent the release of carbon dioxide and small quantities of metals. Moreover, it is estimated that six million tons of ore have to be refined yearly to provide platinum for catalytic converters.[14] On a fundamental level, to view resources and technical solutions as infinite is naive. There are good reasons to doubt the feasibility of developing worldwide an auto-centred transport system like that of Los Angeles and other similar cities.

If one were to set out to produce the most inefficient means of transport the auto might be the outcome. Consider, for example, the facts that the average auto is parked and unused for about 90 percent of its lifetime and that even when it is used, it is nearly empty. In the United States in 1990 the average occupancy for cars was 1.7 persons; for commuters' cars, 1.15 persons. About three-quarters of commuters travel to and from work alone.[15] Research by the Port Authority of New York and New Jersey and the New York City Department of Transportation found that the great majority of cars entering Manhattan during morning rush hours in 1986-1989 carried only a single occupant. Via the George Washington Bridge, 75.8 percent of autos had a sole occupant.

Auto travel feeds on itself. While auto trips that are recreational (as for vacations) or functional (as for going shopping or to work) comprise the majority of all trips, for a while now the fastest growing category has been that of transport-generated trips. These are trips made solely in order to support or to comply with the auto-centred transport system itself. They include trips for servicing the auto, driving around in search of parking space, and chauffeur trips to convey non-drivers.[16]

The auto is inefficient not only because it usually carries only one person but also because that one person is more and more frequently stalled in traffic. For example, one study found that in 1990 the average California driver wasted eighty-four hours a year sitting in traffic congestion. Projections indicate that by the year 2000 the time wasted will climb to 168 hours—or about twenty-one working days—per year. Energy is wasted, as well as time, and both are costly. It is estimated that the average motorist in California pays over $1,000 per year for wasted time and fuel due to congestion.[17] A study of traffic congestion in twenty-nine cities in the United States found that the cost in lost time, fuel, and higher insurance cost was $24.3 billion in 1986, up by 12 percent since 1982. Los Angeles led the list with the most costly traffic congestion.[18]

Although Los Angeles leads the way, other American cities are experiencing increasingly adverse effects from traffic congestion, as the data in Table 2 indicate.

Table 2
Traffic Congestion and Its Cost in Nine U.S. Cities, 1982-87

City	Congestion Index, 1987	Change 1982-87	Per Capita Cost of Congestion, 1987
Los Angeles	1.47	20%	$730
San Francisco	1.31	29	670
Washington	1.25	31	740
Phoenix	1.23	6	510
Houston	1.19	1	550
Atlanta	1.16	30	650
Seattle	1.14	20	580
New York	1.11	4	430
Chicago	1.11	11	340

Adapted from: Office of Technology Assessment, *Delivering the Goods: Public Works Technologies, Management, and Financing*. Washington DC: U.S. Congress, 1991, p. 4.

As a technology the auto did not create contemporary traffic problems any more than use of the horse did in nineteenth century cities. Rather it is the overuse of the auto and the accommodation of social space to it—as a homogenous system of mobility—that is the problem. The problems of the auto are the result of a *system of technology-in-use*. Horses and horse-drawn vehicles also created congestion and pollution problems in nineteenth century cities. Auto-centred transport has compounded these problems by replacing each horse with a greater number of vehicles, producing a level of congestion that defeats the original efficiency of movement of vehicles. As a result, auto-dominated transport uses too many resources and too much energy in order to accomplish too little.

More generally, highly individualized consumption as a pervasive lifestyle, as it exists in Western industrialized societies, results in energy and resource intensity and environmental degradation. The fact is that the single most important cause of the present ecological crisis is to be found in the everyday lifestyles of the residents of industrialized societies. While industrial production has become on the whole more energy efficient, the consumption of energy in the individual sphere, through auto use for example, has increased dramatically in recent decades. Much of this increased consumption has been made possible by the widespread availability of relatively cheap sources of energy. The source of ecological destruction is not to be located simply in the realm of production but in a diffused individualized system of consumption.

It is increasingly apparent that there are limits to the growth of individualized consumption and that auto-centred transport exemplifies the limits. However, the appropriate and feasible alternative is not to eliminate autos but to exercise social control over auto use in judicious ways, to reformulate auto technology, and to diversify transport systems. For such changes to work, attractive alternatives to the auto need to be provided. The auto will remain an oft-used option but it can be made one option among other equally desirable ones. Granted, such a change will be difficult and initially costly, but the potential rewards are great: a considerable reduction in the environmental damage and economic inefficiency created by auto-centred transport and its energy-resource intensity.

NOTES

1. Motor Vehicle Manufacturers Association, *Facts & Figures '92*, Detroit, 1992, pp. 25, 78.
2. Michael Renner, "Rethinking the Role of the Automobile" (Washington, DC: Worldwatch Institute, Paper No. 84, 1988), p. 16.
3. Wolfgang Sachs, *Die Liebe Zum Automobil* (Reinbeck bei Hamburg: Rohwohlt, 1990), p. 150.
4. Diane MacEachern, "Tips for Planet Earth," *San Francisco Examiner*, January 20, 1991.
5. Motor Vehicle Manufacturers Association, *op. cit.*, p. 47.
6. Conservation Law Foundation, "The Automobile: An Environmental Threat" (Boston: CLF Newsletter, Summer, 1990); Krystal Miller, "On the Road Again and Again and Again: Auto Makers Try to Build Recyclable Car," *The Wall Street Journal*, April 30, 1991.
7. Ferdinand Protzman, "Germany's Push to Expand the Scope of Recycling," *The New York Times*, July 4, 1993.
8. Mike Hamer, "Splitting the City," *New Internationalist*, No. 195, May, 1989, p. 11.
9. James B. Sullivan and Paula Montgomery, "Surveying Highway Impact," *Environment* 14 (1972):12-20.
10. Franz Ossing *et.al.*, "Innere Widerspruche und Aussere Grenzen der Lebensweise-Aspekte der Okologische Entwicklung," in Klaus Voy, Werner Polster, und Claus Thomasberger, eds., *Gesellschaftliche Transformationsprozesse und Materielle Lebensweise* (Marburg: Metropolis-Verlag, 1991), p. 362.
11. Lester Brown, "The Future of Automobiles," *Society* 21 (1984):65.
12. Matthew L. Wald, "How Dreams of Clean Air Get Stuck in Traffic," *The New York Times*, March 11, 1990.
13. Gina Kolata, "What If They Closed 42nd Street and Nobody Noticed?" *The New York Times*, December 25, 1990.

14. Greenpeace International, *The Environmental Impact of the Car* (Amsterdam: Greenpeace International, 1991).
15. Deborah Gordon, *Steering a New Course: Transportation, Energy and the Environment* (Cambridge, MA: Union of Concerned Scientists, 1991), p. 20.
16. K.H. Schaeffer and Elliott Sclar, *Access for All: Transportation and Urban Growth* (Baltimore: Penguin, 1975), pp. 115-117.
17. Advisory Commission on Cost Control in State Government, "Getting the Most Out of California's Transportation Tax Dollar" (Sacramento: Joint Publications, 1990).
18. Road Information Program, "The Effects of Traffic Congestion in California on the Environment and on Human Stress," Washington, DC, May, 1990; Road Information Program, "California Congestion Now and in the Future: The Costs to Motorists," Washington, DC, January 1990.

CHAPTER 2

The Ecological and Health Costs of Auto-Centred Transport

The ecological and health effects of auto-centred transport systems range from the obvious to the subtle. Smog and auto accidents are easily linked to the auto but other connections, such as those between the auto and stress and the auto and physical health, are not so easy to establish, in part because any such connection is invisible. In this chapter, after examining the ecological impacts of auto pollution, we turn to the health effects of traffic and of driving; finally, we examine auto accidents and their ideological implications.

Environmental Degradation

The auto waste that has attracted most public concern is the residue from the auto's gasoline-powered internal combustion engine. Less obvious is the impact of the use of resources such as land for paved roads. Paved roads not only consume petroleum in the form of asphalt but also decrease the ground's capacity to retain rainfall, which can increase flooding. Extensive paving disrupts the natural hydrologic cycle, particularly in its depletion of groundwater supplies. The run-off of auto wastes into adjacent lands is enormous.[1] Each year 100,000 tons of fine dust from tire abrasion are generated on the former West Germany's roads and 1 mm of surface is rubbed off the network of roads. Another more obvious impact of auto-centred transport on the environment is the proliferation of auto-related structures, including highway commercial strips and billboards. Auto traffic and its accompaniments can degrade the visual pleasure of physical environments, especially by unsightly land uses.

Although it has these more general consequences for the physical environment, the auto's chief impact consists of the air pollutants it produces. Approximately two-thirds of the carbon monoxide, one-half of the nitrous oxide, and two-thirds of the carbon particulate emissions from human sources are created through traffic.[2] According

27

to Environmental Protection Agency data, in the United States in 1990, road vehicles accounted for 37 percent of the total metric tons of all air pollutants from controllable emissions. This was the largest single source of air pollution, ranking ahead of stationary fuel combustion, industrial processes, solid waste disposal, and other sources. Moreover, the situation promises to worsen. The transport sector is the fastest growing source of carbon emissions. At present growth rates transport carbon emissions will increase 40 percent by the year 2005.[3]

Nitrous oxides and sulphur dioxide from fuel combustion are components (among others) in acid rain, which scars buildings, causes forest and lake damage, and aggravates respiratory disorders in humans. Some fraction of this pollution from fuel combustion which causes acid rain emanates from cars. Additionally, it is estimated that by contributing to ozone production vehicle exhausts have led to as much as 20 percent reductions in crop yields in some areas, along with damage to forests. Chlorofluorocarbons used as coolants in cars may also contribute to the depletion of the ozone layer. Autos produce ozone in the lower atmosphere through the hydrocarbons and nitrogen oxides they emit; they contribute to the destruction of the ozone layer in the upper atmosphere because they emit chlorofluorocarbons.[4] In considering emissions one must take into account both primary emissions that come directly from auto use and secondary emissions that come from fuel storage, extraction, distribution, and manufacturing. Finally, it is important to note the potential global impact of auto-produced pollutants. For instance, it has been argued that exhaust pollution from autos is threatening the self-cleansing capacity of the atmosphere and altering the formation of its cloud patterns.[5]

Technological solutions for reducing emissions have had limited success. While reducing carbon monoxide, sulphur dioxide and nitrous oxides, catalytic converters increase carbon dioxide emissions, which contribute to the greenhouse effect. Also, catalytic converters emit traces of precious metals such as platinum and are effective only at certain speeds. In traffic, converter efficiency declines considerably. They require a great deal of maintenance and soon lose their effectiveness. Furthermore, even though the United States has made strides in creating cleaner cars through governmental regulation, the facts that fleet sizes and fleet mileages are increasing more than offset the gains. The result is a reduction in per car emissions but poorer air quality. Thus, high levels of auto consumption remain a central problem.

Health Effects

Whereas smoking, diet, alcohol use, and exercise get attention as public health issues, the health consequences of auto-centred transport have, in comparison, largely been ignored. A British toxicologist has proposed a slogan: "I won't smoke, if you don't drive."[6] It has been argued that the focus on the contribution of smoking to lung cancer neglects the possible role of air pollution. Also neglected is the synergistic relationship that might exist between air pollution and smoking.[7]

It may well be that in some areas inhaling air pollution is the health equivalent of smoking. For instance, during the summers in Riverside and San Bernardino, California, it is estimated that breathing the air is like smoking one pack of cigarettes a day.[8] Comparisons between smoking cigarettes and second-hand cigarette smoke and "smoking" air pollution have the advantage of shifting the focus from individual lifestyle risks to collective dangers that individuals do not control. It is precisely this collective—or social or systemic—dimension of auto-centred transport that needs more attention.

For humans, auto emissions can contribute to emphysema, lung cancer, and other respiratory disorders. There are numerous empirical examples from around the world that suggest the connections between auto emissions and human health. When inversion layers trap smog in cities like Los Angeles and London, admissions to emergency rooms spike and the deaths from respiratory ailments increase.[9] The winter of 1990-1991 was the most toxic in Mexico City's history. An increase in smog (*nata*), primarily from the emissions of motor vehicles, triggered a 16 percent to 20 percent jump in the incidences of respiratory infections, nosebleeds, and emphysema.[10] An American Lung Association study estimated that vehicular pollution resulted in health costs of at least $4.3 billion and contributed to 120,000 deaths in 1985 in the United States.[11]

There is growing empirical evidence of the harmful effects on human health of the gases released into the air through auto emissions. Carbon dioxide can cause headaches and lead those with coronary heart disease to experience stress.[12] Carbon monoxide can aggravate respiratory and cardiovascular problems.[13] California classifies carbon monoxide as a reproductive toxin that has been linked to low birth weight.[14] New York City cab drivers may have CO levels in their blood so high that their blood cannot be used in transfusions for people with heart disease.[15]

Simon Wolff and C. J. Gillham summarized in 1991 some of the research findings on the possible effects of auto-generated air pollution on health:

> Diesel particulate is a risk factor for lung cancer and contains polycyclic aromatic hydrocarbons which are mutagens and/or carcinogens. In Sydney, it is estimated that 30 lung cancers arise each year as a result of traffic-derived benzopyrene, which is another product of incomplete combustion. Similarly, traffic-derived air pollution has contributed to the increase in lung cancers in Japan and it is estimated that in the United States there are between 586 and 1650 new cancer cases resulting from air pollution each year, based upon the crude risk estimates for the small number of identified combustion-derived carcinogens. In addition to cancer, rates of respiratory illnesses and symptoms are elevated among children living in cities with high motor vehicle-derived particle pollution and total exposure to particulates correlates well with the incidence of chronic obstructive lung disease which is a risk for premature mortality. Total mortality and morbidity from traffic-derived air pollution might thus be very high. Some estimates place the individual risk of death (the annual number of deaths from a specific cause as a proportion of the total population) from car pollution in the United States as high as 1.67×10^4 (i.e. approximately two people per 10,000 die of car pollution each year), which is almost twice as high as the individual risk of death in road traffic accidents in the UK.[16]

Wolff has also published epidemiological evidence linking car ownership with leukemia and lymphoma.[17] The hypothesis is that exposure to benzene from car exhaust and gasoline evaporation contribute to the incidence of the two diseases. While the evidence is tentative, the hypothesis does focus on environmental sources of cancer in a new way. Most research limits itself to industrial and occupational sources of exposure to such substances as benzene.

In addition to dangerous gases, autos emit various metal and mineral particulates. For instance, asbestos particles are rubbed off brake linings and become airborne. Also, as was mentioned earlier, catalytic converters emit traces of precious metals. Even when particulates emitted by autos are not directly harmful to the body, they may help to trigger otherwise only potential carcinogens.[18]

For many years the mining industry mistakenly read the symptoms of black lung disease as being indicative of asthma or individual habits such as smoking.[19] (Of course this mistaken diagnosis also absolved mining companies of any responsibility for the health of their employees.) In a similar vein the chronic respiratory problems generated by smog in some children may be interpreted as symptomatic of colds. In fact, the cause may be pollution, or pollution synergistically acting to increase vulnerability to bacteria and viruses.[20] The effects of pollution are thereby experienced as individual and natural events when in reality they are unnaturally produced and beyond the control of any individual.

Lead is among the most harmful of metals that become airborne through auto use. It is highly toxic and can contribute to brain damage, among other things.[21] Between 1976 and 1986, as the consumption of leaded gasoline decreased in the United States, the average level of lead in the bloodstreams of the population fell by more than one-third.[22] However, a billion gallons of leaded gas are still sold annually in the United States—largely for older cars and farm equipment.[23] Also, U.S. companies continue to export leaded gasoline to developing countries. Thus, there is a double standard for gasoline consumption—one for the developed nations and another less healthy one for developing nations. So, although the consumption of leaded gasoline has decreased in the United States, it is still high in other parts of the world. Roadside dust in Nigeria has been shown to have a higher lead content than leaded paint. Children who live near heavily trafficked streets in Mexico City have higher blood lead levels than those who do not and they are likely to have more neurophysiological-behavioral impairments.[24]

In addition to putting toxic substances in the air, motorized traffic creates other forms of pollution. Perhaps the most insidious is noise pollution, which carries risks for health as well as having an adverse impact on the general quality of life. The noise of traffic on a busy street is rated at about 85 decibels (dBA), while the U.S. Environmental Protection Agency recommends a maximum of 70 dBA for the protection of public health. Although there are louder noises, such as jet take-offs and landings, it is the case that "highway traffic is the major contributor of noise in the United States as a whole."[25] In 1987,

6.6 million residents of housing units in the United States reported to the Census Bureau that noise from heavy street traffic in their neighbourhoods bothered them. While this represented only 7.4 percent of all occupied housing units, it is important to note that traffic noise was more often cited as a problem than was crime. Similar data are reported from other motorized societies. In West German surveys 95 percent of the population felt itself to be burdened by traffic noise; 54 percent had even considered a change of residence because of noise.[26]

Noise pollution produced by traffic is at best a nuisance, at worst a health problem that not only involves hearing loss but also raises stress levels and may contribute to heightened blood pressure. A 1980 West German study showed a relationship between traffic noise and blood pressure. One thousand people were asked if they were under a doctor's care for high blood pressure. The sample was sorted by sex and age, as well as by whether or not respondents lived in areas of high or low traffic density. Those respondents who were not under treatment for blood pressure tended to live in low-density traffic areas, while those who were under treatment for high blood pressure tended to live in areas of high traffic density.[27] While other factors such as genetic inheritance, exercise, and diet are clearly relevant to blood pressure, this study is highly suggestive. Other studies have supported a relationship between noise levels and blood pressure.[28]

In addition to its possible direct bearing on health, studies in various nations have demonstrated that traffic noise produces secondary adverse effects. These secondary consequences include sleep interference, distraction of concentration, interruption of conversation, and psychological distress.[29] Also it has been hypothesized that traffic noise may accelerate the process of age-related deafness or presbycosis.[30]

Holistic analyses of the health consequences of transport systems have yet to be developed. Research, we speculate, would reveal hitherto unnoticed health costs of auto-centred transport. A study comparing the immune reaction in children living in more polluted German cities to those in less polluted ones is suggestive of the potential of such research. This epidemiological study found that the children in the more polluted areas had a relatively more attenuated immune system and lower lymphocyte (T-cell) counts than their counterparts in less polluted areas.[31] If such tentative results eventually mean anything, the implications could be enormous. The effects of traffic-generated pollution on the development of children's immune responses, and its contributions to the incidence of asthma, allergies, and infectious problems might be explored. There is, furthermore, the interesting possibility that the sociopsychological stresses of being in auto-dominated spaces (in addition to, or in synergistic combination with, emissions) have a negative impact on immune responses. Research therefore, needs to focus not only on the health costs of individual emissions (e.g., lead) but also on the possible synergistic effects of two or more emissions acting together. Research, moreover, needs to consider social psychological stressors (e.g., traffic noise) and how these are linked to physiological functions and to the entire complex of auto emissions.

Driving

One acclimates one's mind to the stresses of driving and after a while one may no longer consciously perceive it as stressful. However, though a person's mind may adapt to stress, does the body? Data suggest otherwise. For example, the heart rate of a train passenger is lower than that of a passenger in a private auto. Additionally, driving causes increased levels of stress hormones, blood sugar and cholesterol in the body.[32]

In reviewing the literature on the psychophysical effects of traffic congestion, a U.S. government report concluded:

> Some studies of automobile drivers have shown a significant relationship between exposure to traffic congestion and a variety of adverse physiological reactions. For example, researchers have reported a significant and positive correlation between high traffic volumes and increased heart rates, blood pressure, and electrocardiogram irregularities. Studies have also shown that chronic exposure to traffic congestion, especially over long distances, long waits, and frequent trips, increases negative mood states, lowers tolerance for frustration, and can even lead to more impatient driving habits. Experts in the field point out, however, that most physiological research tends to focus on the short-term reactions of drivers to acute environmental demands rather than on the cumulative behavioral and health consequences of chronic exposure to traffic conditions.[33]

Traffic congestion may also facilitate aggressive behavior in American drivers but American drivers are not unusual in this respect. A Norwegian government study indicated that the impersonality of auto traffic, coupled with the intense competition often manifested in auto congestion, results in the display of an unusual degree of ruthlessness.[34]

One study found that a great deal of involvement in traffic congestion can raise blood pressure, lower frustration tolerance, increase negative mood and aggression in driving. Of course these changes may be moderated by personality style.[35] Field experimental studies of auto drivers have shown a significant relationship between rush hour traffic and chest pain and cardiac arrhythmia, between traffic volume and heart rate, blood pressure and electrocardiogram irregularities, and between commuting distance and blood pressure.[36] Research supports the view that increased traffic congestion results in higher human stress and aggression, contributing to freeway shootings and other projectile attacks, assaults using the auto as a weapon, and roadside conflicts initiated while driving.[37]

Prolonged driving may also affect the body in biomechanical ways. Data have implicated extended periods of driving in a number of body problems, including "motorist's spine" and "driver's thigh."[38] Additionally, persons who drive a car for 20 miles or more a day are at special risk for lumbar disc herniation (lower back injury) and truck drivers suffer a high rate of back injuries.[39] Ultimately, the most pervasive effect of auto driving on the human body may be the general reduction in physical exercise that it fosters.

Fitness in Auto Space

Despite the conventional wisdom that physical fitness is on the increase in the contemporary U.S., the reality is that the rather small percentage of Americans who are physically active is in the mid-1990s no higher that it was in the mid-1980s—about 40 percent. About 60 percent of Americans lead sedentary lives (sedentary equals less than three 20-minute leisure-time physical activity sessions a week). The consequences of lack of physical activity are serious; it is the most prevalent behavioral risk for heart disease, far outdistancing smoking or obesity.[40]

In addition to the fact that driving deprives one of opportunities for physical exercise, it is reasonable to pose the question as to whether or not special spaces adapted to the auto's needs also limit access to other means of remaining fit. Thus, personal physical fitness has become more problematic in contemporary societies not only because levels of physical work have declined, but additionally because the structure of auto space limits opportunities for walking or biking.

A vast compensatory system for becoming and staying fit has emerged—one that is segregated from the web of everyday life. The physical fitness industry provides highly expensive technical equipment that often reproduces natural movements—treadmills, stairmasters, and stationary bikes which stimulate the conditions, respectively, of running/walking, climbing stairs, and cycling. This equipment replicates the physical exercise involved in the natural activity but not the actual *experience*. Fitness has been commodified and, what in reality requires little equipment, technical knowledge or specialized space, has become a complex, expensive and arcane enterprise.

Therefore, it can be argued that the physical fitness of individuals is to a great extent related not only to the nature of work but to the social organization of space. Fitness can be provided by the structure of daily life, as Thomas Boudreau noted: "Good physical space is without a doubt much more assured by proper design of the urban environment, the work environment and the educational system than by the creation of an enormous specialized and parallel system that is exclusively preoccupied with physical activity outside the context of daily life."[41] We would add that the social organization of time, as in the length of work and travel time, are also factors. The fitness industry has flourished because it compensates for the lack of opportunities and time for staying fit that characterize our work and urban environments. The emphasis on specialized fitness techniques such as aerobic exercise and high-tech gyms obscures the more direct and less technically complicated ways of staying fit, such as walking. Walking is made difficult in auto space. Even mall walking, a frequent exercise engaged in by the elderly, requires auto transport to and from a mall. Thus, the auto strongly influences the design of urban spaces, which in turn structure opportunities for physical fitness and access to the means of being fit.

One way to mitigate the auto's indirect but negative impact on physical fitness is to devote more urban space to bicycle and pedestrian paths. (This issue is discussed at greater length in Chapter 9.) Done in a meaningful way, such paths could encourage more people to walk and to bike for short and medium-range trips to work and for other purposes. At a minimum, bicycle and pedestrian pathways could be used for physical exercise and leisure-time activity. There is considerable public support in the United States for the creation of more such pathways. In a 1992 national survey by the Louis Harris Organization, 72 percent of Americans stated that they wanted more bicycle and pedestrian paths. While only 4 percent of those surveyed walked to work and only 1 percent biked, 73 percent said they walked for exercise, 46 percent biked, and 24 percent ran.

Auto Accidents

Death by auto is the most dramatic of its negative effects on health. World Health Organization data reported 142,799 motor vehicle traffic deaths in forty reporting countries in 1988. According to the Census Bureau, in the United States in 1989 there were 19.2 deaths from motor vehicle accidents per 100,000 persons. Auto accidents are by far the leading cause of death for youths aged fifteen to nineteen in the U.S. In fact, more teenagers die from auto traffic accidents than from *all* of the next nine leading causes of deaths combined. The death rate for the second leading cause of teen death in the U.S., homicide, is only about two-fifths of the death rate from auto accidents. In fact, vehicular crashes are the leading killer of Americans aged five to forty-three years. Due to this fact, they are the leading cause of lost years of life expectancy.

Motor vehicle accidents ranked fifth among causes of death for all Americans in 1989; they killed more people than all other accidents, or diabetes, or suicide, or infective disease (including AIDS), or liver disease, or homicide. Additionally, motor vehicle emissions contribute some unknown factor to the pollution that figures into two of the four leading causes of death: malignancies and pulmonary disease.

It is important to note that a goodly proportion of motor vehicle fatalities are not motorists or occupants of autos. According to National Highway Traffic Safety Administration data, nonoccupants comprised 6,440 of the deaths from motor vehicle accidents in the United States in 1991; this represented 16 percent of all motor vehicle deaths. In some other nations pedestrian deaths may be an even larger problem. For example, in Britain about one-third of all deaths on roadways are pedestrians.[42] London has earned a reputation as an especially dangerous city for pedestrians, particularly children and elderly people.

Because of its large population, the size and density of its auto fleet, and the fact that its drivers drive more miles, the United States leads the world in total traffic deaths. Annually, between one-fifth and one-fourth of the world's traffic fatalities are Americans. However, when population and miles driven are standardized, the United States becomes one of the safer countries in which to drive. According to World Health Organization data, the U.S. death rate from motor vehicle accidents per 100,000 people ranked sixth highest among forty reporting nations in 1988; Portugal was first, followed by New Zealand, Hungary, Belgium, and Ecuador. Syria had the lowest death rate, followed by Hong Kong, Chile, Thailand, and Norway. In 1989, among fourteen nations, the U.S. ranked third best, behind Sweden and Norway, in traffic fatalities per 100 million vehicle miles; Spain had the highest fatality rate.[43]

Comparative analysis of auto fatalities is not easy. Definitions vary among nations. Statistics differ with regard to the time period allowed to attribute death to an accident—in many but not all nations it is within thirty days. Furthermore, data are inadequate. In many Third World nations there is no accounting of auto fatalities. In addition to these data collection problems there are problems in interpreting auto fatality data. Variations in auto fatality rates may be due to differences in culture as well as to road and auto safety conditions. In West Germany, for example, "national character" and the absence of speed limits on autobahns have been cited as fatality-inducing factors.[44]

Auto crashes are a major source of bodily injury in the United States. According to the National Safety Council, there were 5.6 million motor vehicle related injuries in 1990, resulting in an economic loss of $95.9 billion. Motor vehicle accidents are the largest single trauma-induced cause of paraplegia and quadriplegia and a major cause of epilepsy and head injury.[45]

In the United States auto safety has improved considerably over time. In the fifty years between 1935 and 1985, the motor vehicle death rate per 100,000 population declined from 28.6 to 19.1; per 100 million vehicle miles, from 15.91 to 2.58.[46] However, auto travel remains considerably more dangerous than travel by other modes. In the United States in 1987 there was one passenger car fatality (auto occupants only included) for every 60.5 million passenger miles, while there was one domestic airway fatality for every 1.5 billion passenger miles; thus, airline fatality rates were about one-twenty-fifth those of passenger cars. In probabilistic terms it is estimated that for an American, over a fifty-year period the risk of death from an airplane crash is one in 20,000; from homicide, one in 300; and from an auto accident, one in 100.[47]

Why auto accidents occur is a complex question. A number of contributory factors have been suggested. Media messages glorify speed and risk taking. Many movie and television car chase scenes convey an exciting and relatively carnage-free image of fast and reckless driving. The screen images are disembodied, as if one were playing a computer game. Advertisements glamorize cars and their speed as images of masculinity and power. Age and sex appear to be significant predictors of accident rates. Young males between the ages of fourteen and twenty-four are at highest risk.[48] Social and cultural factors help to explain why young males are at particularly high risk. Young males are often socialized into taking risks. They frequently disdain the use of seat belts as not being macho.[49]

Economic pressures also contribute to vehicular accidents, especially among truckers.[50] Truck drivers frequently operate under time pressure and have a relatively high rate of drug consumption, especially of stimulants. Because many drivers are self-employed, economic considerations can lead them to drive long hours with unsafe equipment and large payloads. Additionally, truck payloads and size have increased over time, contributing to traffic congestion and accident rates.

Much of the public attention about traffic fatalities focuses on drunken driving. In the United States in 1990, 39.7 percent of road fatalities came from accidents caused by drivers who had a blood alcohol level of 0.1 percent or more, the usual definition of intoxication. This represented a substantial decline from 1982 when 46.3 percent of auto deaths involved intoxication.[51] This decline indicates that the spate of new and stronger laws and public actions, like random roadblocks to check for drunken drivers, have been effective. However, data on alcohol-related auto fatalities are somewhat misleading. For example, the drunken driver is not necessarily *always* the one at fault in accidents. Other estimates place the figure of alcohol-caused fatalities at 25 percent of all auto accident deaths.[52] Many alcohol-related fatalities, furthermore, involve co-factors such as fatigue, inexperience, poorly designed or inadequately lit roads, and unsafe cars.[53]

Campaigns against drunken drivers, it can be argued, weaken individual rights and privacy through the use of intrusive tests. Moreover, by focusing on the driver, these campaigns take needed attention away from the structural problems of autos and roadways, as has been noted:

> To interpret social problems solely in terms of individual irresponsibility is in tune with our times. The

automobile and liquor industries are delighted to blame accidents on the abuse of their products by a small fraction of customers, and to join in public relations campaigns to discourage such abuse. How painless that is compared with making safer cars or admitting that alcohol is a dangerous drug.[54]

Dramatic alcohol-related auto deaths are a newsworthy example of the health costs of alcohol, made even more so by the fact that many persons are innocently and randomly victimized. However, considerably more people die each year from chronic alcohol abuse and under far less dramatic circumstances than from alcohol-implicated auto accidents. This is not to say that drunken driving does not deserve the attention it gets—just that other factors involved in auto fatalities deserve more attention than they get.

One major cause of auto fatalities that deserves more attention is speed. When the United States instituted the 55 mph speed limit in response to the oil crisis in the 1970s, road fatalities declined by about 32 percent. A recent study showed that when the speed limit was raised from 55 mph to 65 mph in the American state of New Mexico in the mid-1980s, the road fatality rate almost doubled within a year.[55] Data from West Germany also support the idea that lower speed limits decrease fatalities. In one study in Buxtenhude, although the number of accidents did not decrease, the number of fatalities did. The number of accidents involving serious injury declined by 30 percent and the number of seriously injured people dropped by 56 percent.[56] A Hamburg study demonstrated that the probabilities of pedestrian injury and death increase with motor vehicle speed.[57] Denmark has had a similar experience—lowered speed limits resulted in fewer road fatalities.[58]

Although the data show that lowering speed limits reduces roadway fatalities, focusing on it does keep the spotlight on the individual driver. Clearly auto drivers have a responsibility to drive safely but concentrating on individual behavior neglects the social, cultural and environmental dimensions of accidents. Car safety has not always been a priority of auto manufacturers. Not only are some cars unsafe (or not as safe as they could be) but some roads are unsafe as well. It is also apparent that some drivers use cars capable of high speeds that are beyond safe limits or the limits of their driving expertise. In many parts of the country the auto is the only available means of transport, pressuring drunken drivers and other impaired persons, such as those with vision problems, into driving. This is changing slowly as programmes and policies are developed to provide alternative transport and designated drivers, at least in situations where drinking alcohol is routine, such as on New Year's Eve.

In addressing the problem of auto accidents most policy still concentrates on changing individual behavior through education or sanctions. However, individuals are hard to reach, to influence, and to control. Traffic penalties are not consistently and rapidly imposed on violators. Since the majority of the populations of the United States and Canada drink and most also drive, it is not cost-effective to monitor and educate all drivers. By contrast an ecological approach would change social and physical environments, produce safer cars, and make alternative ways of travel available to drivers. These kinds of preventive measures are also costly but they offer more promise of effectiveness. However, the political and economic influence of the auto industry seriously limits the government's capacity to prevent auto accidents, especially but not solely in the United States. In West Germany, for example, it is the auto industry and private racing clubs that most actively oppose speed limits.[59]

Ultimately, then, death by auto is a social and political problem as well as one of individual negligence. In discussing auto accidents in Britain, John Adams concluded:

> The underlying cause of the growth in traffic deaths since the War has been the increase in traffic. This increase has been fostered, and is still being fostered, by a wide range of government initiatives, the most prominent being the lavish assistance provided for the car industry and the even more lavish expenditure on the road programme; it has been the policy of both conservative and labour governments, almost completely unopposed in Parliament, to promote the principal cause of traffic accidents.[60]

Perhaps Adams oversimplifies the issue and ignores the resistance to traffic growth demonstrated by some members of Parliament. Nonetheless, he describes a problem to which we shall return later—that by continuing to support the entrenched economic interests of auto-centred transport, policy makers also end up encouraging its environmental, health, and ecological hazards. Thus, as Matthew Wald has noted about the auto pollution problem in the United States:

"The degree to which cars are culpable and the comparative ease of cleaning up tailpipes and smokestacks seem to vary according to factors like how many auto plants a Congressman has in his district."[61]

NOTES

1. Otto Ullrich, "The Pedestrian Town as an Environmentally Tolerable Alternative to Motorized Travel," in Rodney Tolley, ed., *The Greening of Urban Transport: Planning for Walking and Cycling in Western Cities* (London: Belhaven Press, 1990), p. 99.
2. Otto Ullrich, "Die Kontraproductivitat des Automobils," in Jobst Kraus, Horst Sackstetter, und Willi Wentsch, eds., *Auto, Auto Uber Alles?* (Freiburg: Dreisam Verlag, 1987), pp. 152-155.
3. Michael R. Eaton, "What Climate Change Means for Transportation Policy in California," in Robert L. Deen, ed., *The Alternatives to Gridlock: Perspectives on Meeting California's Transportation Needs* (Sacramento: California Institute of Public Affairs, 1990), p. 102.
4. Eric Mann, *L.A.'s Lethal Air* (Los Angeles: Labor/Community Strategy Center, 1991), p. 12.
5. Tim Thompson, "Where Have All the Clouds Gone?" *Earth Island News* 7 (1992):40-42.
6. Personal correspondence.
7. Simon P. Wolff, "Air Pollution and Cancer Risk?" Correspondence, *Nature* 356 (1992):471.
8. Mann, *op. cit.*, p. 6.
9. Michael Renner, "Rethinking the Role of the Automobile" (Washington, DC: Worldwatch Institute, Paper No. 84, 1988), p. 35.
10. Christine Gorman, "Mexico City's Menacing Air," *Time* Magazine, April 1, 1991, p. 61.
11. Alexandra Allen, "The Auto's Assault on the Atmosphere," *Multinational Monitor* 11 (1990):23.
12. Deborah Gordon, *Steering a New Course: Transportation, Energy and the Environment* (Cambridge, MA: Union of Concerned Scientists, 1991), p. 62.
13. Jean-Philippe Barde and Kenneth Button, "Introduction," in Jean-Philippe Barde and Kenneth Button, eds., *Transport Policy and the Environment* (London: Earthscan Publications, 1990), pp. 1-2.
14. Mann, *op. cit.*, p. 13.
15. Paul Wachtel, *The Poverty of Affluence* (Philadelphia: New Society Publishers, 1989), p. 56.
16. Simon P. Wolff and C.J. Gillham, "Public Health versus Public Policy? An Appraisal of British Urban Transport Policy," *Public Health* 105 (1991):219.
17. Simon P. Wolff, "Correlation between car ownership and Leukaemia: Is non-occupational exposure to benzene from petrol and motor vehicle exhaust a causative factor in Leukaemia and lymphoma?" *Experientia* 48:301-304 (Basel: Birkhauser Verlag, 1991).
18. Mann, *op. cit.*, p. 17.

19. Barbara Ellen Smith, "Black Lung: The Social Production of Disease," *International Journal of Health Services* 11 (1981):343-359.
20. Mann, *op. cit.*, p. 22.
21. Merck Manual, "Lead Poisoning," (Rahway, NJ: Merck, Sharp and Dohme Research Laboratories, 1982), p. 1879.
22. Renner, *op. cit.*, p. 37.
23. Philip Hilts "California to Test Children for Lead Poisoning," *The New York Times*, October 12, 1991, p. 7.
24. Kenny Bruno, "Not getting the Lead Out," *Greenpeace*, October-December, 1991, pp. 18.
25. Frederick P. Stutz, "Environmental Impacts," in Susan Hanson, ed., *The Geography of Urban Transportation* (New York: The Guilford Press, 1986), p. 329.
26. Till Bastian und Harold Theml, *Unsere Wahnsinnige Liebe Zum Auto* (Beltz: Psychologie Heute/Taschenbuch, 1990).
27. Institut fur Angewandte Umweltforschung, *Der Auto Knigge* (Reinbeck bei Hamburg: Rowohlt Verlag, 1990).
28. Bastian und Theml, *op. cit.*
29. Sonja M. Hunt, "The Public Health Implications of Private Cars," in Claudia Martin and David V. McQueen, eds., *Readings for a New Public Health* (Edinburgh: Edinburgh University Press, 1989), pp. 100-115.
30. Ad Hoc Group to the Environment Committee of OECD, "Automotive Air Pollution and Noise: Implications for Public Policy," in Ralph Gakenheimer, ed., *The Automobile and the Environment: An International Perspective* (Cambridge, MA: The MIT Press, 1978), pp. 402-404.
31. Ernst Gerhard Beck und Pavel Schmidt, "Verkehr und gesundheit in Frankfurt," in Tom Koenigs und Roland Schaeffer, eds., *Fortschritt vom Auto* (Munchen: Raben Verlag, 1991), pp. 57-74.
32. A.A. Robinson, "The Motor Vehicle, Stress and Circulation System," *Stress Medicine* 4 (1988):173-176.
33. U.S. General Accounting Office, *Traffic Congestion: Trends, Measures and Effects*, Washington, DC, 1989, p. 68.
34. Hakon Stang, *Materialized Ideology: On Liberal and Marxist Power Analyses, Westerness and the Car* (Oslo: University of Oslo, Trends in Western Civilization Program No. 12, 1977), p. 19.
35. University of California Wellness Letter, "When Rush Hour Never Ends," 4:1-2. Berkeley, 1988.
36. Daniel Stokols and Raymond Novaco, "Transportation and Well-Being," in Irwin Altman, Joachim Wohlwill, and Peter Everett, eds., *Transportation and Behavior* (New York: Plenum Press, 1981), pp. 85-125.
37. Road Information Program, "The Effects of Traffic Congestion in California on the Environment and on Human Stress," Washington, DC, May, 1990.
38. Samuel Homola, *Backache: Home Treatment and Prevention* (West Nyack, NY: Parker Publishing Co., 1968).
39. National Institute on Disability and Rehabilitation Research, "Low Back Pain," *Rehab Brief* 9:9. Washington, DC, 1987.
40. Jane E. Brody "Personal Health," *The New York Times*, February 3, 1993.
41. Thomas J. Boudreau, "Physical Activity, Health and Social Policies," in Ferdinand Landry and William Orban, eds., *Physical Activity and Human Well-Being* (Miami: Symposium Specialists, 1978), p. 249.
42. William E. Schmidt, "Britain Puzzles Over a Peril: Crossing the Street," *The New York Times*, November 25, 1991.

43. Motor Vehicle Manufacturers Association, *Facts & Figures '92*, Detroit, 1992, p. 91.
44. Bastian und Theml, *op. cit.*
45. Joan Claybrook, *Retreat from Safety* (New York: Pantheon, 1984).
46. Carol A. MacLennan, "From Accident to Crash: The Auto Industry and the Politics of Injury," *Medical Anthropology Quarterly* 2 (1988):234.
47. "Threats: A Comparison," *The New York Times*, June 18, 1991.
48. Susan B. Baker, Stephen Teret and Eric M. Daub, "Injuries," in S. R. Levine and A. Lilienfeld, eds., *Epidemiology and Health Policy* (New York: Tavistock, 1987), pp. 177-206.
49. Elizabeth Horton, "Why Don't We Buckle Up?" *Science Digest* 93 (1985):22.
50. J. Peter Rothe, *The Trucker's World: Risk, Safety and Mobility* (New Brunswick, NJ: Transaction Publishers, 1991).
51. Ronald Smothers, "Employers Becoming Targets of Suits in the Fight to Halt Drunken Driving," *The New York Times*, December 24, 1991.
52. H. Laurence Ross and Graham Hughes, "Drunk Driving: What Not to Do," *The Nation* 243 (1986):663-664.
53. Joseph R. Gusfield, "Risky Roads," *Society* 28 (1991):10-16.
54. Ross and Hughes, *op. cit.*, p. 664.
55. Margaret Gallagher *et. al.*, "Effects of the 60 MPH Speed Limit on Rural Interstate Fatalities in New Mexico," *Journal of the American Medical Association* 262 (1989):2243-2245.
56. Gerd Hickmann und Klaus Dieter Kaser, *Trau keinem uber Tempo 30* (Stuttgart: Grunen im Landtag von Baden-Wurttemberg, 1988), p. 15.
57. Dieter Seifried, *Gute Argumente: Verkehr* (Munich: C.H. Beck, 1991).
58. Gallagher *et.al.*, *op. cit.*
59. Institut fur Angewandte Umweltforschung, *op. cit.*
60. John Adams, *Transport Planning: Vision and Practice* (London: Routledge and Kegan Paul, 1981), p. 263.
61. Matthew L. Wald, "How Dreams of Clean Air Get Stuck in Traffic," *The New York Times*, March 11, 1990.

CHAPTER 3

The Social Inequalities of Auto-Centred Transport

Cultural beliefs about the connections between individual freedom and automobility tend to obscure the role of social inequalities that diminish access to cars. Despite pervasive motorization a lot of people cannot afford a car, or find auto-dependence financially burdensome, or are not capable of driving a car. The auto and its spaces are apparently built to the specifications of one kind of person, as Edward Relph noted: "Modern landscapes seem to be designed for forty-year old healthy males driving cars."[1]

Despite the fact that auto-dominated transport is seen as democratic, in fact it disenfranchises many people. The young and the elderly, people with disabilities, women, and poor people are disproportionately excluded. Being transport-disadvantaged is clearly not a status that is equally or randomly distributed among groups in societies. A major empirical study of transport in Buffalo in the mid-1970s found that females, the elderly, the unemployed, and low-income persons were disproportionately carless.[2] The researchers also estimated that 49 percent of the U.S. population was carless in 1970. Of this 49 percent, 20 percent lived in households without cars and 29 percent did not drive because they were too young or too incapacitated by old age, even though they lived in households with cars. It is from this kind of data that John Adams generalized: "Estimates of the percentage of the population ever likely to qualify as car drivers, even given the improbable assumption of universal affluence, suggest that there will always be a minimum of 40 percent who can never have full, participating rights in a car-owning 'democracy'."[3] In the United States the 40 percent minimum amounts to about 100 million people. In most other nations the carless proportion of the population is even higher. For example, in West Germany it has been estimated that the auto-disenfranchised represent about 50 percent of the population.[4]

Just as auto transport limits access to many citizens, mass transit expands transport access. In 1984, 40 percent of all transit trips in the United States were made by riders from households earning less than

$10,000 a year; these households represented 25 percent of all households. In the same year women accounted for 62 percent of transit trips. Somewhat surprisingly, the aged are not over-represented among transit riders.[5] This is probably due to the fact that the aged are less likely to travel to work because many are retired. African-Americans are also more dependent on transit than are other Americans, probably because they are disproportionately represented in poor populations. A study in Baltimore found that 29 percent of trips to work by African-Americans were made by bus and 65 percent by auto; for other Americans in that city, only 9 percent of trips to work were by bus, while 87 percent were by auto.[6] According to the Census Bureau, for the United States in 1987, 29 percent of African-American households were without a car, truck, or van, while only 11 percent of all households were without a vehicle.

The Poor

According to data from the Census Bureau, in 1987, in the United States, only 11 percent of all occupied housing units were without a car, truck, or van; of households below the poverty line 38 percent were without a vehicle. In 1989, while 84.4 percent of all families in the U.S. owned at least one vehicle, 51.6 percent of families with incomes below $10,000 owned a vehicle.

While it is commonly recognized that poverty prevents many people from owning an auto, it is less commonly recognized that lack of access to an auto and to public transit is a contributing factor to unemployment and poverty. Although physical access to jobs (determined by a combination of worker and job locations, and available transport) historically has been socially maldistributed, changes in recent decades have given poor people special difficulties. Two students of these changes noted: "Postwar changes in urban ecology and transportation systems, while conferring significant improvements on the majority have almost certainly caused a *relative* deterioration in the access to job opportunities enjoyed by a significant fraction of the poor."[7]

The move to an auto-dominated transport system has penalized the poorest workers, adding yet another burden to their lives, as Glenn Yago noted:

> Skewing transportation toward highway spending has resulted in an unequal distribution of transportation

access on the basis of race, sex, income and class. Since
the McCone Commission first pointed to rail transit
abandonment as a probable cause of the Watts riot in
Los Angeles, the issue of access to transport in
metropolitan regions has been raised periodically, suggesting how the lack of physical mobility limits social
mobility.[8]

The conventional wisdom is that the middle class is the primary
source of mass transit subsidies. In fact, since mass transit is financed
principally from regressive taxes such as sales taxes, the burden falls
disproportionately on the poor. Additionally, the middle class is the
principal beneficiary of the newer mass transit systems such as the
California Bay Area's Rapid Transit, which largely serves middle
class commuters who travel from suburbs to San Francisco or Oak-
land to work.

The location of work opportunities has become decentralized as
jobs have been increasingly sited in suburbs and exurbs. In fact, the
decentralization of jobs into urban fringe areas led the massive suburbanization of the population of the United States in the mid-twentieth century.[9] Thus, there is a large and growing mismatch between
the residences of the urban poor and the location of jobs for which
they qualify. In the United States between 1960 and 1980 two-thirds
of all new jobs were located in suburban areas.[10] Access to these jobs
is difficult for the poor who reside in central cities. They cannot afford to relocate to the suburbs and public transport to the suburbs is
inadequate. Public transit predominantly serves the traditional commuter who travels from suburb to city in the morning and from the
city to suburb in the evening. Public transit service is lacking for the
reverse commuting done by the urban poor, which is city-to-suburb
in the morning and suburb-to-city in the evening. Also, the best
developed public transport is that which connects more affluent
residential suburbs with the core of the central city business district;
such paths often bypass poor areas. Thus, in the U.S. since World War
II, urban deconcentration and the development of auto-centred
transport have resulted in longer journeys to work for the
workingclass and minorities. Blue-collar and minority workers travel
farther and longer to work than the average worker, regardless of
residence.[11]

While it is extremely difficult for inner city poor persons to secure
decent jobs in suburbs, it is even more difficult for them to hold on to

the jobs. An example is the difficulties encountered in an on-the-job training programme for young male inner city "unemployables" in San Diego, most of whom were African-American and Latino. The researchers found that far from having less trouble with the law, their "incidence of arrests during the job was nearly double what it was before the job."[12] The chief source of the new problems the young men had with the law was transport. The men had a long reverse commute to make that was virtually impossible to do by public transit. Consequently, the number of the men owning cars rose after recruitment into the programme. This resulted in a sizeable increase in traffic citations and other problems with the law. Because the men were poor the cars they could afford were old ones and in bad repair—referred to by some as "ghettomobiles." Thus, they were more likely to be stopped for problems like malfunctioning tail lights and mufflers. Also, the situation was complicated by the fact that these were groups of young minority males travelling in beat-up cars into areas where they were not usually seen. They were prime targets for police suspicion. Furthermore, after being pulled over for a minor traffic infraction the men would often have their cars searched. Sometimes the search revealed small amounts of illegal drugs. The general public just does not recognize the difficult transport problems faced by poor persons, especially those who are also members of minority groups. These problems are compounded by auto-centred transport systems.

Those who can afford to own a car must also be able to bear the costs of its operation. According to data from the Bureau of Labor Statistics, vehicle purchases, gasoline and motor oil represented 11 percent of total expenditure for all consumer units in the U.S. in 1990, more than twice as much as health care expenditure. The costs of transport as a proportion of total personal expenditure has more than tripled in the United States since mass transit declined in the 1930s.[13] This increase places a special burden on the poor. According to 1988 data from the U.S. Census Bureau, poorer families have fewer vehicles that are driven fewer miles and consume less fuel than do better-off families. Despite these facts, in 1990, auto transport consumed a considerably higher *proportion*, over twice as high, of the incomes of poorer families than of the incomes of better-off families. In other nations a similar relationship exists between income level and proportion of income spent on auto transport. For example, in West Germany, those with low incomes spend 26.4 percent of their income on auto transport; those with middle incomes, 12.9 percent; those with high incomes, 7.5 percent.[14]

The costs of automobility are not the only way in which it disadvantages the poor. The deleterious health effects of auto pollution are differentially distributed within the population. Poor and minority households have higher-than-average exposure to air pollution because in many nations they are disproportionately concentrated in and near city centres, areas where traffic is most dense. In the U.S. in 1992, according to data from the Environmental Protection Agency, 57 percent of Latinos and 46 percent of African-Americans lived in areas polluted by carbon monoxide, compared to 34 percent of whites who lived in such areas. Autopsies done at the University of Southern California on 100 youths who died of violence or accidents showed that 80 percent had noticeable lung tissue abnormalities and 27 percent had severe lung lesions. Poor nutrition, smoking and a history of frequent infections may have contributed to these lesions. Nonetheless, the fact that all the youths were lower-class Latinos living in highly trafficked and polluted central Los Angeles could have also been a factor.[15] In cities like Los Angeles clean air has become a commodity that only the more affluent can afford.

Like the effects of pollution and other health costs of auto-centred transport, mortality from accidents is also socially distributed along class lines. For example, there are the 1970-72 data collected by the British Office of Population Censuses and Surveys. The mortality rate from all motor vehicle traffic accidents for men aged 15-64 was 84 percent higher for the two lowest social classes (out of a total of five classes) than it was for the two highest social classes. Among pedestrians only, the mortality from motor vehicle traffic accidents was six times higher for the lowest two social classes than it was for the highest two classes. Data from 1979-80 and 1982-83 from the same British Office demonstrated that child mortality from motor vehicle accidents showed the same social class disparities. Children of the two lowest social classes had a mortality rate from traffic accidents that was 2.3 times the mortality rate for children of the two highest classes. For child pedestrian mortality, the difference was even greater. Children of the two lowest social classes had a mortality rate from motor vehicle traffic accidents that was 3.2 times higher than the rate for children of the two highest classes.[16] The higher mortality rates for the lower social classes may be attributed to a number of factors, including the probabilities that members of the lower classes drive in more heavily trafficked areas that are not as well organized for traffic safety and that they drive older, less safe vehicles. The higher mortality rate for child pedestrians of the lower social classes may be due to the probabilities that they are more dependent on walking, less likely to be accompanied by an adult caregiver, and more likely to walk in areas that are not safe.[17]

Women

In the 1920s the auto provided those women who could afford it with the means to expand the horizons of their physical and social worlds. Some women used the car as a means of recruiting other women to the suffragette movement. The auto was a means of connecting widely dispersed rural homes to a community and thus freed many women from isolation. While in some respects the auto could be used as such a liberating technology, it did not free women from a gendered division of labour; ultimately, it simply extended the sphere of the home outward.

Today's urban transport is modulated by gender issues. The secondary position of women in the labour force is an important factor affecting their travel patterns. Because women's work is regarded as less important than men's work, because it often commands a lower wage, and because women have greater domestic responsibilities than men do, women tend to work closer to home and more often to use public transport. Women are less likely than men to have a driver's license. For example, in West Germany only 35 percent of license holders are women; just 50 to 55 percent of women have licenses, compared to 77 percent of men.[18] In Britain only one-third of women have licenses and only one-fourth have access to an auto when they need it.[19] According to the Department of Transportation, in the United States in 1991, 48.7 percent of drivers were females, up from 39.6 percent in 1963.

In addition to having less access to autos, women have different attitudes toward them than do men. In one West German survey significantly more men than women would let no one else drive their car.[20] In the United States, surveys show that an overwhelming majority of males would not give up their cars no matter how much mass transit was available, whereas the majority of women would give up their cars.[21] Another survey found that getting a license was equally important for girls and boys but unlike boys, girls were willing to use public transport after getting a license.[22] Additionally, the desire to drive at high speed is primarily a masculine one. According to a national poll in the United States, the average male claims to have driven over 100 miles per hour at some point, while only a small minority of women say that they have driven over 100 mph. The average woman claims that the fastest speed at which she has driven is 82 mph, while it is 106 mph for men.[23]

Additionally, research has demonstrated that "women are more, often significantly more, pro-transit and anti-car than men."[24] In West Germany in 1982, men used environmentally friendly transport (walking, biking, mass transit) for 42 percent of their trips, while women did for 60 percent of their trips.[25] For all journeys to work in the United States in 1985, women workers drove alone in their cars less frequently than men and women more frequently used public transit or walked. This is despite the fact that women are more concerned than men with the personal safety of public transit.[26] It is not clear whether women's attitudes about autos and public transit are an adaptive response to the fact that they have fewer options than men do, or whether these attitudes simply reflect personal preferences.

In the United States the increased homogenization of transport along with the dispersal of functional areas has affected women's work in the home. What is often touted as the transformation of household work into consumption of commodities rather than their production was facilitated by the auto. Rather than lessening home work, however, the auto actually transformed it. In the case of transport, "households have moved from the net consumption to the net production of transportation services, and housewives have moved from being the receiver of purchased goods to being the transporters of them."[27] Prior to auto hegemony, goods (at least necessities) were located not far from home and were often delivered. By the 1920s the burden of transport had shifted from the seller to the buyer. Thus, transport costs were externalized for the seller—they were shifted to the consumer.

Studies indicate that in the 1930s women spent about two hours a week on shopping. Some thirty years later the figure was eight hours a week. Time spent on all transport actually increased substantially.[28] Thus, being a chauffeur has become a principal role for the modern middle-class mother. As noted by Ruth Cowan, the auto is the medium through which the contemporary mother does "much of her most significant work" and in which she can most often be found.[29] The woman's role as driver functions to reconnect the community fragmented by automobility by providing links between home, on the one hand, and school, leisure sites, shopping, and friends, on the other hand.

Male domination of the world of the auto is indicated by the fact that it was not until 1991 that "the first truly comprehensive social history of the female driver" was published.[30] It was a welcome rejoinder to the cultural link between masculinity and driving—a link that sustains such negative stereotypes as the "woman driver"— clumsy, incompetent, and even dangerous. This stereotype lives despite its lack of empirical support. For example, U.S. Census Bureau data for 1989 demonstrated that, in fact, the least safe drivers were elderly men, followed by young men. The safest drivers were middle-aged women. The social history of female automobility by Virginia Scharff, while refreshing and revealing, uncritically accepts the world of the auto.[31] In reality, as our analysis demonstrates, auto-centred transport has been a mixed blessing for women.

Can there be an ecological and feminist perspective on transport? Presently, the auto creates a certain dilemma for some ecofeminists: "While the car constitutes a major environmental hazard, for women, at least in the short term, demanding 'equal access' to the car is an important assertion of their right to independence, mobility and physical safety."[32]

Jane Jacobs provided a feminist perspective to the literature on cities, although that was not her purpose.[33] She observed an ecology of neighbourhoods that was filled with a complex of activities like shopping, children playing, and so forth. These activities and the general quality of life in urban neighbourhoods have been adversely influenced by auto-centred transport, which is driven by the ideologies of primarily male city planners. Jacobs' perspective of a "lived domesticity" is one that could be used to improve city and transport planning.[34] Presently, transport policy is a heavily male-dominated field in which those who are auto mobile are prevalent. For example, of the leading figures in West German transport science only 1.3 percent are women.[35] This contributes to the fact that the interests of children and other non-motorized categories of people are under-represented in present policy making.

There is at the very least a fresh orientation towards transport among feminist Greens. In the face of the given gendered division of labour, this orientation emphasizes changes that will make women's transport needs a priority.[36] Examples include placing child care centres in proximity to workplaces and creating child-friendly social spaces and public transport—illustrative of the nurturance of a feminized urban space. This would further include urban spaces in which the routes to various activities would be shorter and more accessible to bicyclists, pedestrians, children, and adults caring for children. Mass transit and public spaces in general would be more woman user-friendly; for example, they would be made safer and with more and better public facilities, such as toilets and resting places.

A transport policy that includes a feminist orientation could address such interests, as well as give greater emphasis to softer, and less emphasis to harder, forms of mobility. Softer forms make less impact on other people and on the environment; walking and cycling are good examples. Harder forms make greater impacts on and carry greater risks to oneself, to others and the environment, as well as consuming more resources and energy; the auto is the best example.

The Disabled

The limits that a system based on individualized use of autos imposes on individual freedom and mobility are nowhere so apparent as in the case of citizens who are physically or mentally impaired. With the greying of the populations of industrialized societies and the capacity of medical technology to allow people with impairments to live long lives, this issue will become increasingly relevant. The goal of barrier-free public transport has been raised successfully by disability rights groups and has profound implications for an auto-centred transport system.[37] Paraplegics, as well as those who are sight impaired and others are generally excluded from driving. However, at the same time, mass transit systems often remain inaccessible to them.

Disability rights groups, with their emphasis on providing expanded means of mobility and access, raise the most profound and fundamental issues for transport systems. Many people with disabilities have special physical needs—they have non-standard bodies, so to speak. Such bodies require different transport modes and spaces; certainly they require a transport system that is more heterogeneous than our present one. The most democratic transport system is one that can accommodate the needs of the widest spectrum of bodies; one that allows people who use wheelchairs or are sight-impaired to move about freely. Even though the technological means for building such a transport system exists, it has yet to be developed. It is in this sense that disability rights movements can pose the most radical and progressive challenges for transport policy.

The Young and the Elderly

Perhaps since the dependence and relative powerlessness of children is taken for granted in all areas of life, their special problems with regard to automobility go unnoticed. Since they cannot yet participate in a system of automobility, children are dependent on being chauffeured by their elders, or must make do with often inadequate mass transit, or with walking and biking—both of which are most difficult and somewhat dangerous in auto space. Thus, it is not surprising that an auto driver's license represents an important rite of passage in industrial cultures. Since spatial arrangements are taken for granted and children are powerless, the child's disadvantage in the politics of space remains uninteresting for adults and adult city planners. Yet the inability of children to move safely through auto space and the auto's appropriation of spaces in which children play, particularly poor children in inner city areas, are important forms of social inequity.

Independent geographic mobility has long been used by child development experts as a measure of human maturation. In the 1940s, even slow-maturing children were expected to be able to go to familiar places on a bus, or to go downtown, getting on and off by themselves, by the time they were 9 years old. With today's auto-centred transport, many youths do not have their first solo excursion beyond their neighbourhoods until they are permitted to drive.[38]

In an empirical study of British children aged seven to fifteen years, comparing 1990 to 1971, it was found that the space usable by children had been reduced considerably. The principal reason given by parents for the decreased independent mobility of their children was increased street traffic. The analysis by the researchers concluded that "the increase in the personal freedom and choice arising from widening car ownership has been gained at the cost of freedom and choice for children."[39] The result has been increased parental escort of school children, especially in autos, at a considerable increase in cost—between 10 billion and 20 billion pounds in 1990.

The problem of children's mobility and safety being reduced by autos has been confronted in some local areas. For example, in Odense, Denmark, a major restructuring of roadways has been going on since 1981. The most common changes have been the creation of slow-speed zones, road narrowings, and separate pedestrian and cycle paths. Reported accidents were reduced by 85 percent as a result of the changes.[40]

At the other end of the life cycle, elderly persons face different problems with automobility than do children. Surveys over recent decades show that transport is one of the two most serious problems faced by the elderly—the other is health and health care.[41] In 1987, according to Census Bureau data only 11 percent of all occupied housing units in the United States were without a car, truck, or van, but 24 percent of units occupied by the elderly (65 years and over) were without a vehicle.

The elderly face substantial physical, financial, and environmental obstacles to auto travel. Of these three sets of problems it is the environmental ones, including how roadways discourage older drivers, that are most amenable to amelioration. Additionally, the elderly face extraordinary environmental barriers to other means of travel. Public transit is often not accessible and walking is made more dangerous by traffic conditions that favour the auto, including wide roads that have brief green lights for cross streets. Also, while walking is a viable form of transport and exercise for the elderly, pedestrian facilities are inadequate or nonexistent in many parts of the United States. Additionally, personal safety while travelling is a far greater concern for women and for elderly persons than it is for men and for younger persons. This is a prime factor that leads many women and elderly to shun public transit, especially subways.

One of the few examples of sensitivity to the transport needs of the elderly is the retirement community. In the design of these planned communities, bicycles, adult tricycles, and pedestrian movement are favoured.

Conclusion

The inequities of any transport system can be conceptualized on a number of levels. What disadvantages are there for different kinds of participants? To what extent are special abilities and resources required in order to be fully mobile in a given system, for instance, the ability to drive and the availability of an auto? Does a system favour particular forms of mobility to the disadvantage of others? Are some citizens effectively disenfranchised by the requirements of a given system? How does the dominance of one means of transport shape the politics of space—who gets to use what space for what purpose?

On another level one may ask how one's location in various social hierarchies—for example, those based on social class, age, and gender—affect access to, or the cost of participating in a given transport system. How will one's social location shape how much of the socioenvironmental costs of a given transport system one will be forced to bear?

The conventional wisdom is that accessibility to autos is so common in modern societies so as to leave out no sizeable groups of people. For example, Werner Polster and Klaus Voy contend that auto ownership in West Germany is so widespread that only a small minority of people has no access to an auto.[42] It is true that about two-thirds of adults in West Germany own an auto. However, there are several problems with this reasoning. One-third of the adult population *is* a sizeable minority—to which all non-adults must be added. Also, as the demographic structure of society changes to include a larger elderly population the one-third minority is likely to increase. Furthermore, as a system, auto-centred transport does not distribute the costs of auto ownership equitably. For example, auto noise and pollution tend to be concentrated geographically, with the most auto-dependent populations in the suburbs suffering less from these costs and the least auto-dependent populations in the inner cities suffering more.

Polster and Voy, as does Scharff, view the auto as contributing to the emancipation of women. However, they fail to recognize gendered sources of inequity in an auto-centred system. Perhaps the biggest source of inequity is women's secondary position in the paid labour force, which leads to women carrying the burden of household transport—ferrying children and shopping. Thus, while the auto has contributed to women's geographic, social, and political emancipation, that contribution may have topped out. Additionally, the auto has done little to mitigate the secondary position of women in the labour force.

At first glance, auto-centred transport systems are highly democratic and help to level social differences. While there is certainly truth to this, there are major unexamined questions with regard to the democracy of auto ownership. Autos are costly to buy and to operate, they impose their social and environmental costs unequally, and they dominate the social organization of space to the disadvantage of many people. The poor, the elderly, the young, women, and the residents of inner cities are the principal groups who are disproportionately disadvantaged.

Furthermore, the auto has an additional negative impact on group relations in contemporary societies. The infrastructures of auto space are used to promote the segregation of classes and races in contemporary cities, at least in the United States. The built environment of the modern city consists largely of freeways, parking lots, and skyscrapers (see Chapter 7). The skyscrapers, whether residential or commercial, are made highly secure through the elaboration of private security forces, sophisticated surveillance technology and telecommunications, and fort-like constructions. These bunker cities add significantly to the personal isolation of the individual and the spatial apartheid of social groups. Mike Davis analyzed how the processes of redevelopment in Los Angeles have created a fortress city in which, for example, freeways become moats that function as physical barriers between the territories of African-Americans, Latinos, and Anglos.[43] While clearly not the most important factor involved in this situation, the auto is a key technology in fostering and sustaining it. As Peter Calthorpe has noted, "the auto allows the ultimate segregations in our culture—old from young, home from job and store, rich from poor and owner from renter."[44]

NOTES

1. Edward Relph, *Rational Landscapes and Humanistic Geography* (London: Croom Helm, 1981), p. 196.
2. Robert E. Paaswell and Wilfred W. Recker, *Problems of the Carless* (New York: Praeger, 1978), pp. 2, 44, 170.
3. John Adams, *Transport Planning: Vision and Practice* (London: Routledge and Kegan Paul, 1981), p. 89.
4. Helmut Holzapfel, "Steigende Mobilitat—Raum gewinn oder Raum vernichtung?" in Jobst Kraus, Horst Sackstetter, und Willi Wentsch, eds., *Auto, Auto Uber Alles?* (Freiburg: Dreisam Verlag, 1987), pp. 111-119.
5. Gordon J. Fielding "Transit in American Cities," in Susan Hanson, ed., *The Geography of Urban Transportation* (New York: The Guilford Press, 1986), p. 236.
6. Susan Hanson and Margo Schwab, "Describing Disaggregate Flows: Individual and Household Activity Patterns," in Susan Hanson, ed., *The Geography of Urban Transportation* (New York: The Guilford Press, 1986), p. 175.
7. John F. Kain and John R. Myer, "Transportation and Poverty," in Harold Hochman, ed., *The Urban Economy* (New York: W.W. Norton, 1976), p. 181.
8. Glenn Yago, "U.S. Lacks Transportation Policy," *In These Times* 9 (1985):7.
9. John F. Kain, "The Distribution and Movement of Jobs and Industry," in James Q. Wilson, ed., *The Metropolitan Enigma: Inquiries into the Nature and Dimensions of America's "Urban Crisis,"* (Garden City, NY: Doubleday/Anchor, 1970), pp. 1-43.
10. Michael Renner, "Rethinking the Role of the Automobile," (Washington, DC: Worldwatch Institute, Paper No. 84, 1988), p. 47.
11. Glenn Yago, "The Sociology of Transport," *Annual Review of Sociology* 9 (1983):171-190.

12. Harland Padfield and Roy Williams, *Stay Where You Were: A Study of Un-employables in Industry* (Philadelphia: J.B. Lippincott Company, 1973), p. 130.
13. Yago, 1985, *op. cit.*
14. Institut fur Angewandte Umweltforschung, *Der Auto Knigge* (Reinbeck bei Hamburg: Rowohlt Verlag, 1990), p. 45.
15. Eric Mann, "L.A.'s Smogbusters," *The Nation* 251 (1990):257.
16. *Health on the Move,* "The Policy Statement of the Transport and Health Study Group" (Birmingham: Public Health Alliance, 1991), p. 20.
17. Mayer Hillman, "Health Transport Policy," in Peter Draper, ed., *Health Through Public Policy* (London: Merlin Press), pp. 82-91; Alison Quick, *Unequal Risks: Accidents and Social Policy* (London: Socialist Health Association, 1991).
18. Institut fur Angewandte Umweltforschung, *op. cit.*, p. 210.
19. Women and Transport Forum, "Women on the Move: How Public is Public Transport?" in Cheris Kramarae, ed., *Technology and Women's Voices: Keeping in Touch* (New York: Routledge and Kegan Paul), pp. 116-134.
20. Wolfgang Sachs, *Die Liebe Zum Automobil* (Reinbeck bei Hamburg: Rohwohlt, 1990).
21. Adrienna Gianturco, "Die Verkehrspolitik der USA unter Feministichen Aspecten," in Paul Beekmans *et. al.*, eds., *Welche Freiheit Brauchen Wir? Zum Psychologie der AutoMobilen Gesellschaft* (Berlin: VAS in der Elefanten Press, 1989), p. 131.
22. R. Stoddart, "Erfahrung of Young Drivers," in J. Peter Rothe, ed., *Rethinking Young Drivers* (British Columbia: Insurance Corporation of British Columbia, 1987), pp. 131-198.
23. George Gallup, Jr. and Frank Newport, "Americans Do Love Their Cars," *San Francisco Chronicle*, May 6, 1991.
24. Sandra Rosenbloom, "Women's Travel Issues: The Research and Policy Environment," in *Women's Travel Issues: Research Needs and Priorities* (Washington, DC: U.S. Department of Transportation, 1978), p. 22.
25. Rolf Monheim, "Policy Issues in Promoting the Green Modes," in Rodney Tolley, ed., *The Greening of Urban Transport: Planning for Walking and Cycling in Western Cities* (London: Belhaven Press, 1991), pp. 134-158.
26. Larry G. Richards and Ira D. Jacobson, "Perceived Safety and Security in Transportation Systems as Determined by the Gender of the Traveller," in *Women's Travel Issues: Research Needs and Priorities* (Washington, DC: U.S. Department of Transportation, 1978), pp. 441-478.
27. Ruth Schwartz Cowan, "More Work for Mother: Technology and Housework in the U.S.A.," in Les Levidow and Bob Young, eds., *Science, Technology and the Labour Process: Marxist Studies* (Atlantic Highlands, NJ: Humanities Press, Volume 2, 1985), p. 98.
28. *Ibid.*, p. 104.
29. Ruth Schwartz Cowan, *More Work for Mother: The Ironies of Household Technology from the Open Hearth to the Microwave* (New York: Basic Books, Inc., 1983), p. 84.
30. Joe Queenan, "Drive, She Said," *The New York Times Book Review*, March 17, 1991, p. 12.
31. Virginia Scharff, *Taking the Wheel: Women and the Coming of the Motor Age* (New York: The Free Press, 1991).
32. Judy Wajcman, *Feminism Confronts Technology* (University Park: The Pennsylvania State University Press, 1991), p. 135.

33. Jane Jacobs, *The Death and Life of Great American Cities* (Baltimore: Penguin Books, 1965).
34. Marshall Berman, *All That is Solid Melts into Air: The Experience of Modernity* (New York: Penguin Books, 1988), pp. 322-323.
35. Ulrike Lichtenthaler/Reutter und Ute Preis, "Frauen Unterwegs-Wege fur eine weibliche stadt," in Paul Beekmans *et. al.*, eds., *Welche Freiheit Brauchen Wir? Zum Psychologie der AutoMobilen Gesellschaft* (Berlin: VAS in der Elefanten Press, 1989), pp. 114-128.
36. Paul Beekmans *et. al.*, eds., *Welche Freiheit Brauchen Wir? Zum Psychologie der AutoMobilen Gesellschaft* (Berlin: VAS in der Elefanten Press, 1989).
37. Peter E.S. Freund and Meredith B. McGuire, *Health, Illness, and the Social Body: A Critical Sociology* (Englewood Cliffs, NJ: Prentice Hall, 1991).
38. K.H. Schaeffer and Elliott Sclar, *Access for All: Transportation and Urban Growth* (Baltimore: Penguin, 1975), p. 111.
39. Mayer Hillman, John Adams, and John Whitelegg, *One False Move—A Study of Children's Independent Mobility* (London: Policy Studies Institute, 1990), p. 106.
40. Ole Nielsen, "Safe Routes to School in Odense, Denmark," in Rodney Tolley, ed., *The Greening of Urban Transport: Planning for Walking and Cycling in Western Cities* (London: Belhaven Press, 1990), pp. 255-265.
41. Frances M. Carp, "Improving the Functional Quality of Housing and Environments for the Elderly through Transportation," in Thomas O. Byerts, Sandra C. Howell, and Leon A. Pastalan, eds., *Environmental Context of Aging* (New York: Garland Press, 1979), pp. 127-146; Frances M. Carp, 1988, "Significance of Mobility for the Well-Being of the Elderly," in *Transportation in an Aging Society* (Washington, DC: National Research Council, Special Report 218, 1988), pp. 1-20.
42. Werner Polster und Klaus Voy, "Eigenheim und Automobil-Materielle Fundamente der Lebensweise," pp. 263-320 in Klaus Voy, Werner Polster, und Claus Thomasberger, eds., *Gesellschaftliche Transformationsprozesse und Materielle Lebensweise* (Marburg: Metropolis-Verlag, 1991).
43. Mike Davis, *City of Quartz: Social Struggles in Postmodern Los Angeles* (London: Verso, 1990).
44. Peter Calthorpe, "The Post-Suburban Metropolis," *Whole Earth Review*, No. 73, Winter, 1991, p. 45.

CHAPTER 4

The Globalization of Auto Hegemony

Since its introduction in the latter years of the nineteenth century the auto has become a global commodity. Today, the number of autos produced daily in the world is approaching the number of babies who are born each day. The auto was popularized in North America and Western Europe, where it was first patented in 1886. There were only 8,000 autos in the United States in 1900, one for every 9,500 persons; by 1930 the auto fleet was up to 23 million, one for every 5.3 Americans. Since then the U.S. auto market has slowly reached saturation (it is now overwhelmingly a replacement market); in 1991 there were 145 million autos, one for every 1.7 persons.[1] While the auto is now a global commodity, its diffusion remains highly uneven, as was noted in Chapter 1. In addition to discussing the twentieth century diffusion of the auto in this chapter, we give attention to the two major world areas that remain unsaturated by auto-dominated transport—the Third World and the former centrally-planned economies.

Diffusion of the Auto

The auto's diffusion in the twentieth century was based on two major innovations—one in the realm of production and the other in the realm of consumption. On the production side, mass production of the auto was made possible by Henry Ford's combination of the assembly line technology with the division of labour scheme of Frederick Taylor.[2] Taylorism, or "scientific management," divided the tasks of production into their most minute and mundane operations and then standardized their optimal performance by workers. It represented a major transition from old-style craft production to new-style mass production. Ford's achievement in this area set the pace for all of twentieth century industrial expansion and it was important enough to gain the appellation of Fordism. On the consumption side the major innovation was in marketing; it was made by the manager of Ford's chief competition, Alfred P. Sloan at General Motors. Sloan introduced the two major selling strategies of the auto industry: annual styling changes and different products for targeted market segments or sub-groups of the population. Both of Sloan's strategies remain major stimulants of consumer demand for autos.[3]

Sloan's innovation of the yearly model helped to stimulate consumption through surface changes that each year became obsolete. Such stylistic changes, including increased size, have shaped the use of auto technology. Karal Marling observed that "in practice then, a business once ruled by engineering took on the trappings of the dressmaker's salon, the notion of the obsolescence of a serviceable product was transferred from the clothing of the upper class to the single most important industrial product made in America."[4] The flux of style and the changes not only gave designers a new role but affected the use of the technology itself—for instance, less durable cars were built.

While one should not overstate its role, advertising has played an important role in promoting car ownership, especially in its early history. The market for auto consumption in the United States began to approach saturation in the late 1920s. In 1926, market research showed that those who could afford to own a car already owned one. By 1927, car sales and production dropped sharply for the first time. Thus, it was no coincidence that it was during the 1920s when the auto industry became one of the heaviest advertisers in magazines, newspapers and other media, as it has continued to be since then.[5] Such advertising is a primary way to stimulate consumer demand for autos. Individualism is a generic theme in auto advertisements while other appeals may be pitched to the particular *zeitgeist*. Magazine advertisements for cars in the late 1920s and the 1930s (the Great Depression) stressed comfort and dependability, though the appeal of the freedom of the open road was also a theme. Many advertisements of the 1950s (the Baby Boom years) appealed to family values (e.g., station wagons) while others emphasized sexual appeal.[6] Commercials of the 1960s appealed to youth and freedom while in the 1970s the small practical car briefly asserted itself in response to the oil embargo. However, the 1980s saw a return to affluent, streamlined, and high-tech images—cars were advertised as icons of sexuality, aggression, and even spirituality.

The United States became the world locus of automobility not only because of the innovations of Ford but also because of the dispersion of its population at the time. Although the auto's history began in Western Europe during the latter quarter of the nineteenth century, auto transport really took off in the United States in the first quarter of the twentieth century. This was due in large measure to the fact that the U.S. population was considerably more dispersed (living in small towns and on farms) than that of the comparably industrialized nations of Western Europe—Germany and Britain. It was not until the 1920 census that the urban population of the U.S. became a majority—and then only about 51 percent of the nation's people lived in cities and suburbs. Moreover, at the time, the U.S. had the poorest rural and intercity transport system among industrialized nations. Rail travel has never been as widespread in the U.S. as it has been in Western Europe: "Even in their heyday around 1920, the U.S. railroads on a per capita basis carried only a third of the passengers of the British and German railroads, or a fifth of the passengers of the Swiss system."[7]

The combination of a dispersed and growing population, on the one hand, and inadequate rail transport, on the other hand, presented a unique niche in which the auto flourished. This niche was the market exploited by Ford and other U.S. auto makers, who realized its mass potential: "The automobile, while invented in the city and used there as a rich man's toy, grew to prominence as a mature everyday transportation mode in rural areas and from these invaded the city and transformed it."[8]

Currently seven nations in the developed world dominate the realm of automobility: France, Italy, Sweden, Britain, Japan, Germany, and the United States. These seven nations account for the great majority of auto production and auto consumption and they are home to all the transnational auto companies.[9] The auto more than any other commodity has been the basis of the extension of capitalism throughout the world in the twentieth century. Transnational auto corporations have successfully extended their reach into the Third World and have the potential for repeating that success in Eastern Europe and the former Soviet Union.

The Ford Motor Company established its first international subsidiary in Canada in 1903 and it was the first auto producer to become a successful transnational corporation. Before World War I the Ford Company had production facilities in Canada, England, and France. By 1929 Ford was assembling autos in twenty-one nations and General Motors in sixteen; the two companies dominated the world market. In 1929, North America accounted for 89.5 percent of world passenger car production, Western Europe accounted for 10.3 percent, and centrally planned economies accounted for 0.2 percent.[10]

By 1938 nearly one-fourth of Ford's production and a bit less than one-fifth of GM's was in other nations.[11]

The post-World War II period has witnessed further internationalization of auto production and consumption, as the reconstructed industries of Europe and Japan joined American companies in spreading around the globe, especially in the Third World. By 1973 TNC's were directly responsible for about 90 percent of the over one million autos produced in the Third World—in Argentina, Brazil, India, and Mexico.[12]

European and Japanese auto production has continued to grow, as has Third World production. Between 1950 and 1991, the share of world motor vehicle production held by the U.S. fell from 75.7 percent to 19.0 percent. Europe's share of world motor vehicle production rose between 1950 and 1991 from 18.8 percent to 37.9 percent, Japan's share rose from 0.3 percent to 28.5 percent, Canada's share rose from 3.7 percent to 4.1 percent, and all other countries (except the U.S.) rose from 1.5 percent to 10.5 percent.[13] Japan's auto industry has eclipsed the U.S. industry in productivity and now represents the leading edge in production technology. The Fordist mass production system pioneered in the United States has been outperformed by the Japanese model of just-in-time inventory, batch production, and lean manufacturing. Currently, for example, each GM worker produces about thirteen cars a year while each Toyota worker produces forty-five a year.[14]

The globalization of auto production since the 1960s has involved the following principal processes: (1) decline of U.S. dominance; (2) integration of worldwide operations; (3) competitive interpenetration of markets; (4) the geographic separation of operations. The result is that today "nearly identical cars are assembled at various sites using components produced in different countries," enabling auto TNC's "to take advantage of local production conditions to maximize worldwide profits."[15] Thus, Toyota and Honda are, in the mid-1990s, developing the first truly global manufacturing system in the auto industry. The goal is to be able to make "world cars" anywhere that can be sold anywhere. One example is the Toyota plant in Kentucky that makes cars with steering on the right for shipment to Japan and Britain.[16]

Two areas of the world remain unsaturated markets for the auto—the Third World plus Eastern Europe and the former Soviet Union. In the more developed First World, largely in Western Europe and North America, there were only about two persons per car in

1990. In the less developed Second World, comprised of the formerly centrally-planned economies of Eastern Europe and the U.S.S.R., there were about eleven persons per auto. In the developing nations of the Third World—the bulk of Africa, Asia, and Latin America— there were about sixty-seven persons per auto. Thus, auto density in the Third World is only about one-thirtieth what it is in the First World, largely because much of the Third World remains poor and economically underdeveloped; in a word, cars are too costly. In the Second World, the former centrally-planned economies, auto density is only one-sixth what it is in the First World. Lower auto density in the former CPE's is due to two interrelated factors: lack of stimulation of consumption owing to political decisions and a somewhat lower overall level of development. Cars were not promoted there.

By the end of the 1970s, the auto markets in the United States and Northwestern Europe were saturated and since then it has been in the Third World, Eastern Europe and the former Soviet Union where the potential for new markets exists. The potential is substantial, as one analyst noted: "Analysts expect the European car fleet to double in the next twenty years and more than double in Asia and Latin America."[17] As an example of the possible volume of auto sales there are 100 million middle-class Indians who can now afford inexpensive compacts.[18] The fastest growth rates in auto consumption are in the Third World. In Latin America the number of passenger cars has been increasing at an annual rate of 14 percent; in Asia, 15 percent; in Africa, 7 percent. By comparison the number of cars has been increasing at annual rates of 6.5 percent in North America and 3.5 percent in Europe.[19]

The Third World

As indicated earlier, there are enormous discrepancies in car consumption between North and South. For most Third World citizens the auto is not an economically feasible means of transport. The growth in auto consumption in the Third World has been restricted to the relatively small elite and middle-class sectors. Auto consumption by these classes has had an adverse impact on the availability of public transport options for the masses. The historic pattern of rather thoughtless direct transfer of technology such as the auto from North to South has been a problematic undertaking, in which the major gain to the South has been learning what mistakes to avoid. Three transport specialists noted in their review of such mistaken efforts:

It is apparent that solutions from developed countries are often transplanted to developing countries with little adaption or consideration for the differences in needs, values, resource availability, climate, etc. Such transplants may typically use imported technology based on the capital/labor mix optimal in developed countries, require skills, foreign exchange, or other resources that are in short supply, and fail to take advantage of resources that are really plentiful. The blame for such uncreative transfers of solutions from developed countries may often lie with the imported consultants and experts, although the developing countries may also insist on "modern" solutions (e.g., jet airliners, and automated factories), that they associate with the developed state. While developing countries undoubtedly can learn much from the developed ones, the most useful lessons may often be the negative ones, i.e., what mistakes to avoid.[20]

Unfortunately, the learning that results from the effort to implant developed technology comes at some cost to Third World nations, including material and social damage to local infrastructures.

The damage done by the inappropriate transfer of technology has added considerably to the transport problems of Third World nations. The general nature and consequences of transport problems in Third World cities were itemized by the World Bank in 1986:

Most of the cities in the developing countries face severe transport problems. Road congestion is spreading, the movement of people and goods is slowing to a crawl, and transport costs are escalating. The result has been a serious decline in productivity and city efficiency, a drain on city and national budgets, and a strain on urban institutions. The transport crisis also takes a human toll. Statistics indicate that traffic accidents are a primary cause of death in the developing world.[21]

Of course there are causes in addition to the inappropriate transfer of technology behind Third World transport problems. Third World cities face more serious transport problems than do cities in the rest of the world for other reasons as well, including a lack of resources, relatively weak central governments, and rapid unmanaged growth.

The problems of traffic congestion in Third World cities may be greater than they are in the cities of the developed world. Auto traffic in the Third World is confined to rapidly growing urban areas, creating massive congestion and pollution. For example, by 1980 Mexico City had more autos than New York City, and Sao Paulo more than London.[22] It is conventionally known that cities like Los Angeles in the developed world have very high pollution levels. In fact, Mexico City considerably outdistances Los Angeles in levels of auto-generated air pollution. World Bank data show that in 1989 Mexico City was exposed to 4.4 million tons of all man-made pollutant emissions and that 76 percent were attributable to motor vehicles. In 1985, Los Angeles was exposed to 3.5 million tons of pollutants, 63 percent of which were produced by motor vehicles.[23] Older, poorly-maintained autos that use lower-quality fuel are more likely to be driven in Third World countries. The principal plaza in Mexico City is one example of the damage done by the wholesale adoption of auto-centred transport in the Third World. What used to be a popular and pleasant place to walk and talk is now "filled with deafening traffic and the air is blue with car exhaust—trying to walk is more dangerous than driving."[24]

Research has demonstrated that there is a general worsening of urban air quality in the Third World. According to one World Bank researcher worsening conditions in Third World cities will affect about one-eighth of the world's population in the near future: "Without effective measures to curb pollutant emissions from motor vehicles, some 500 million city dwellers in developing countries will become exposed to unhealthy and dangerous levels of air pollution by the turn of the century."[25] Already, it is estimated that 60 percent of the residents of Calcutta have pollution-related respiratory disorders.[26]

Although data is lacking it is probably the case that death by auto accident is more common in the Third World than it is in developed nations—if deaths are standardized for auto use rates. The mix of types of traffic in Third World cities—streets are clogged with pedestrians and animal-drawn vehicles as well as motorized vehicles—and their inadequate (for auto traffic) roadways contribute to accidents:

> Death on the highways is common at all ages—and not, as in the West, as the result of accidents between

cars, which are items of extreme luxury in Rwanda. Of course, the overloaded taxi-buses routinely cut blind corners along the twisting Chinese-built north-south highway, and every few days one will end up in a tangle of metal with another car. Yet most accidents are with pedestrians; the peasants use the paved, single-lane highway as a footpath through their densely populated hills. They do so even at night when they become invisible, wrapped in dark clothes and leading brown cattle, and they do not seem to understand the power of several tons of hurtling steel.[27]

Such accidental deaths are another adverse consequence of the direct transfer of auto technology to Third World nations without adequate regard for local conditions.

Mobility is a particular problem for poorer people in Third World countries. There, the increasing cutbacks in the public sector because of debt repayment, coupled with population growth in urban areas that outdistances the availability of public transport, deprives many people of any form of mobility except walking. The burden of developing an auto-centred transport system falls on the poor but benefits the more affluent: "In much of the Third World, the resources of entire nations are marshalled to build and maintain a transportation system that serves only a disparately small share of the population."[28] In the Third World the elitist nature of automobility is becoming more and more apparent. The promise of freedom and mobility that the car helped to fulfil for many ordinary people in the United States and Europe is not accessible to most Third World citizens, whose needs are for food, shelter, and far less expensive means of transport.

According to the United Nations, the use of petroleum and other resources and the need to import a great deal of material contributes to the foreign debts of Third World nations:

> For non oil-producing, non-industrialized developing countries which represent the vast majority of developing countries, petrol consumption by automobiles represents well over 50 percent of the total petroleum consumption. Energy consumption by these countries contributes largely to their foreign currency disbursements and to their balance of payment deficits.[29]

An extreme example is Haiti, where one in 200 people owns a car, yet at least one-third of the country's imports are fuel and transport equipment.[30]

Passenger cars in the Third World use a large share of the public infrastructure but offer limited capacity to carry people. In 1980, Mexico City had 1.6 million cars and 18,500 buses. The buses accounted for 51 percent of all motorized trips and the autos accounted for only 19 percent.[31] Overall, autos in Mexico City comprise 97 percent of total transport units but make only 16 percent of the total trips. This is a highly energy-inefficient system. Autos use 66 percent of total gasoline consumption while public transport uses less than 22 percent.[32]

Not only do many Third World governments subsidize auto transport and the auto industry at the expense of alternatives, so do world banking institutions. Of the amount that the World Bank loaned for urban transport projects in the Third World in 1972-85, 49 percent went to roads, 17 percent to buses, 16 percent to rail systems, 12 percent to road traffic management, 5 percent to road and rail technical assistance, and 1 percent to pedestrian facilities.[33] Non-motorized forms of travel such as improved bicycles (e.g., by using light metal) and carts have received virtually no subsidy. Thus, alternative transport, which is viewed as "backward," is sacrificed to the auto. Yet, in Third World nations, bicycles are a source of jobs, foreign exchange, and generate entrepreneurial activities such as vending, scrap collecting, and delivery services. Bicycle manufacture and maintenance are labour intensive enterprises. Bicycles also contribute to small scale business in economically developed nations and their contribution could be expanded.[34]

Because of government support for the wholesale introduction of auto technology, many Latin American cities have become caricatures of auto-centred cities in the United States.[35] Cities such as Caracas have almost unimaginable journeys to and from work (up to seven hours per day), elaborate freeways without adequate feeder arterials that result in massive congestion, and highways that stop abruptly at the edges of old city centres because of lack of space. These cities could benefit from improved bus service, bicycle and jitney use, and other less energy-resource intensive modes of transport.

The growth of auto-centred transport in the Third World brings into sharp relief issues of social inequality, the inappropriate use of transport technology, and the limits of globalizing such an energy-resource intensive and environmentally unfriendly system. The ideal of a motorized world built in the image of Southern California is simply not materially feasible on a global scale:

> The American experience, desirable or undesirable, is not repeatable, because the conditions in which it occurred are not repeatable. The cities of the world that exist now and which were built before significant numbers of their inhabitants owned cars, have, with few exceptions, neither the undeveloped land, nor the fuel, nor the money necessary to follow the American example.[36]

The continuing diffusion of auto-centred transport systems into the Third World is a major contributor to its ongoing social and fiscal crises. Yet the system is seen as an icon of modernity.

Governments in Third World countries are eagerly adopting the auto as a primary means of transport. Auto mobility is viewed as a sign and means of economic development. Malaysia's experience with its government's "National Car Project" in the 1980s is an example of the huge costs involved in developing an auto industry. Overall, Malaysians have paid more than $200 million so that 1 percent of them can drive a Malaysian-made auto.[37] The auto is an upmarket product that costs more than the average Malaysian house. In addition to sinking funds into production of the car, the government allocated billions to new road and bridge construction, while cutting expenditure for rail and bus transport. Despite this public investment (and government taxation of other, imported, cars), the Malaysian car faces immense challenges and is now under Japanese management. Local critics argue that the experience demonstrates the folly of industrial mega-projects for poor and small nations.

While most urban centres in the Third World have allowed free rein to the auto some cities have restricted its use. One successful example of diversifying transport in the Third World is Curitiba, Brazil, a city of 1.6 million. Beginning in the 1970s, the city adopted a series of transport-related measures, including improved bus transit, cycleways and pedestrian ways, and integration of transport and zoning policies, in which higher densities were encouraged along major arterials and a mix of jobs, homes, and services were included in local areas. Additional policies have included traffic calming schemes and infill, in which new development is sited in the existing city rather than sprawling outward. Several improvements have been attributed to these policies, including the facts that Curitiba's rate of accidents per vehicle is now the lowest of Brazilian cities and its gasoline consumption per vehicle is 30 percent less than in other Brazilian cities of its size. Finally, residents of Curitiba spent about 10 percent of their incomes on transport, one of the lowest such rates in Brazil. This is despite the fact that the city's auto ownership rate is high by Brazilian standards—second only to Brasilia's.[38]

However, efforts to curtail auto use and to recast auto technology in order to reduce pollution and other social costs need to focus on the heart of the problem: the industrialized nations of the North. To cite just one example, carbon dioxide is the most important component of the gases causing the greenhouse effect. The United States, Japan, and Germany account for 30 percent of the world's CO_2 emissions, while containing only 8.5 percent of the world's population. China, India, and Indonesia, the most populous Third World nations, account for only 14.5 percent of world CO_2 emissions, while having 41 percent of the world's population.[39]

The Case of East Germany

Before reunification West Germany was considerably more auto-dependent and less public transit oriented than was East Germany. For example, in 1983, public transport trips per person were 540 in East Berlin and 389 in West Berlin—28 percent less.[40] In West Germany, there were 2.1 people per car in 1988; in East Germany, 4.6.[41] A different, denser social organization of space, together with higher costs of automobility and cheap mass transit had dampened but not inhibited the growth of automobility in the former East Germany. Before reunification East Germany had reached levels of automobility that approximated that of its Western counterpart in the 1960s and early 1970s. Since the 1960s, East Germany had been moving towards a transport system based on the auto as the primary means of mobility. As real income rose so did automobile ownership. Even prior to reunification East Germany had developed some of the changes in the structure of space that the auto facilitated in West Germany.[42] The large cities of the former German Democratic Republic did not differ significantly from their Western counterparts with regard to highway structure and satellite settlements at the urban periphery.[43] Nonetheless, until now, cars in Central and Eastern Europe were primarily used for social and recreational purposes, not for commuting.

Despite the pre-reunification rhetoric the course of East German transport development was more similar than different to that of West Germany.[44] Indeed, except for the socialist ideal of subsidizing basic material necessities (food, shelter, transport), East German socialism was not opposed to automobility, nor had it developed any systematic socialist transport policy.[45] This particular example of socialism failed to provide a vision or concrete illustration of a pleasurable and efficient mass transit—or of any ecologically friendly transport system. One major difference that existed between East and West Germany may be that East Germany failed to give any consideration to the social and ecological consequences of transport and other technologies adopted from the West. In West Germany there has been at least some attention given to protecting the environment and current comparisons of East and West Germany give evidence of this fact.

The story of the Trabant, East Germany's now notorious auto, is illustrative of former East/West differences. Reunification imposed strict fees on the Trabi because it lacks a catalytic converter. Those owners who can sell, do, while others must pay a fee to junk the car. It is not easy to junk because it is made of a lot of plastic that defies recycling. Also, the Trabi has become the symbol of the cheap and unattractive products of the former centrally-planned economies. It has no power devices, gadgets, or buttons; its seats are stiff; its transmission is manual and requires some forceful pressure to operate. Despite all its shortcomings, the Trabi demonstrated some positive aspects. The car's cheapness made it widely available and it is functional auto transport that uses only a two-piston engine.[46] Its two-stroke engine uses less fuel than Western European cars. The average gasoline consumption in Eastern Europe in 1990 was 8.7 litres per 100 km, compared to Britain's usage, which is close to the Western European norm, of slightly less than 10 litres per 100 km.[47]

The passenger car, it has been suggested, may be perceived as meeting psychosocial needs of individual empowerment. The urge towards automobility in the former East Germany may meet a hunger for autonomy fuelled by the former oppressive political structure.[48] As it is in the West, automobility is linked with the idea of personal freedom in the East. Thus, this desire, together with the release of a more general consumerist fervour, may inhibit East Germans from considering alternative means of empowerment and from socializing transport in a way that democratizes mobility and reduces environmental hazards.

The mass transit infrastructure that existed in East Germany, probably equal to that in West Germany in the early 1960s, was subsequently allowed to deteriorate immensely, partly because of diversion of resources to the military sector. Post-reunification constraints on public spending may result in a neglect of public transit. Along with rising transit fares, the greater availability of private cars, and declining quality of mass transit, a spiral of decline may be set into motion with a resultant dramatic increase in private car use for commuting and shopping. As a consequence, traffic congestion and pollution will increase, especially in cities not designed for auto traffic.

Transport planning has become a more important issue in local Berlin politics since reunification. City and state planners are moving to extend the well developed freeway system of West Berlin (where the last tram ran in 1967) into the East. In 1992 the principal focus was the Overbaum Bridge, at the former wall, over which city leaders wished to extend West Berlin's inner ring freeway. The beginning of construction prompted demonstrations by local community groups on both sides of the bridge—Friedrichshain in the East, Kreuzberg in the West. The demonstrators protested against the highway construction, arguing that it would degrade their local neighbourhoods, and demanded instead that the city extend the tram line from the East across the bridge into the West.

Economic planning for the new Eastern Germany tends to favour the development of automobility. There are numerous efforts to set up auto production facilities in the East and the sale of Western-produced cars is booming. As a result of their differing courses before reunification, from the perspective of entrepreneurs in Eastern Europe and the former Soviet Union, auto markets remain underdeveloped there. Recent reports contrast booming car sales in reunified Germany with declining sales in other car manufacturing countries.[49] East Germans bought one million used cars from the West in 1991 alone.[50] Dealers in the eastern part of the country expect to sell 700,000 new cars per year through the 1990s.[51] In all of Eastern Europe there are about 100 million potential customers for autos.[52]

The West German auto industry plans to invest 10 billion deutschmarks in East Germany by 1994, creating production sites, distribution points, service centres, and about 1,000 dealerships.[53] New autobahns in the east on the scale of those in the west are being planned. A new highway that will connect Dresden with Prague will have six to eight lanes and carry 90,000 vehicles per day. Local environmentalists are opposing the new roadway because it "would ravage one of the most beautiful parts of Germany," would create "decades of pollution and traffic problems," and "symbolizes a commitment to the automobile as the best form of transportation."[54] The economic interests of West German auto firms that are seeking to economically colonize East German production are not necessarily healthy ones for the transport, ecological, or even the economic interests of East Germany.

However, there is reason for optimism. Eastern Germany does possess a good mass transit infrastructure; while rails need repair, not many new lines need to be developed. Also, the East Germans have accumulated an impressive body of know-how in rail car construction. It may make economic sense to build upon this expertise, rather than to focus on creating a local auto industry. Perhaps East Germany could develop a market for exporting mass transit vehicles, especially rail cars.[55]

We have focused on East Germany but it is only an example of the probable proliferation of auto-centred transport systems into much of Eastern and Central Europe, as well as the former Soviet Union. In Poland, for instance, it is estimated that car ownership will double by the year 2010.[56] To avoid the problems that plague auto-centred transport in Western Europe and North America, the transport policies of both Eastern European and Third World nations need to be reoriented away from auto-centredness to diversification, emphasizing those modes that minimize energy-resource consumption and environmental degradation, and maximize democratic access. While the problems of auto-centred transport are large in countries like the United States, they promise to be even greater in Eastern Europe and in the Third World, if only because those areas of the world lack sufficient economic resources and public pressure to ameliorate the impact of auto hegemony. It appears that Eastern European nations are at a juncture where they can or cannot opt to imitate the mistakes of the West. Unfortunately, many Third World nations have already made the decision to imitate.

In conclusion, the problems of automobility are now global. While local solutions can certainly emerge, the political and economic contexts of the international market eventually surface as barriers. For instance, in the fall of 1989, the French took the Dutch to the European Court claiming that Dutch limits on auto emissions made the sale of French cars in the Netherlands impossible. Common Market agreements, the French argued, were being violated. The French won the case. This is an example of how individual states have become weaker in relationship to the growing power and mobility of transnational capital.[57] National car emission regulations can be over-ridden by the prerogatives of international trade.

NOTES

1. Motor Vehicle Manufacturers Association, *Facts & Figures '92*, Detroit, 1992, p. 25.
2. Frederick Winslow Taylor, *The Principles of Scientific Management* (New York: Harper, 1911).
3. For more detailed histories of auto production and marketing see: James J. Flink, *America Adopts the Automobile, 1885-1910* (Cambridge, MA: The MIT Press, 1970); James J. Flink, *The Automobile Age* (Cambridge, MA: The MIT Press, 1988); David Gartman, *Auto Slavery: The Labor Process in the American Automobile Industry, 1897-1950* (New Brunswick, NJ: Rutgers University Press, 1986); Karl Ludvigsen and David Burgess Wise, *The Encyclopedia of the American Automobile* (New York: Exter Books, 1982); John B. Rae, *The American Automobile: A Brief History* (Chicago: The University of Chicago Press, 1965); James P. Womack, Daniel T. Jones, and Daniel Roos, *The Machine that Changed the World* (New York: Macmillan Publishing Co., 1990).
4. Karal Ann Marling, "America's Love Affair with the Automobile in the Television Age," *Design Quarterly* 146 (1989):7.
5. *Ibid.*
6. Todd Gitlin, "We Build Excitement," in Todd Gitlin, ed., *Watching Television* (New York: Pantheon Books, 1986), pp. 137-143.
7. K.H. Schaeffer and Elliott Sclar, *Access for All: Transportation and Urban Growth* (Baltimore: Penguin, 1975), p. 41.
8. *Ibid.*, p. 39.
9. Alan Altshuler *et. al.*, *The Future of the Automobile: The Report of MIT's International Automobile Program* (Cambridge, MA: The MIT Press, 1984).
10. *Ibid.*, pp. 16, 19.
11. George Maxcy, *The Multinational Automobile Industry* (New York: St. Martin's Press, 1981), p. 87.
12. *Ibid.*, pp. 114-115.
13. Motor Vehicle Manufacturers Association, *op. cit.*, p. 11.
14. Doron P. Levin, "Experts Doubt Cutbacks Will Save G.M.," *The New York Times*, December 23, 1991.
15. Norman J. Glickman, "Cities and the International Division of Labor," in Michael Peter Smith and Joe R. Feagin, eds., *The Capitalist City: Global Restructuring and Community Politics* (Oxford: Basil Blackwell, 1987), p. 70.
16. Jane Perlez, "Toyota and Honda Create Global Production System," *The New York Times*, March 26, 1993.
17. Robert Schaeffer, "Car Sick, Automobiles Ad Nauseam," *Greenpeace* 15 (1990):14.
18. *Ibid.*
19. Motor Vehicle Manufacturers Association, *Facts & Figures '90*, Detroit, 1990, p. 37.

20. Everett C. Carter, Himmat S. Chadda, and Paul M. Schonfeld, "A Comparison of Transportation Planning in Developed and Developing Countries," *Transportation Quarterly* 38 (1984):79.

21. World Bank, *Urban Transport: A World Bank Policy Study*, Washington, DC, 1986, p. 1.

22. *Ibid.*, p. 46.

23. Asif Faiz *et. al.*, "Automotive Air Pollution—Issues and Options for Developing Countries" (Washington, DC: World Bank, 1990).

24. Wayne Ellwood, "Car Chaos," *New Internationalist*, No. 195, May, 1989, p. 6.

25. Asif Faiz, "Motor Vehicle Emissions in Developing Countries: Relative Implications for Urban Air Quality," in Alcira Kreimer and Mohan Munasinghe, eds., *Discussion Papers #168* (Washington, DC: World Bank, 1992), p. 183.

26. Michael Renner, "Rethinking the Role of the Automobile," (Washington, DC: Worldwatch Institute, Paper No. 84, 1988), p. 36.

27. Bruce E. Fleming, "Another Way of Dying," *The Nation* 250 (1990):448.

28. Renner, *op. cit.*, p. 6.

29. United Nations, *Urban Transportation with Particular Reference to Developing Countries* (New York: Department of International Economic and Social Affairs, 1989), p. 27.

30. Renner, *op. cit.*, p. 52.

31. World Bank, *op. cit.*, pp. 46-47.

32. Timothy Campbell, "Resource Flows in the Urban Ecosystem—Fuel, Water, and Food in Mexico City" (Berkeley: Working Paper No. 360, Institute of Urban and Regional Development, University of California, 1981).

33. World Bank, *op. cit.*, p. 39.

34. Mary Morse, "Autocracy is Being Exported to Third World," *Utne Reader*, July-August, 1990, pp. 15-16.

35. Rainer Dombois, "Autos und Autoindustrie in der Dritten Welt," in Jobst Kraus, Horst Sackstetter und Willi Wentsch, eds., *Auto, Auto Uber Alles?* (Freiburg: Dreisam Verlag, 1987), pp. 137-140.

36. John Adams, *Transport Planning: Vision and Practice* (London: Routledge and Kegan Paul, 1981), p. 47.

37. Halinah Todd, "The Proton Saga Saga," *New Internationalist*, No. 195, May, 1989, pp. 14-15.

38. Marcia D. Lowe, "Shaping Cities," in Lester Brown, ed., *State of the World* (New York: W.W. Norton, 1992), pp. 127-128; Mac Margolis, "A Third-World City that Works," *World Monitor* 5 (1992):42-50.

39. Sylvia Nasar, "Cooling the Globe Would be Nice, but Saving Lives Now May Cost Less," *The New York Times*, May 31, 1992.

40. Marcia D. Lowe, *Alternatives to the Automobile: Transport for Livable Cities* (Washington, DC: Worldwatch Institute, Paper No. 98, 1990) p. 17.

41. Motor Vehicle Manufacturers Association, 1990, *op. cit.*, p. 37.

42. Winfried Wolf, *Neues Denken oder Neues Tanken? DDR Verkehr 2000* (Frankfurt am Main: ISP Verlag, 1990).

43. Werner Polster und Klaus Voy, "Freie Fahrt fur FreieBurger—Auto-Mobilisierung der Nation," in Arthur Heinrich und Klaus Naumann, eds., *Alles Banane-Ausblicke auf das endgultige Deutschland* (Koln: Papy Rossa Verlag, 1990), pp. 114-131.

44. Wolf, *op. cit.*, p. 23.

45. Polster and Voy, *op. cit.*

46. John Tagliabue, "Klunkers Go Kaput," *San Francisco Examiner*, January 20, 1991.
47. Malcolm Ferguson, "Factors Influencing Atmosphere Emissions from Road Traffic in Central and East Europe," Paper presented at Conference, "Tomorrow's Clean and Fuel-Efficient Automobile: Opportunities for East-West Cooperation," Berlin, March 25-27, 1991.
48. Micha Hilgers, "Auto-Mobil oder das Selbst im Strassenverkehr: Zur Psychoanalyze des Automobilmissbrauchs," *Universitas* 46 (1991):541-556; Wolf, *op. cit.*
49. Ferguson, *op. cit.*
50. Alan Durning, *How Much is Enough?* (New York: W.W. Norton, 1992).
51. Stephen Kinzer, "Long-Stifled Dresden Debates Highway to Prague," *The New York Times*, January 2, 1992.
52. Schaeffer, *op. cit.*
53. *This Week in Germany*, "German Car Industry to Invest DM 10 Billion in East," May 24, 1991, p. 5 (New York: German Information Center).
54. Kinzer, *op. cit.*
55. Marcia D. Lowe, "Rediscovering Rail," in Linda Starke, ed., *State of the World* (New York: W.W. Norton, 1993), pp. 120-138.
56. Ferguson, *op. cit.*
57. Katherine Yih, "The Red and the Green: Left Perspectives on Ecology," *Monthly Review* 42 (1990):16-28.

PART TWO

Deconstructing Auto Hegemony

CHAPTER 5

THE IDEOLOGY OF AUTOMOBILITY

In order to envision changes to a more environmentally friendly, less space and resource-energy intensive transport system, one must first consider the factors that contribute to maintaining the present system. Most people view individualized uses of the car as natural, inevitable and desirable. There are fears that attempts to impose speed limits, raise gasoline taxes or in any other way to limit the use of the car will inhibit freedom and mobility; to those who hold these fears such action smacks of totalitarianism. This collection of beliefs can be characterized as what André Gorz once called the ideology of the motor car.[1] Indeed, beliefs and sentiments about freedom and mobility are salient factors in sustaining the dominant role of the individual passenger car in our system of transport. In addition to the material factors relevant to understanding auto hegemony, including the structure of auto space, in this section we look at cultural beliefs and sentiments that surround the auto, particularly beliefs about its efficacy as an agency of freedom and mobility.

Ideologies operate most effectively when their assumptions become taken-for-granted features of culture. They come to be taken for granted when they are embodied in various material and cultural forms. For instance, rush hour radio traffic reports reaffirm the centrality of the auto and its "natural" place in our daily lives as the predominant—even the only reasonable—means of mobility. Preston Schiller has suggested that these reports be treated as a form of auto advertising.[2] In a similar fashion, Dennis Wood has suggested that maps, although representations of general spatial arrangements, in fact serve particular interests and naturalize certain ideas about transport:

> North Carolina *does* publish the *North Carolina Public Transportation Guide*—a highway map-like document displaying intercity bus, train and ferry routes—but it printed 15,000 copies of the most recent edition, less than a hundredth as many maps as it printed of its highways. Not an advertisement, the public transpor-

tation map was produced without the assistance of the Department of Commerce. Could this be why, unlike the highway map among whose blond hikers, swimmers, golfers and white-water enthusiasts no blacks appear, blacks figure so prominently on the public transportation map? Here blacks buy intercity bus tickets, get on city buses, and in wheel chairs get assisted into specially equipped vans. The reek of special assistance is like sweat: "many of you have requested information on how to make your trip without using a private automobile. Because of these requests ..." But there is nothing of this tone on the highway map. There was never any *need* to have requested a highway map: it, after all, is ... *a natural function of the state.*[3]

Highway maps thus naturalize the fact that car-centred transport is preferred, marginalizing an awareness of alternative modes.

The auto and all that it represents is an integral part of North American and European culture. Individualism and mobility are important values that buttress automobility. The auto is the principal instrument of geographic mobility and it secures a high degree of privatism and freedom of choice for the individual. He or she can travel alone in an environment that reflects his or her personal taste.

Mobility and Freedom through Power and Speed

The car is perceived as affording the driver a high level of freedom of choice as to when and by what route he or she travels, as well as the destination of travel. An editorial in *The Economist* called the car the "greatest mobile force for freedom in the rich democracies," a liberator of women, and a device that transformed a locally bound worker into a free yeoman.[4] Indeed, the auto represents an icon of freedom of movement and is seen as a great equalizer among citizens. The degree of motorization of a country is often taken as a measure of its democratization:

We live in a dirt crazed, unruly society. And ... some of that madness can be traced to the machine in the driveway. It maims people and kills them. It fouls the air and clogs the streets. But love it or hate it ... the auto ... has been our great emancipator and it is not coin-

cidental that the ownership of such a device is discouraged in totalitarian societies. A mobile population
is a population essentially out of control of centralized
governments.[5]

In fact it was Hitler's fascist regime that promoted the autobahn
(which became a model for the U.S. interstate highway system) and
the Volkswagen, making automobility into a "folk right" in Germany.
Autos are limited to the elite in many totalitarian or undemocratic
societies probably not so much for reasons of social control but for
economic reasons, and because of poorly managed production and
distribution.

Geographic mobility seems to be an especially prized value of
North American culture. It has played a role in a number of analyses
of U.S. civilization, including Frederick Turner's celebrated frontier
thesis.[6] For a nation of seemingly boundless land, populated largely
by relatively recent immigrants, geographic mobility has been a fact
of life and it has been tied to social mobility. The United States has always had a frontier and does so even today—in Alaska.

Another significant way in which the auto resonates with the U.S.
experience lies in the aversion to political remedies for social problems
and the preference for technological and geographical fixes. The auto
itself was once seen as a technological cure for environmental
problems caused by horses, including their ubiquitous germ-laden ex-
creta. Today, the auto provides a means by which urban ills, including
widespread poverty, inter-group social conflict, and sociopsychic
stress, can be escaped. Henry Ford himself capsulated this technological strategy for dealing with social problems when he said: "We shall
solve the city problem by leaving the city."[7] Indeed, with the help of
the auto, Americans did leave the cities for greener pastures, thereby
contributing to the decline of cities. Of course, this phenomenon has
taken place in many nations, for example, in Germany. Some critics
there have argued that in West Germany population movement to
greener, socially more encapsulated and homogenous spaces on the
urban periphery, contributed to ecological deterioration.[8]

The auto was heralded for providing not only individual
mobility but family mobility as well. By the 1940s the car was
marketed not just as a car but as a family car. It made the whole family
mobile. The car was invested with a domestic imagery and designed
in such a way as to embody the image. A Ford sales brochure in 1949
declared that "the Ford is a living room on wheels!"[9] The personally

owned auto provided a substantial chunk of private property—like "owning one's own home."[10] Of course the mobile home is the quintessential home on wheels, a uniquely American hybrid of home and auto.[11] The trailer home was popularized in the 1920s and since then has become immobile—less than 3 percent ever move from their first location today.[12] The trailer home has been replaced on American roads by the recreational vehicle. The RV combines what the auto and trailer provided in two separate units.

Recent innovations in digital displays and computers have enhanced the imagery of power and speedy mobility of cars:

> Mentally seated before their instrument panel with its exotic computer graphic displays and indulged by a host of unseen robotic servants, we begin to sense the control and opportunity gadgetry affords. This is the stuff of Mittyesque daydreams with their erotic fantasy settings and myths of manly adventure. It isn't just speed and safety, it's sex drive and self-image.[13]

Some drivers are developing this new capacity to unusual lengths. Many Californians, for example, are increasingly using power converters which plug into dashboard cigarette lighters, automobilizing virtually any household appliance, including televisions and hair dryers. Considering the fact that most Californians spend more time idling in traffic than they do on vacations, the increasing use of the car as a home is by no means eccentric.[14]

Assumptions about gender made by auto producers demonstrate the role of social ideology in the development of auto technology. Virginia Scharff indicated that the introduction of the electric self-starter was delayed because of the commonsense assumption among car makers that men would scorn such feminine accessories and preferred the manly effort of the hand-cranked start. The "creative possibilities of the car culture" Scharff argued have been stifled by such assumptions.[15] We would add that such factors may have contributed to inhibiting the potential of transport culture in general, including the development and popularization of softer means of mobility, safe and comfortable mass transit, and denser communities that are more oriented to community and familial life.

What is most frequently overlooked by those who uncritically espouse the freedom and mobility of driving are the social controls that any transport system brings with it. Furthermore, these controls also affect those who do not drive, as in the impact of traffic rules on pedestrians. Spaces in which children can play or in which people can wander without heeding traffic are constrained and shaped by the prevailing traffic patterns. It is not only the auto. All modes of transport bring specialized forms of social control with them, as John Adams has pointed out:

> Developments in transport and communications have already necessitated many social controls. Speed limits, blood alcohol limits, driving tests and licenses, parking restrictions, laws to regulate noise and fumes, laws permitting the compulsory purchase of land for transport developments, compulsory vaccination, and the vast apparatus of customs and immigration are only a few of the most obvious social controls made necessary by increasing mobility.[16]

Controls over individual mobility become after a while so obvious as to be unnoticed. Thus, they become a taken-for-granted feature of the social landscape.

One implicit assumption of auto ideology is the tendency to equate physical movement with political freedom. Note for example the significance of the word "freeway." It may denote a road that is free of tolls, traffic lights, and stop signs but it also resonates with "freedom." While freedom of movement is significant and a primary dimension of personal liberty, the equation of movement and freedom is equivocal. One can argue that *access*, not movement, is the correct aim of transport.[17] One may never leave home and yet have access to all the benefits of a good life. We get water in our taps without fetching it and food and entertainment can be delivered to the home. Decreased access may therefore be more of a problem than lack of mobility. Nonetheless, many people believe that the mere possession of an auto provides them with freedom. We will say more about this later when we discuss the structure of space and access. Meanwhile, we turn our attention to cultural connections between the auto and individualism.

Individualism

The auto is not just a means of transport but a technical object which embodies in its basic structure certain taken-for-granted cultural meanings. These meanings of the auto include a mastery over time and space and above all, personal independence and individuality. The auto is one of the many commodities in modern technical development that reflects a more general tendency towards design for individual use. The self-steered vehicle along with television, personal computers, and other devices are meant for private, independent consumption that does not depend on the rhythms or needs of others, and minimizes or even eliminates interaction with others. The built-in individual user quality of commodities serves an economy in which consumers become an interchangeable and atomized aggregate—a mass market. The auto represents the one commodity of the industrial age that holds out the greatest promise of individual liberation through the possession of things.

A U.S. General Accounting Office report concluded that the preference for private vehicles is an expression of American individualism.[18] It claimed that the sense of freedom is enhanced by driving one's own car, and that the overwhelming majority of all trips are made by car because of its quality as a personalized form of transport. As we have discussed, while such ideological motivations figure into car use, what this report neglected is the fact that most everyday activities *have* to be carried out by auto, since public transport and other options are woefully inadequate or impractical.

The auto is the choice for many people not necessarily because it is preferred but because it is the only choice. Auto ownership and daily use are anything but irrational in most parts of the United States. It is the only option given the social arrangement of space and the absence of alternative means of transport. Even when there are alternatives to auto transport, they may not be rational choices. In the present context, from the point of view of the individual, car ownership, despite its costs, is more efficient and flexible than poor quality or non-existent public transport or other alternatives.

The popularity of the auto is only partly based on the fact that spatial arrangements favour its use. The auto is a useful symbol for individuals and is a vehicle for individual self-presentation. In this respect, Jonathan Raban noted:

> Cars have had to carry an excessive burden of symbolism; they have been decked out with every sort of frippery, used as promiscuously as tailors' dummies to promote a style. The car is a special simulacrum of the

self; it goes where its owner goes; it forms his outer suit, his most visible and ubiquitous expression of choice and taste; it is most often seen briefly, on the move—like the citizen himself, it has to make its message plain in an instant.[19]

Thus, when cruising around in cars, teenage boys can display their masculinity. (Later we will discuss the fact that the auto is not restricted to being a symbol of masculinity.) The car embodies the speed and power its driver commands. The issue of control and individual autonomy is highlighted in a comment by racing car driver Emerson Fittipaldi: "Outside my car I feel I am nothing; in it everything changes, and I feel the virile master of the world and of destiny."[20] For many people the auto is the ultimate symbol of technological progress with which they are intimately familiar. This icon is the symbol of unstoppable force, an embodiment of an ideology that equates technical progress with freedom and acts as a symbol of unfettered individualism.

The ideology of automobility projects an image of the lone individual unencumbered by social constraint. Consider, for example, a new 1993 television show in the United States that was based upon and named after a car—the Viper. The show will feature a Lone Ranger private detective who drives around a futuristic city. His car will have several non-standard extras, including a battering ram and a missile-launch system.[21] However much one may aspire to be a Lone Ranger as a driver, one is never really detached from the vagaries of energy costs and other social contingencies. Similarly, the individual driver is seldom an isolated monad traversing an open empty space. Individuals generally find themselves located in a constraining matrix of traffic. The General Accounting Office has documented the fact that traffic congestion is growing and auto speeds are slowing in the United States.

The auto does allow individuals to be their own drivers and to come and go as they please. However, as its use spreads, new social controls (speed limits and traffic lights), new constraints (the presence of many other individual drivers), and new dependencies (on energy) emerge. Thus, the social reality of driving is constrained by schedules, the rhythms of movement of others, and social controls. The image of the free-wheeling individual who is dependent on no one, while persisting as part of the ideology of auto-centred transport, is being gradually eclipsed by reality. However, the image remains a potent sales weapon. It shares similarities with that single most successful of all advertising images—the "Marlboro Man"—as well as with what Todd Gitlin called the "lone driver."[22]

At the opening of an award-winning (from *Advertising Age* in 1990) car commercial, we see a crowded expressway. A voice says, "If I could afford a sport sedan, the road would belong to me, *Bob*." The perspective shifts to the driver's point of view. We see a sign, "Bob's expressway," with a lane empty except for Bob's car, and an adjacent lane that is congested. Another sign reads, "Yield to Bob," and one over a toll lane announces itself as *"Bob's* lane." The green light signals, "Go Bob," and a policeman directing traffic waves Bob through, clearly impressed by Bob's auto. A "no parking except Bob" sign appears and Bob pulls up next to it. A policeman comes over. "Oh, it's you, Bob," he notes with a deferential salute. A voice-over concludes: "Introducing the new Nissan Sentra, because rich guys shouldn't have all the fun."

Bob's—every*man's*—life as a driver is transformed through a commodity that allows him and only him to transcend limits of time, space, and traffic rules, not to mention the constraints of social class. Bob's fantasy is not only profoundly individualistic but anti-social and anti-democratic as well, with a touch of *shaden freude* as we see his fellow drivers crowded into an adjacent lane. The contradiction between the individual and the social are masked over. After all, what would happen to spatial and other resources if this everyman's dream came true for everyone? The belief that status can be purchased through a motorcar camouflages the realities of social class, as well as the fact that everyone simply cannot have fun in the form of the limitless privileges that Bob possesses. This commercial condenses and amplifies social meanings that are integral to the ideology and utopian fantasies of automobility.

In his essay on the social ideology of the motor car, Gorz argued that private autos are luxuries like private beaches that society cannot make available to everyone. There are not enough beaches to provide one for each person. The illusion the ideology of the motor car supports is "that each individual can seek his or her own benefit at the expense of everyone else."[23] Gorz argued that the more widespread the use of fast vehicles in society, the more time people spend on travelling to meet needs. Auto-centred transport dramatically raises the issue of individual freedoms in a collectivity. If every human in the world cannot own their private beach, then private ownership of beaches must be limited because their number is naturally finite. As more and more people use the auto for everyday purposes, the freedom of individual drivers decreases.

The individual right to travel at speed has only recently become an issue of social debate. In West Germany there has been a continuing battle over appropriate speed limits. It is a hotly debated issue which has led to demonstrations and counter demonstrations. Those who wish to limit speeds to, for instance, 100 kilometres per hour on autobahns and 30 kmph on side streets, argue that reduced speeds lower the rate of auto fatalities. As we pointed out in Chapter 2, there is evidence to support this assumption. Evidence also suggests that lower speed limits decrease noise, fuel use, emissions, stress and the amount of space needed by cars, since braking distances are also reduced.[24] Limiting speeds in side streets allows for their safer use by children and pedestrians.

Attempts to impose speed limits on West Germans have been seen by some as reflecting a socialist asceticism more appropriate to the former East Germany. Additionally, popular cultural images of mass transit associate it with the Welfare State and socialism, while automobility is equated with individuality and wealth.[25] The *Allgemeine Deutsche Automobil Club* is the second largest (after the American Automobile Association) auto club in the world. Using the motto, "free driving for free citizens," they have campaigned against the imposition of a 100-kmph speed limit on the West Berlin autobahn.[26] The ADAC, while approving lower speed limits in some residential areas, argued that these be established on a restricted basis and the speed limit be 40 kmph, not 30 kmph.[27] Thus, the equation of mobility and freedom is extended to one of speed and freedom.

Speed *is* the premier cultural icon of modern societies. Aldous Huxley is reputed to have remarked that it is the only novel sensation of the twentieth century.[28] As early as 1929, the Russian writer Ilya Ehrenburg noted hyperbolically the powerful appeal to the human psyche that auto speed had: "The automobile has come to show even the slowest minds ... that the heart is just a poetic relic, that a human being contains two standard gauges: one indicates miles, the other minutes."[29] Speed symbolizes manliness, progress, and dynamism. Slowness on the other hand signifies old, weak, backward, sick, unproductive and feminine.[30] The thrill of speed is a combination of fear and pleasure, and control versus lack of control. The desire to drive at high speed is decidedly gender modulated, as discussed in Chapter 3.

There is a lot of resistance to downsizing and slowing autos. An editor of a car magazine complained that the obsession with energy efficiency would "put all of us who love cars into devices that looked and ran like enclosed riding lawnmowers."[31] Such psycho-aesthetic desires for size and power coincide with the fact that such vehicles are more profitable. As Barry Commoner has argued, style and profit considerations, more so than function or social need, combine to shape the design of cars with the result that they are greater in necessary size and power ("minicars make miniprofits").[32] Thus, despite gains in the early 1970s in fuel efficiency, the United States still lags behind Europe and Japan. The U.S. auto industry continues to oppose fuel efficiency improvements, arguing that "tiny" cars would force "full size" models, which are more profitable, out of production.[33] "Tiny" gives a negative spin to small cars, while "full size" gives a positive spin to large cars. This is just one small example of the propaganda that is produced about autos—propaganda rooted in considerations about profitability.

Fast movement is connected to the ideas that time is a scarce commodity and that time and space are things to be transcended or to be compressed. Speed then has a strong affinity with modern production's focus on the rate of time use, which determines productivity. But it is not so clear that with greater speed we actually do more in our daily lives. For one thing, congestion has made the speed of the auto virtually useless in central cities. In fact, we often travel more in order to do many of the same activities that were previously done with less travel time.

Pleasure and Sexuality

In an analysis of the meaning the auto has in the lives of auto workers, M.D. Moorhouse pointed out that it is a commodity that brings not only mobility but pleasure.[34] Working on and maintaining cars as well as racing them is for many a form of pleasure, in which traditionally masculine skills are displayed.

It is by now a cliché to say that Americans have a love affair with their cars. What does this mean? On one level it signifies the psychosexual symbolism of the auto. Thus, a 1993 ad for a car stated: "So you've lusted after one. Perhaps caught a glimpse on a highway somewhere or drooled over its V10 and curvaceous body at an auto show."[35] On another level it simply means strong attachment based on potent feelings, perhaps especially for men—and not only

American men. In one West German survey 35 percent of men would let no one else drive their car, whereas 16 percent of women expressed this feeling.[36] In the United States, a survey has shown that 70 percent of males would not give up their cars no matter how much mass transit was available, whereas the majority of women would give up their cars.[37] A survey in Canada found that getting a license was equally important for girls and boys but unlike boys, girls were willing to use public transport after getting a license. Many of the girls did not want to drive in snow, during rush hours, and on freeways.[38]

The auto is more than a purely masculine symbol; it is unusual in its capacity to project both feminine and masculine imagery, to carry erotic appeal for both women and men. In no other city is the auto used as a pleasurable aspect of a general lifestyle more than in Los Angeles. Angelenos speak of public transit as if it were an alien experience. In this extremely auto-centred city, both the inadequacy of public transit and the stigma attached to its use reach their acme.[39] The auto-lives of Angelenos has been featured recurrently in movies and fiction. One example cited by Peter Hall is Joan Didion's heroine in *Play It As It Lays*, a woman who "turns to the freeways for sustenance":[40]

> Again and again she returned to an intricate stretch just south of the interchange where successful passage from the Hollywood onto the Harbor required a diagonal move across four lanes of traffic. On the afternoon she finally did it without once braking or once losing the beat on the radio she was exhilarated, and that night slept dreamlessly.[41]

This passage also indicates the very real pleasure that can come from mastering skilful manoeuvres of the auto.

It has been argued that the erotic appeal of the auto is based on a combination of feelings of self-enclosed regression, omnipotence, and control.[42] Driving can be an onanistic experience in which the driver extends his power manifoldly without intercourse with others in a self-enclosed womblike capsule. The person's power is amplified by a light touch on the gas pedal. The inner space of an auto is not unlike the simulated environment that can be created by a computer ("virtual reality"). Both environments provide their inhabitants with a sense of control. The world outside the auto assumes the appearance of a film, like the image on a computer screen—something distant, alien, and a bit unreal.

However gender versatile it has become, the auto traditionally has been used as a masculine symbol. Auto shows have traditionally been events in which feminine sex appeal is used to sell products. Although there has been a moderation of the uses of female bodies in recent years, the practice continues. In 1991, of the 250 models used in Detroit auto shows only 15 percent were male, up from virtually zero percent in the early 1980s. A journalist described this use of the female form to sell cars:

> At Cadillac's exhibit, the female models don't talk, period. That's because the GM luxury car division purposely chooses "high-fashion models" who pose silently next to cars on rotating platforms, wearing full-length evening gowns with "jewel-toned" accents—and plenty of cleavage.[43]

As early as 1917, Stephen Bayley pointed out, Dadaist Francis Picabia was showing the components of auto engines as highly erotic, in drawings of valves and guides, and of carburettors.[44] In 1926, e.e. cummings was describing the operation of a new auto as like making love, in his poem, *xix*. In 1929 Sinclair Lewis's Sam in *Dodsworth* was describing his new car in arguably sexual terms: "The engine bulked in front, under a proud hood over two feet long, and the steering column was not straight but rakishly tilted."[45]

One may of course argue with such deep psychological explanations and view them as the convenient projections of auto critics. Nonetheless, they do suggest that our love affair with the auto is linked to our desires and not simply to rational choice. To some degree a car is not just a car! The most functional of autos—racing cars, for instance—are not simply utilitarian machines but embody a certain look. A Porsche designer claimed that the car has "the winning look that weapons have." The appearance of cars—their form and look—comes from airplanes "or busts, bottoms and the other pleats, tucks, depressions and protuberances of the body."[46]

The irrational and ideological aspects of people's relationships with cars show that the preference for the auto is not merely based on rational and instrumental grounds. The cultural values of automobility find their psychic analogue in a masculine psychology of mastery and control, which embodies the culture of speed, power, and the conquest of nature. The imagery of auto advertising associates the car with a combination of animal vitality and technical precision. Thus, auto technology to some extent is anthropomorphized to produce gendered images of natural animal power.[47]

It is also the case that driving can become a vehicle for the expression of gender-related aggression. A study of young drivers suggested that aggressive driving is not deviant behaviour but rather a way of over-conforming to masculine values.[48] The auto can serve as a symbol, especially for males, of rebellion against parental authority and risky driving can be seen as a normal part of teenage masculine subculture. Gender-related insults include the typically masculinized or macho reactions to traffic situations; for example, feeling angry or competitive when one is simply passed by another vehicle.

An integral part of teenage masculine subculture is risk-taking. Young men account for a disproportionate share of auto accidents and fatalities, of citations for speeding and reckless driving and of drunken driving.[49] For young people, particularly males, one's first car and license are rites of passage to adulthood and manhood. Getting a license is experienced as a major turning point in an adolescent's biography. Of course one must add that the car is not just a symbol for young people but also a necessary material means of gaining freedom and overcoming exclusion and dependence in the auto-dominated social spaces of modern society. For men, in particular, it is an expression of self-worth and of carefreeness. In fact, it has been argued that for some the auto may act as a substitute for older sources of identity derived from work, religion, and position in the community.[50] It may also fulfil fantasies of power, attractiveness, dominance, superiority and aggression.

Conclusion

In summary, individual mobility, freedom, and personal pleasure are widely recognized as major rewards of automobility. Alternatively, there is little attention given to the problems of automobility or to the possibility of alternate arrangements. In this sense we can speak of an ideology of automobility, which clouds and mystifies social realities. People generally do not challenge the existing spatio-temporal arrangements which constrain them. These arrangements appear as natural givens not subject to change. Our dissatisfaction with these arrangements may be perceived as our personal failure. Complaints or challenges to such arrangements will not be understood by those immersed in auto space and culture. Margret Eder recalled an anecdote about her child who ran into a parked car with her bike.[51] The driver wanted damages but Eder replied that she would not pay since she does not get money from the car owners who appropriate play space. The owner of the car understood nothing of this and probably thought she was mad.

It is important to keep in mind that these ideological assumptions, explicitly or implicitly, are shared even by transport planners. Indeed, it is such assumptions that are integral to the windshield perspective of many planners and officials. This perspective leads them to assume that people do not want alternatives to personalized auto transport and that their "love affair" with the auto makes change impossible.

In the first decade of this century few would have imagined the eventual extent of the auto's hegemony in transport. One result is that our subjective experiences of daily life have been radically affected by the nature of "auto space," an issue to which we now turn our attention.

NOTES

1. André Gorz, *Ecology as Politics* (Montreal: Black Rose Books, 1980).
2. Preston Schiller, "Turn Off the Traffic Rap!" *Auto-Free Press* 4 (1993):6.
3. Dennis Wood, *The Power of Maps* (New York: The Guilford Press, 1992), p. 107.
4. "The Unfinished Revolution," *The Economist*, January 25, 1986, pp. 12-13.
5. Cited in: Robert Schaeffer, "Car Sick, Automobiles Ad Nauseam," *Greenpeace* 15 (1990):16.
6. Frederick Jackson Turner, *The Frontier in American History* (New York: Holt, Rinehart and Winston, 1962).
7. Cited in: James J. Flink, "Three Stages of American Automobile Consciousness," *American Quarterly* 24 (1972):462.
8. Franz Ossing *et. al.*, "Innere Widerspruche und Aussere Grenzen der Lebensweise-Aspekte der Okologische Entwicklung," in Klaus Voy, Werner Polster, und Claus Thomasberger, eds., *Gesellschaftliche Transformationsprozesse und Materielle Lebensweise* (Marburg: Metropolis-Verlag, 1991), p. 367.
9. Peter Marsh and Peter Collett, *Driving Passion: The Psychology of the Car* (London: Faber and Faber, 1986), p. 11.
10. Helmut Frank, "Mass Transport and Class Struggle," in Enne de Boer, ed., *Transport Sociology: Social Aspects of Transport Planning* (Oxford: Pergamon Press, 1986), pp. 211-222.
11. Heather Mackey, "Home on the Range," *The San Francisco Bay Guardian*, February 6, 1991.
12. Allan D. Wallis, *Wheel Estate: The Rise and Decline of Mobile Homes* (Oxford: Oxford University Press, 1991).

13. Donald J. Bush, "Emotive Power," *Design Quarterly* 146 (1989):27.
14. Peter O'Rourke, "Changing Driver Behavior: The Safety Dimension," in Robert L. Deen, ed., *The Alternatives to Gridlock: Perspectives to Meeting California's Transportation Needs* (Sacramento: California Institute of Public Affairs, 1990), pp. 43-44.
15. Virginia Scharff, *Taking the Wheel: Women and the Coming of the Motor Age* (New York: The Free Press, 1991), p. 61.
16. John Adams, *Transport Planning: Vision and Practice* (London: Routledge and Kegan Paul, 1981), p. 233.
17. *Ibid.*, p. 195.
18. *Traffic Congestion: Trends, Measures and Effects* (Washington, DC: U.S. General Accounting Office, 1989), p. 26.
19. Jonathan Raban, *Soft City: The Art of Cosmopolitan Living* (New York: E.P. Dutton & Co., Inc., 1974), p. 100.
20. Cited in: Hakon Stang, *Materialized Ideology: On Liberal and Marxist Power Analyses, Westerness and the Car* (Oslo: University of Oslo, Trends in Western Civilization Program No. 12, 1977), p. 18.
21. Jeff Pelline, "Dodge Viper to Have Its Own TV Show," *San Francisco Chronicle*, May 3, 1993.
22. Todd Gitlin, "We Build Excitement," in Todd Gitlin, ed., *Watching Television* (New York: Pantheon Books, 1986).
23. Gorz, *op. cit.*, p. 70.
24. Institut fur Angewandte Umweltforschung, *Der Auto Knigge* (Reinbeck bei Hamburg: Rowohlt Verlag, 1990), pp. 186-187.
25. Siegfried Reinecke, "Der Mass aller Dinge: Autoculture und Medienkurse," in Paul Beekmans *et. al.*, eds., *Welche Freiheit Brauchen Wir? Zum Psychologie der AutoMobilen Gesellschaft* (Berlin: VAS in der Elefanten Press, 1989), p. 46.
26. Klaus Staeck, *ADAC Cade* (Gottingen: Steidl Verlag, 1990).
27. Rolf Monheim, "Policy Issues in Promoting the Green Modes," in Rodney Tolley, ed., *The Greening of Urban Transport: Planning for Walking and Cycling in Western Cities* (London: Belhaven Press, 1991), pp. 134-158.
28. Stephen Bayley, *Sex, Drink and Fast Cars: The Creation and Consumption of Images* (London: Faber and Faber, 1986), p. 31.
29. Cited in: Wayne Ellwood, "Car Chaos," *New Internationalist*, No. 195, May, 1989, p. 5.
30. Gerd Hickmann und Klaus Dieter Kaser, *Trau keinem uber Tempo 30* (Stuttgart: Grunen im Landtag von Baden-Wurttemberg, 1988), p. 10.
31. Cited in: Matthew L. Wald, "Where All that Gas Goes: Drivers Thirst for Power," *The New York Times*, November 21, 1990.
32. Barry Commoner, *Making Peace with the Planet* (New York: Pantheon Books, 1990).
33. Doron P. Levin, "Detroit's Assault on Mileage Bill," *The New York Times*, May 11, 1991.
34. M.D. Moorhouse, "American Automobiles and Worker's Dreams," *Sociological Review* 31 (1983):403-426.
35. Matt De Lorenzo, "Viper Brings Wide Grins," *San Francisco Chronicle*, February 5, 1993.
36. Wolfgang Sachs, *Die Liebe Zum Automobil* (Reinbeck bei Hamburg: Rohwohlt, 1990).
37. Adrienna Gianturco, "Die Verkehrspolitik der USA unter Feministichen Aspecten," in Paul Beekmans *et. al.*, eds., *Welche Freiheit Brauchen Wir? Zum*

Psychologie der AutoMobilen Gesellschaft (Berlin: VAS in der Elefanten Press, 1989), p. 131.
38. R. Stoddart, "Erfahrung of Young Drivers," in J. Peter Rothe, ed., *Rethinking Young Drivers* (British Columbia: Insurance Corporation of British Columbia, 1987), pp. 131-198.
39. Sara Rimer, "L.A.'s Phantom Toll Bus," *International Herald Tribune*, July 8, 1992.
40. Peter Hall, *Cities of Tomorrow: An Intellectual History of Urban Planning and Design in the Twentieth Century* (Oxford: Basil Blackwell, 1988), p. 282.
41. Joan Didion, *Play It As It Lays* (New York: Farrar, Straus & Giroux, 1970), p. 16.
42. Gudrun-Axeli Knapp, "Auto-Erotik: Sexualisierung und Sexismus," in Jobst Kraus, Horst Sackstetter, und Willi Wentsch, eds., *Auto, Auto Uber Alles?* (Freiburg: Dreisam Verlag, 1987), pp. 106-108.
43. Neal Templin, "Fewer Sexy 'Accessories' at Car Shows," *San Francisco Examiner*, January 20, 1991, p. 3.
44. Bayley, *op. cit.*
45. Sinclair Lewis, *Dodsworth* (New York: Harcourt, Brace and Co., 1929), p. 1.
46. Bayley, *op. cit.*, pp. 43, 109.
47. Gudrun-Axeli Knapp, "Auto-Erotik: Sexualisierung und Sexismus," in Paul Beekmans *et. al.*, eds., *Welche Freiheit Brauchen Wir? Zum Psychologie der Auto-Mobilen Gesellschaft* (Berlin: VAS in der Elefanten Press, 1989), pp. 61-74.
48. Stoddart, *op. cit.*
49. Jerry Kunz, "The Car—the Driver: Their Relationship in America," Unpublished, 1985.
50. Micha Hilgers, "Auto-Mobil oder das Selbst im Strassenverkehr: Zur Psychoanalyze des Automobilmissbrauchs," *Universitas* 46(1991):541-556.
51. Margret Eder, "Man kann doch nicht das Atmen verbieten," in Jobst Kraus, Horst Sackstetter, und Willi Wentsch, eds., *Auto, Auto Uber Alles?* (Freiburg: Dreisam Verlag, 1987), pp. 43-46.

CHAPTER 6

The Phenomenology of Automobility

Driving and living in auto space—space that is largely dedicated to auto use—have certain unique phenomenological aspects. These phenomenological aspects can be analyzed from a two-fold perspective: The character of the subjective experience of driving the auto, and the subjective experience of placelessness that resonates from automobility. It is only by considering these inner aspects that we can fully understand both the sources as well as the more subtle consequences of auto hegemony.

The Subjective World of the Auto

Our love affair with the auto is partly a result of becoming immersed or embedded in an auto world with its culture and activities, and the social spaces in which these are located. This process of subjective engagement involves becoming familiar with a world, expecting certain pleasures from it, and developing typical ways of relating to it. These typical ways may include a tendency to take the world of the auto for granted over time. Experiences in that world which we initially find troublesome, intrusive, or uncomfortable may recede from the forefront of our awareness as we become inured to them. In addition to changes in the way we apprehend events and surroundings, there are intrinsic features of experiences which influence our subjectivity by limiting how we notice what we are doing and where we are doing it. Social and physical activities, furthermore, make demands on our consciousness. They may require a certain subjective state from us. For example, driving demands that we be wide awake and alert to auto-motion relevant features of our environment. Sleeping or daydreaming are clearly inappropriate.

The subjective experience of automobility is invariably described in terms of pleasure, excitement, mastery, and similar positive feelings. Stephen Friedman described one aspect of the personal pleasure of driving in a dense urban space:

> Every city driver knows the thrill of racing against a light at a familiar intersection. And then there are the joys of covering large urban distances without stopping, thanks to luck, timing, and intimate knowledge of traffic patterns and the progressively timed lights on a particular route. How many mini-grand prix take place during the morning commute, and does the marathon drive have any of this quality.[1]

Such satisfaction from driving is real but it probably does not represent the conscious experience of most drivers most of the time. For one thing, the *grand prix* quality of driving that Friedman describes is more self-enhancing for males and is part of the primarily masculine oriented car culture. Furthermore, much of our bodily experience of environments is not fully conscious. The stress of driving can take its toll on the body without being consciously perceived.

Nonetheless, Friedman captures elements of subjectivity overlooked by many critics of automobility. Other observers have commented on the excitement of driving on the Los Angeles freeways and how for some drivers driving is a means of feeling alive.[2] Human-machine interactions can be experienced as a particular form of sensuous, energizing, relaxing, and self-enhancing pleasure. Parents sometimes take babies for a ride in a car in order to rock them to sleep or to soothe them. Riding in a car can be a rhythmic and relaxing experience, akin to sitting in a rocking chair. Apart from the ideological meanings that valorize speed, the experience of speedy motion also may be physiologically arousing—a kind of high which like many highs may be addictive for some.[3] It is unlikely, however, that such experiences predominate in the mundane tasks of driving to work and to shop.

When driving (and even when walking in auto space) one's subjective state continually must be geared to managing the demands of auto machinery and auto traffic. Both driver and pedestrian must maintain a wide awake and alert subjective relationship to their surroundings. As more and more space is appropriated by the auto, the demand for this instrumental, diligent, wide awake state of being becomes the rule. This leaves less psychosocial space and time for other states of mind, including playfulness and altered states of consciousness such as daydreaming. The imposition of a particular kind of subjectivity while driving or walking in traffic represents one of the more subtle forms of social control that accompanies auto-centred transport. It is in this sense that we can speak of a politics of subjectivity.

In order to illustrate the psychic dimensions of the "civilizing process"—one that involves increasing self-control—Norbert Elias used the analogy of different road systems. On the one hand, in the country roads of a simple warrior society there is little traffic and the primary danger is from human and other predators. Such a system requires a subjective readiness to fight or to flee and the ability to give free vent to one's emotions. On the other hand, "Traffic on the main roads of a big city in a complex society of our time demands a quite different moulding of the psychological apparatus."[4] Here, there is a complex flow of traffic to be navigated and attended to—with signals, pedestrians, cyclists and other vehicles. Self-control and a state of vigilance are essential. A loss of self-control can be lethal. While this analogy oversimplifies, it does illustrate a subjectivity that has come to be taken for granted in our society. Ironically, it has also been argued that in a society in which self-control is so pervasively necessary, the auto may function as one of the last "free spaces," a means of freedom and refuge from civilization.[5] Resistance to mass transit or to car pooling may come partly from the fact that "car time" for many people is one of the only occasions that they can be alone for an appreciable length of time.

Even if there are subjective refuges in automobility, the constant vigilance and self-control that it requires are not the natural conditions of consciousness. The rather narrow band of consciousness—and its constancy—demanded by successful automobility poses problems for humans. For example, in a transport system as homogenized as ours, what alternatives to driving are there for those who choose to get high or tipsy but then must get home? As one critic of auto-centred transport observed: "Is it really beyond our capacity to arrange the kind of life where we can drink a bottle with our friends and not have to worry about consequences more serious than falling down and skinning a knee?"[6] What happens to the elderly person who is impaired or someone who is daydreaming when they try to negotiate auto space?

The issue of whether or not people should or should not get high (on substances or activities) or daydream is one issue. How safely one can do this in the context of a particular mode of transport is another issue. In the debates about drunken driving few have defended people's rights to get drunk or have criticized the lack of transport alternatives. That drunken driving is dangerous and that pilots and engineers who get high are more likely to cause accidents are self-evident facts. What is not apparent is the taken-for-grantedness of the need for a more general sobriety in a technological society. Automobility requires all drivers to be their own pilots. Our increasing reliance on the auto makes sobriety, wide awakeness, and the optimal functioning of our biomechanical bodies, unquestioned norms demanded of anyone who wishes to have full freedom of movement.

Of course not everyone can function optimally at all times. That is one direct or manifest reason why there are auto accidents. However, the indirect or underlying reason is the auto-centred transport system that demands such ideal human functioning. With regard to this issue, one observer noted:

> When each individual is driving their own two-ton machine, our safety is dependent upon the mental state of all the other individuals behind the wheel. Competition for road-space and the need for momentary decisions makes constant vigilance essential. The reorganization of communities around the auto means we have to drive at all different times of day, no matter what our state of mind might be right then: fatigued from the day's work, angry at the boss's remarks, upset over breaking up with one's lover, tipsy after a few beers at one's favorite tavern or spaced-out from a couple [of] joints. Momentary lapses by individual drivers are inevitable.[7]

The focus of most discourses on auto accidents has been on the role of alcohol-impaired subjectivity. While alcohol and various sources of chemically-caused psychomotor incompetency certainly merit attention, other more mundane sources of distraction and interference with the appropriate driver-pedestrian oriented subjectivity tend to be excluded from discussion of auto accidents.

However, what can be called normal distraction (as opposed to chemically-induced distraction) is an important factor in auto accidents. The National Highway Traffic Safety Administration ranked inattentive driving, which includes talking, eating, etc., when driving, as the fourth most common in its list of eleven reasons for fatal crashes in the United States in 1991. Additionally, Peter Rothe has observed that normal emotional arousal contributes to auto crashes:

Almost all the young drivers felt comfortable on the day of the drive. Yet, significant variables could be highlighted which may indicate some form of temporary emotional instability. To illustrate, aroused emotions arising from sporting or recreational events, anxieties caused by school or work activities, aggressions resulting from romance problems, tensions because of car and weather conditions, resentments because of negative circumstances like having sprained an ankle, and thoughts about mental escape caused by poor work days may have influenced the driving act. Further, attention to passengers, the radio and/or cassette player, upcoming events and surroundings possibly contributed to the crashes.[8]

What is significant here is that to participate (even as a pedestrian) in an auto-centred system, one cannot be distracted by emotions or thoughts during one's travel time. Daydreaming, tiredness, the intrusion of personal troubles must be held at bay in an auto-oriented subjectivity.

In a court decision in the United States, an employer was held liable for a fatal car crash caused by a young and overtired employee. The plaintiff claimed that an employer can be held negligent for allowing a worker who has been working for an unreasonable length of time to drive. Some argued from the employer's perspective that an assessment of tiredness was a subjective one. One exclaimed, "What next? What about an employee who leaves work mad and then causes an accident?"[9] This court case is not unlike the ones that have held bar owners responsible for the sobriety of their driving customers. Such cases bring the issue of auto-oriented subjectivity to the fore but they shift responsibility for the demands of auto driving from drivers onto other individuals. They do not examine the *social* contexts and demands of transport technology and space. The assumption of wide-awakeness to the exclusion of other states of mind, and the inability to see this assumption as the result of socially constructed conditions, are integral features of the culture of automobility.

Most discourse on drunken driving reaffirms a certain kind of morality by conflating the issue of being drunk with the issue of safety. In this conflation the question of the freedom to be drunk does not surface as an important issue.[10] The right to Dionysian abandon or the opportunities for such abandon are not addressed. Since we devalue and trivialize (and fear) activities that alter consciousness in these ways, the idea of a freedom for people to get drunk or stoned while not putting others at risk seems strange. Yet the modes by which we transport ourselves are not unrelated to how dangerous various altered states of consciousness may be. A daydreaming pedestrian in a mass transit-, bicycle-, and walking-oriented transport system can still be a risk to himself or herself or to others, but in an auto-centred transport system the risk is greatly multiplied. Thus, according to National Safety Council data, in 1989 in the United States, 6,600 pedestrians and 800 bicyclists were killed by motor vehicles; many more were injured.

A critical phenomenology of driving and auto space must also address the following question: How do people experience the harmful and noxious consequences of auto hegemony? One answer is that they adapt and the consequences are not so much denied as pushed out of the centre of awareness. They come to be less noticed. One study showed residents of Los Angeles slides of landscapes that ranged from clear to smoggy and found that the longer people had lived in Los Angeles, the less likely they were willing or able to notice pollution.[11] When one of this book's authors first arrived in Los Angeles for a visit, the pollution created headaches, tearing eyes and other symptoms. Within a few days, not only had the bodily symptoms disappeared but the "mind-body" had adapted. Awareness of the pollution was minimized—at least on the surface of consciousness. What seems to happen is not only that the noxious features of the environment become less noticeable but that one's recollection of experiences in other, cleaner spaces fades.

Auto pollution illustrates how one may not notice one's own contribution to societal problems. Modern technology creates side effects that are not readily visible. Auto pollutants, for instance, may be spatially displaced; that is, they eventually become invisible to the naked eye as they "disappear" into the atmosphere or are carried elsewhere. The effects on health are slow and cumulative and many of the diseases that might be associated with auto pollution take decades to appear, as is the case with the empirical connections between smoking cigarettes and lung cancer, or between alcohol abuse and cirrhosis of the liver. The result is thus a temporal and spatial displacement of effects, making them less visible. As the number of pollutants increases (for example, through new additives to gasoline) new interactions of side effects may not emerge or be noticed for decades. These effects are not visible to the human eye but are detectable by longitudinal, experimental, or epidemiological research. Furthermore, while the tolls from much industrial pollution and from most environmental disasters are readily measured, the ecological costs of a socially pervasive lifestyle of individual consumption—costs which are diffuse and incremental—are less readily measured. Our subjective experience is simply unable to grasp the totality of effects, including our own contributions, of an auto-centred transport system.

Automobility also apparently contributes to our tendency to repress our conscious experience. For example, Dennis Hayes described daily life in Northern California's Silicon Valley, in which commuting is an integral part of everyday activities. As a response to traffic congestion, commuters turn inward and encapsulate themselves in their cars; they surround themselves with stereos or drugs to block out "the special pain of not getting somewhere fast."[12] There is a term used to describe the ways in which drivers turn their cars into electric nests—"carcooning."[13]

There are other, more speculative, consequences for subjectivity from being transported by motorized contrivance. For instance, by being regularly transported, do young persons lose some of their ability to develop cognitive maps of extended life space and a sense of distance and place? Although this issue is not restricted to the auto, the auto is central to it. Does the increased confinement facilitated by auto hegemony (because streets become dangerous, for example) atrophy our awareness of the texture and horizons of natural environments? In an auto-centred transport system children are to some degree housebound by auto-dominated space, as are older and disabled persons (as discussed in Chapter 3). A British Department of Transport road safety slogan—"one false move and you're dead"—highlighted the dangerous nature of streets for children. Despite children having television as a window to the world, is it possible that their experiences of spaces have become simulated and fragmented?

Many discourses on the use of the auto and other technologies (e.g., telecommunications) which compress time and space view them as enhancing expanded horizons and increasing contact with people at a distance—creating what has been called the "global village."[14] However, on the other side of this picture is the fact that these technologies may be used as tools to help people construct social realities which isolate them from other worlds and allow them to remain in their own enclaves. Spatial segregation, through the use of malls, freeways, and residential and corporate fortresses guarded by private security officers serve to isolate people and to restrict them from contact with people of other social groups.[15] As already noted, Mike Davis has analyzed how redevelopment in downtown Los Angeles reinforced the spatial apartheid of Anglos, African-Americans, and Latinos through the construction of moat-like freeways.[16]

Auto-centred transport has helped facilitate the further segregation of people into communities segmented along social class and racial lines. Of course the auto is not intrinsically a means of segregating populations. In the American South a white man fearing that the auto would promote integration was said to have advocated taking it away from blacks or at least creating a separate system of roads.[17] Yet in the past few decades, the auto, more than rail and other transport modes, has facilitated the movement of largely white and middle-class people from inner cities to encapsulated suburbs. While rail originally made this segregation possible, the auto, along with computers, television, and other telecommunications technologies, have accelerated the process. The result is an increase in the degree to which natural social contact with others is limited while the illusion of being "in touch" is maintained.

Placelessness

Car traffic allows people to mix and assemble without ever meeting.[18] There are often advantages to travelling with others without actually meeting them. Friedman argued that the popularity of the car may hinge partly on the fact "that it's such an effective filter in dealing with the incredible abundance of the city"; a car can be "a private box and public stage."[19] Though such experiences can be seen as contributing to the erosion of community, serving as substitute pseudo-relationships, and as severing contact with the natural and social environments, they need not be seen as altogether problematic. This is especially true in a society that values privacy or a society in which random contact with others is threatening or overwhelming.

While the physical structure of space in a society does not automatically create street culture and public use, it can either stimulate or inhibit them. Broadly speaking, a physical feature of pedestrian space that stimulates use is *complexity*, whereas auto space promotes simplicity. Thus, an environment that is "comfortably stimulating from a car becomes monotonously boring on foot, while what is interesting on foot becomes chaotic in a car."[20] At the higher speeds of auto travel, gradual curves, long views, wide symmetrical spaces, and low complexity are preferable. However, for the slower speed of the pedestrian, the opposite is true. Furthermore, while for the driver the visual is by far the most important sensory data, for the pedestrian non-visual features are also important; for example, smell and hearing. Of course it is not just speed in auto space but the commercialization of our experiences that engenders a sense of flatness, of sameness of environment, and of not being able to distinguish image from reality. This mode of apprehending the world constitutes the essence of the postmodern experience.

The appreciation of space and architecture constructed for the needs of auto transport played a key role in demarcating postmodern from modern society.[21] This appreciation was heralded by the publication of *Learning from Las Vegas* by Robert Venturi and his associates in 1972, in which parking lots, billboards, and other auto-associated structures were hailed as forms of architectural communication. The functionalism of modernism gives way to the symbolism of postmodernism in this analysis. Architecture in the "auto landscape becomes symbol in space rather than form in space."[22] Subsequently, roadside structures have been taken seriously as architectural forms—not only signs but motels and fast-food outlets as well.

In addition to contributing to the postmodern sensibility, the spread of the auto as the primary mode of transport has catalyzed the deterioration of vital public space. The accommodation of space to motion in an enclosed capsule has contributed to a loss of meaning for public spaces: "The technology of modern motion replaces being in the street with a desire to erase the constraints of geography."[23] Public space is no longer seen as a place in which to do many things but as essentially meaningless, except as something to pass through. In an auto-centred transport system, movement is measured by the time it takes to move from an originating point to a destination. Los Angeles serves as the prototype of the urban "vision of the citizen as motorist" as Jonathan Raban has noted:

> ... changed scale of speed and distance gave rise to a
> city ... in which individuals were perceived as
> voyagers: the neighborhood and the street were
> replaced by the super-highway, and the old supportive
> systems in which one knew who one was by the reflec-

tions given back by familiar faces from next door or the corner shop gave way to the bold, curt announcement of identity made by the motor car.[24]

The predominant effect of auto-centred transport has been to transform the psychosocial significance of place into the simple functionality of space. Auto transport, even more so than rail and air transport, has precipitated the transformation of place into space because only the auto has become a routine and personal means of conveyance. It is not only the quality of auto use ("personal") that sets it apart from other motorized modes in this respect; it is the intensity (routinization) of auto use as well.

Space as something to pass through may be an especially American sensibility. The American sense of rootlessness and mobility is mirrored in the landscape which an auto-centred transport system helped to construct. American suburban-exurban landscapes lack clear boundaries or centres and are protean, in their sense of being amorphous.[25] There is an unusual quality of homogeneity to American-built landscapes. Malls or shopping strips in California can hardly be distinguished from those in New Jersey or Kentucky. Such homogeneity may not penetrate the conscious awareness of the traveller—it can remain unnoticed. Yet it structures the experiences of place and travel. The tourist's fascination with commodified nostalgia and quaintness seems to express an American desire for roots.[26]

The authors of *The View from the Road* have described the auto driver's detachment from the environment well:

> The modern car interposes a filter between the driver and the world he is moving through. Sounds, smells, sensations of touch and weather are all diluted in comparison with what the pedestrian experiences. Vision is framed and limited; the driver is relatively inactive. He has less opportunity to stop, explore, or choose his path than does the man on foot. Only the speed, scale, and grace of his movement can compensate for these limitations.[27]

Thus, automobility contributes to the deauthentication of sense experience. It is impossible to absorb in real time the full sensory experience of driving. Photography can be used to catch what the driver actually sees. A noteworthy example of this kind of work is Alison Smithson's; she compiled a visual and written diary of auto travel from London to Wiltshire.[28] It is a revelation to see from the outside the limitations of a motorist's visual field. One does not get the same sense of constricted panorama when one is behind the wheel.

Perhaps place is of importance to humans because we are bodily beings—physically grounded on the surface of the earth. The need for an existential ground can be found even among nomads, who have a home base and who are intimately anchored to a few possessions and to their social networks. Homeless street people, burdened with shopping bags, layers of clothes and what seems to be a surplus of belongings, appear as irrational unless we understand that these objects may serve as a grounding physical anchor and a material connection to the world. Some trends in ecology like bioregionalism speak of a desire to recapture a natural sense of place.[29] While difficult to document, it can be argued that many, Americans especially, yearn for such a place, perhaps because American history has been so characterized by social mobility (upward, downward, and lateral) and geographic mobility. The auto both facilitates and expresses this movement.

The built environments of auto space—the sameness of high-speed freeways, vast parking lots—contribute to the *dis*-experience of where we actually are in space. This sense of placelessness is a principal source of the existential alienation experienced in city life. The postmodern city has surpassed our powers to map. This is a theme that began with the work of Kevin Lynch and continues with that of Fredric Jameson: "The alienated city is above all a space in which people are unable to map (in their minds) either their own position or the urban totality."[30]

As well as being a source of our simultaneous yearning for nature, community and stability, placelessness may be a cause of the ecological destructiveness of our way of life. Perhaps "rootedness in place promotes a more efficient use of energy, space and environment than today's place relationships, which emphasize social mobility and the frequent destruction of unique places."[31] Of course such a critique of automobility risks very conservative implications. Mobility may detract from community but it also frees people from a tyranny of place (and culture) and opens the horizons of their experience. German Greens argue that in valuing home space through the promotion of bioregionalist, locally-oriented, small-scale communities and in giving less priority to high speed movement, there is a danger of returning to a hermit-like notion of community, with its accompanying provincialism and ethnocentricity. Thus, while German Greens stress the need to revalue the spatially near, to devalue mobility and speed for their own sake, and to emphasize the quality of travel as opposed to its quantity, they do not suggest a return to a pre-industrial *Gemeinschaft* society.[32]

Our position is that unrestricted geographic mobility is not an unqualified good, if only because resources are limited. The German Greens emphasize local mobility over rapid movement across large distances.[33] Travel over long distances is not excluded; in fact, by reducing long travel for tasks such as shopping, long distance travel for other purposes (e.g., education) may be more available. While there is value in seeing new and distant places there is also value in greater appreciation of one's immediate surroundings. The alternative to auto hegemony need not be a place-bound, provincial immobility which narrowly turns inward, fears anything different or new, and breaks with the outside world. It is important to strive, as did Frances Willard, an American feminist and Christian socialist, for the goal of making "the whole world homelike."[34]

In conclusion, it is important to analyze the significance of place for the human condition, especially for ecology, community and individual ontological security. In a number of ways auto-centred transport has been instrumental in transforming the existential significance of place into the functional use of space. We continue our analysis of this transformation in Chapter 7 by focusing on the structure of urban physical space that has been fostered by auto-centred transport.

NOTES

1. Stephen Friedman, *City Moves: A User's Guide to the Way Cities Work* (New York: McGraw Hill, 1989), p. 238.
2. Edward Relph, *Place and Placelessness* (London: Pion Ltd., 1976), p. 130.
3. Stephen Bayley, *Sex, Drink and Fast Cars: The Creation and Consumption of Images* (London: Faber and Faber, 1986), pp. 31-32.
4. Norbert Elias, *Power and Civility* (New York: Pantheon Books, 1982), p. 233.
5. Till Bastian, "Auto-Mobilitat," *Universitas* 46(1991):515-516.
6. Wolfgang Zuckermann, *The End of the Road* (Post Mills, VT: Chelsea Green Publishing Co., 1991) p. 135.

7.   Tom Wetzel, "The Case Against the Auto," *Ideas and Action*, No. 14, Fall, 1990, p. 18.
8.   J. Peter Rothe, "Erlebnis of Young Drivers Involved in Injury Producing Crashes," in J. Peter Rothe, ed., *Rethinking Young Drivers* (British Columbia: Insurance Corporation of British Columbia, 1987), pp. 116-117.
9.   Cited in: Amy Stevens, "Bosses Fret They May Be Liable for Tired Workers on Road Home," *The Wall Street Journal*, April 16, 1991.
10.   Craig Reinarman, "The Social Construction of an Alcohol Problem," *Theory and Society* 17 (1988):91-120.
11.   Alan Weisman, "L.A. Fights for Breath," *The New York Times Magazine*, July 30, 1989.
12.   Dennis Hayes, *Behind the Silicon Curtain: The Seductions of Work in a Lonely Era* (Montreal: Black Rose Books, 1990) p. 39.
13.   Alan Durning, *How Much is Enough?* (New York: W.W. Norton, 1992).
14.   Marshall McLuhan, *Understanding Media: The Extensions of Man* (New York: New American Library/Signet, 1964).
15.   Marshall Berman, *All That is Solid Melts into Air: The Experience of Modernity* (New York: Penguin Books, 1988).
16.   Mike Davis, *City of Quartz: Social Struggles in Postmodern Los Angeles* (London: Verso, 1990).
17.   Dan Rose, *Black American Street Life: South Philadelphia, 1969-1971* (Philadelphia: University of Pennsylvania Press, 1987), p. 52.
18.   Henri Lefebvre, *Everyday Life in the Modern World* (New York: Harper & Row, 1971), p. 100.
19.   Friedman, *op. cit.*, p. 237.
20.   Amos Rapoport, "Pedestrian Street Use: Culture and Perception," in Anne Vernez Moudon, ed., *Public Streets for Public Use* (New York: Van Nostrand Reinhold Company, 1987), p. 88.
21.   Peter Hall, *Cities of Tomorrow: An Intellectual History of Urban Planning and Design in the Twentieth Century* (Oxford: Basil Blackwell, 1988), p. 300.
22.   Robert Venturi, D.S. Brown, and S. Izenour, *Learning from Las Vegas* (Cambridge, MA: The MIT Press, 1972), p. 110.
23.   Richard Sennett, *The Fall of Public Man* (New York: Vintage Books, 1978), p. 14.
24.   Jonathan Raban, *Soft City: The Art of Cosmopolitan Living* (New York: E.P. Dutton & Co., Inc., 1974), pp. 100-101.
25.   Relph, *op. cit.*, pp. 133-135.
26.   Dean MacCannell, *The Tourist: A New Theory of the Leisure Class* (New York: Schocken Books, 1976).
27.   Donald Appleyard, Kevin Lynch, and John R. Myer, *The View from the Road* (Cambridge, MA: The MIT Press, 1964), p. 4.
28.   Alison Smithson, *AS in DS: An Eye on the Road* (Delft: Delft University Press, 1983).
29.   See: Kirkpatrick Sale, *Dwellers in the Land: The Bioregional Vision* (San Francisco: Sierra Club Books, 1985).
30.   Kevin Lynch, *The Image of the City* (Cambridge, MA: The MIT Press, 1960); Fredric Jameson, "Postmodernism, or the Cultural Logic of Late Capitalism," *New Left Review* 146 (1984):89.
31.   David Seamon, "Afterword," in Ann Buttimer and David Seamon, eds., *The Human Experience of Space and Place* (New York: St. Martin's Press, 1980), p. 194.
32.   Andrew Dobson, *Green Political Thought* (London: Unwin Hyman, 1990).

33. Gerd Hickmann und Klaus Dieter Kaser, *Trau keinem uber Tempo 30* (Stuttgart: Grunen im Landtag von Baden-Wurttemberg, 1988).
34. Cited in: Dolores Hayden, "Capitalism, Socialism and the Built Environment," in Steven Rosskamm Shalom, ed., *Socialist Visions* (Boston: South End Press, 1983), p. 71.

CHAPTER 7

Auto Space

The concept of a social space—that space and its uses are socially constructed—has become since the late 1960s an increasingly significant factor in analyses of our civilization. European theorists in particular, notably Manuel Castells, David Harvey, and Henri Lefebvre, have developed formulations to explain the complex relationships between social space and class conflict, and between social space and the round of daily life.[1] In the 1980s and 1990s, the flip side of this coin—the idea that society is spatially constructed as well—has been elaborated. Thus, society's workings are now analyzed as being in some measure a product of spatial arrangements.[2] The contemporary exposition of this two-way direction of the relationship between society and space can be read in the work of Mark Gottdiener, David Harvey, Fredric Jameson, Henri Lefebvre, and Edward Soja.[3] It has been the auto, more centrally than any other technology, that has provided for the alterations of social life which underlie the burgeoning interest in the connections between the organization of society and of space. The transformation of urban space by the auto and all of its accouterments has profoundly reconfigured social life in the twentieth century.

To understand the key role the auto has played in transforming social space, it is important first to recognize that for automobility to function with all the personal mobility and flexibility that it can provide, much more is involved than the privately owned car.[4] The following are the necessary accessories of automobility: (1) a qualified driver; (2) an extensive network of roadways; (3) a legal, social, and technical system of operational controls that manage traffic; (4) ample storage facilities for autos when they are not in use; (5) an elaborate supporting infrastructure of service, repair, junking, and fueling facilities; and (6) production and distribution facilities. It is a fact of life in the twentieth century that the auto and its myriad accouterments have come to constitute the principal material for the built environments of urban areas. It is in this broad context that one can speak of a structure of auto space.

The spaces of urban areas have increasingly come to be dominated by auto traffic and an auto infrastructure, and this dominance is "taken for granted." The sovereignty of the auto and its needs in the city is relatively recent. As Wolfgang Sachs has documented, in its early days the auto was met with popular and legal resistance.[5] A Parisian writing in 1896 threatened to shoot the next auto driver who endangered his peace and security. After walking in Paris in 1924, the prominent architect of modernism, Le Corbusier, commented: "I think back twenty years to my youth as a student, the road belonged to us then; we sang in it, we argued in it, while the horse-bus flowed softly by"; later in his life Corbusier was to view the street as "a factory for producing traffic."[6]

Today the auto is the single most important influence on the configuration of urban spaces. The architect Peter Calthorpe has described some of the details of this influence:

> The car is now the defining technology of our built environment. It sets the form of our cities and towns. It dictates the scale of streets, the relationship between buildings, the need for vast parking areas, and the speed at which we experience our environment. Somewhere between convenience and congestion, the auto dominates what were once diverse streets shared by pedestrians, cyclists, trolleys, and the community at large.[7]

The auto requires many dedicated spaces. Although the uses of space by autos may appear to be random or unsystematic, in fact they comprise a structure. It is this general structure of auto space to which we now turn our attention. We shall examine the impacts of auto-centred space with regard to two aspects of contemporary social life: urban deconcentration and family life.

Urban Deconcentration: The Dispersed City

In its early heyday the auto provided a source of extraordinary and unprecedented mobility and pleasure. However, what was at first a chosen form of transport eventually became a needed one— as basic a need as food, shelter, or clothing in many cases. As the consumption of autos proliferated, the spatial and social patterns of society changed, and the auto was transformed from a choice into a requirement. Joseph Interrante has described this transformation:

> What began as a vehicle to freedom soon became a necessity. Car movement became the basic form of travel in metropolitan consumer society. However, there was nothing inevitable about metropolitan spatial organization or people's uses of cars upon that landscape. The car could have remained a convenience used for recreation and cross-movement outside areas serviced by railroads and trolleys, while people continued to use mass transit for daily commutation. Car travel could have remained an option offering certain distinct advantages; instead it became a prerequisite to survival. Moreover, this dependence upon the automobile was not the outcome of a corporate manipulation of consumer needs. Rather, it resulted from *reconstitution* of transportation needs within the spatial context of metropolitan society—a reorganization of the physical and social environment which the car facilitated but did not require.[8]

Thus, the massive changes in the twentieth century urban landscape, including the rise of metropolitan areas, were fuelled by auto consumption. In 1922, only 135,000 homes in suburban areas of sixty U.S. cities were beyond the reach of public transport; by 1940 it was 13 million.[9] As auto use grew, the sites of the daily round of social life became more dispersed, making the auto a necessity. It is in this way that the auto contributes to what Sachs has called an "exploding radius of activity" in contemporary life.[10]

The built environment that resulted from these changes is the highly decentralized city surrounded by sprawling suburbs and exurbs—the corporate city, to use David Gordon's term.[11] The corporate city is characterized by a downtown given over to high-rise office buildings, parking lots, and related structures. The streets of this downtown are often deserted at night, as commuting workers are in their suburban homes and former central business district functions have moved to outlying suburbs and to airport areas. The corporate city emerged in the auto age and its mediums—expressways, parking lots, malls, and commercial strips—dominate land space. The overall structure of the city is characterized by horizontal and diffuse sprawl, giving rise to the term, "fragmented metropolis."[12]

Los Angeles is the quintessential twentieth century corporate city that came of age with the auto, and the term fragmented metropolis was first applied to it. However, older cities also have been made over in the image of the corporate city by the political and socioeconomic forces of the twentieth century. Because of historical reasons and the timing of their redevelopment, most of these older cities, such as Detroit, are in worse shape—physically, socially, and economically—than the newer corporate cities such as Los Angeles. The term, "the centrifugal city," has been applied to Detroit to denote the process through which economic decentralization and population fragmentation have led to the central city's decline.[13]

The spatial feature most associated with auto hegemony is sprawl, a word which means "to spread irregularly." The auto facilitated and now sustains a pattern of settlement that is spread out diffusely over a large area. This is a pattern quite different from the concentrated and focused pattern of the pre-auto city. The auto's speed and flexibility make the more remote areas outside cities accessible. The development of limited-access highways and faster autos pushed the edges of metropolitan areas farther and farther from the centre. However, while limited-access highways are efficient as roadways for private vehicles, they discourage public transit. An example is Route 128, the first limited-access highway built to circle a major U.S. city. Opened in 1947, Route 128 "not only provided a positive means to turn the Boston suburban region over to the automobile, but it also created an effective barrier to the development of circumferential local bus transit."[14] Promoted by the auto, urban sprawl is now dependent on it because urban sprawl is low density and discontinuous, connected by narrow ribbons or strips of development. It maximizes the use of land and distances between points. As Samuel Wallace has noted: "Sprawl is a gluttonous use of land and stems from a combination of causes, including poor or nonexistent land use planning, which can sometimes be traced to lack of public regulation outside municipalities, independence of decision-making by land users, land speculation, and auto transit."[15]

Urban sprawl has been fostered by certain political and economic forces. The political economy of mature capitalism has been undergoing a major transformation in the last quarter of the twentieth century. In broad terms this transformation centres on a transition from capital accumulation rooted in concentrated, industrial mass production (Fordism) to one rooted in deconcentrated, flexible production, including home and informal (the underground economy) production and production in far-flung rural and Third World areas. Decentralized flexible accumulation depends upon the technologies of telecommunications, computers, and the auto and other motorized vehicles, as well as on high-speed air transport. These technologies make it possible for production to be done by a highly decentralized labour force, the basis of urban sprawl. The auto makes it possible for workers to live a great distance from their jobs and to work in a variety of schedules. Also, auto transport externalizes the cost of getting to and from work—the individual worker (and society, through mass transit) rather than the firm must bear this cost.

The dispersal and geographic mobility of post-Fordist production, according to Harvey, represent part of a new round of time-space compression.[16] The basis of Fordist time-space compression and greater capital accumulation was Taylorism (see Chapter 4) and the assembly line, both of which served to divide production into specialized routine actions and concentrate it into factories, enabling intensified productivity through economies of scale. More production was compressed out of available time and space. Thus, goods and skills become more rapidly obsolete, tasks change more rapidly, and capital turnover speeds up.[17] The present round of deconcentration allows for the flexibility of moving production units great distances in order to maximize profitability (by lowering labour cost and other costs of production) to rural areas as well as to the fringes of urban areas, and to the Third World. The fixity of Fordist production is replaced by the impermanence and fluidity of flexible production. This is a primary factor in the rise of exurban sprawl and the continued decline of central cities. Distance is compressed by speedy transport and time is compressed by telecommunications. Ironically, at the same time that production has become more decentralized, management and financial functions are still concentrated geographically—in corporate headquarters—and organizationally—in large transnational corporations.

New downtown corporate and commercial centres are material representations of flexible worldwide production, in which space is grotesquely distorted. A prominent example of such developments is Bonaventura in Los Angeles. Jameson has commented on the social implications of the "hyperspace" created by such built environments: "... this last mutation in space—postmodern hyperspace—has finally succeeded in transcending the capacities of the individual human body to locate itself, to organize its immediate surroundings perceptually, and cognitively map its position in a mappable external world."[18] The postmodern hyperspace engendered by contemporary built environments features towering high rise buildings with outsized internal atriums and external plazas. The buildings are sheathed in a reflective glass skin and house high speed elevators. All of these features collaborate to create non-referent spaces: One is easily lost or confused in a maze of vertical levels and horizontal passageways, all of which are similar in appearance. The result is a placeless dissociation. While conducive to auto technology, such built environments are estranging to pedestrians. As has been noted, their "effect is particularly alienating; where mirror-glass oppresses, hyperspace dominates, pedestrians get excluded or lost."[19]

In the most extreme example of postmodern auto-centred environments, simply crossing the street is made into a torturous driving manoeuvre:

> If you want to cross the street to visit another business, you do the following: you get in your car; risk your life by driving out into the constant traffic; go half a mile to the next turning place; risk your life to join the opposite stream of traffic; drive a half mile back to the driveway opposite where you started and turn into the car-park. But of course, in this city, people do not cross the street.[20]

The auto-centred development of cities features such contradictions as this one.

What we are witnessing in our cities, writ large, is a generic and dynamic process of capitalism—uneven development. Behind urban restructuring is the movement of capital to maximize profits. Thus, the growth of suburban and exurban areas and the deterioration of central cities are driven by capital investment and capital flight. The heightened mobility of capital, which is the basis of uneven development, means that it can be moved with accelerated speed and over greater distances today. The result is that areas of the world compete intensely for limited capital investment. The ways of attracting investment are lower labour costs (including non-existent or ineffective labour unions), tax breaks and tax incentives, and free or cheap land. The competition for capital investment produces winners and losers, and the older central cities of the U.S., on the whole, have been losers.

The auto has been a key in extending and intensifying the growth of the urban fringe, although it was light rail which originally created the urban fringe in the last half of the ninteenth century. The first suburbs were developed along rail and trolley lines to facilitate the movement of the traditional commuter, who travels from a suburban home to a central city job. It was the elimination of electric rail (see Chapter 8) that allowed the auto to dominate the traditional commuting pattern, and "in turn the automobile allowed the suburbs to sprawl more freely, and farther, than mass transit could ever have done."[21] It is important to note that auto-based sprawl is class-biased because of the costs of owning and using an auto, and the lack of low-cost housing in suburbs. Class (and racial) segregation is a salient feature of urban sprawl in the United States and it is in some measure an outcome of planning. A vivid example of this comes from the work of noted planner Robert Moses. He built his parkway bridges in New York too low for buses. The beaches and parks at the end of the parkways would be accessible only to car commuters.[22]

In addition to the availability of the auto there were at least three other preconditions for the expansion of suburbs—roads, restrictive zoning, and cheap financing for homes. All three of these preconditions were made possible in the United States by government. The 1956 Federal Highway Act marked the onset of widespread suburban freeway construction. Zoning already had been incorporated as a local government policing function in the first quarter of the twentieth century. The 1949 Federal Housing Act greatly increased the funds available to the Federal Housing Authority; the money went to low-cost financing of suburban homes, most notably new tract developments. These tract developments took on a generic name from their prototype—Long Island's Levittown.

Although it is a generic process of capitalism, uneven development does not take the same form or course in different eras and locales. As Michael Smith has pointed out, there are meaningful differences in the current processes of uneven development in two leading centres of world capitalism—the United States and Europe:

> ... the particular forms of uneven development [in the U.S.]—sprawling suburban development, widespread urban fiscal stress, extreme class segregation of

residential communities, and pronounced population deconcentration of affluent communities to the hinterlands—are not found in their same form in the other advanced capitalist states. In Europe, for instance, suburban sprawl is less pronounced; centralized state structures finance a larger share of local government budgets, thereby mediating local fiscal stress; uneven development tends to be more pronounced within central cities than between cities and suburbs; and the upper strata are less anti-urban in lifestyle and residential location.[23]

The two peculiarities of uneven development in the United States—sprawl and anti-urbanism—are additive factors in fostering greater automobility in the U.S. than in Europe. Other factors (discussed in Chapter 4) include the sheer availability of land in the U.S. and its frontier history.

The compression of space and acceleration of time in contemporary production contributes to a continuous destruction and reconstruction of urban areas. To use Marshall Berman's term, "all that is solid melts into air."[24] Spatial arrangements are continually transformed as new structures and transport infrastructures are built that facilitate production, the movement of workers, and the interests of developers who seek to valorize spaces. All of this change—what Joseph Schumpeter referred to as the "creative destruction" of capitalism—is not done in the framework of long range plans that account for social needs, but in the temporal framework of short-term profit considerations.[25]

An important feature of post-World War II development in the United States was that in contrast to before, when residential development followed infrastructure (e.g., schools, pre-existing transport), it was no longer "infrastructure bound" and could occur "randomly."[26] Three-quarters of the growth between 1980 and 1986 occurred in suburbs. Much of this growth was unplanned; for instance, it did not consider access to work and the availability of mass transit.[27] The assumptions of planners are that everyone owns an auto and that the auto can overcome any local distance.

In the latter part of the twentieth century, the auto has fostered four other suburban commuting patterns in the United States—to join the traditional pattern of suburb to central city. They are: (1) radial commuting, from one suburb to another; (2) reverse commuting, from central city to suburb; (3) local commuting within the same suburb; (4) extended commuting from non-metropolitan areas to central cities and suburbs and from central cities and suburbs to non-metropolitan areas. All four of these new patterns were made possible and are sustained by the auto. In most cases there is no alternative available to the auto. Public transit between suburbs, within suburbs, and from city to suburb in the morning and back in the evening is virtually nonexistent, as are other alternatives to the private auto, such as car pooling, walking, or cycling. Public transit still focuses on the traditional commuter; its services are structured for the suburban resident to travel to the central city in the morning and then home in the evening.

Modernist urban landscapes were built to facilitate automobility and to discourage other forms of human movement. Indeed, there is little social space for human activity outside buildings. The shopping mall has become a substitute for public squares and other forms of communal space. Malls are privately owned commercialized spaces built around use of the auto. They are rationalized so as to facilitate maximum consumption; for example, seats often are not comfortable so as to discourage sitting and talking. Malls and similar spaces differ from streets, which are public and are not subject to corporate control. Thus, the privatization and individualization of transport through use of the auto has been paralleled by the rise of privately controlled public spaces such as malls.

The dominance of the auto in urban areas has contributed to the decline of street life: "Because even the pedestrian is treated as someone going to and from a car, we miss or ignore opportunities to design spaces that promote truly public modes of seeing and moving."[28] Suburban communities encourage a turning inward to private worlds. Outside of one's home these private worlds consist of mini environments—favoured restaurants and malls, etc. Movement between these private worlds is through dead public spaces by car; hence, drivers in suburban landscapes often develop "environmental blinders."[29] Dead public spaces inhibit alternatives to the auto as well as opportunities to exercise and to socialize. Accommodations to auto traffic sacrifice public spaces used for resting, playing, pausing, and interacting. Sidewalks are viewed as "pedestrian movers" and many suburbs do not even build them. Even in areas where pedestrian travel is the dominant mode of transport, space is disproportionately allocated to auto use. For instance, in midday Manhattan two-thirds of all travel is on foot but only one-third of transport space is available to the pedestrian.[30] Another study of a midtown Manhattan area showed that only 22 percent of the people were in vehicles but they occupied 66 percent of the available space.[31]

The effects of auto hegemony on urban space were succinctly summarized by Jane Jacobs over a quarter century ago:

> Traffic arteries, along with parking lots, filling stations and drive-in movies, are powerful and insistent instruments of city destruction. To accommodate them city streets are broken down into loose sprawls, incoherent and vacuous for anyone on foot. Downtowns and other neighborhoods that are marvels of close grained intricacy and compact mutual support are casually disembowelled. Landmarks are crumbled or are so sundered from their contents in city life as to become irrelevant trivialities. City character is blurred until every place becomes more like every other place, all adding up to no place. And in the areas most defeated, uses that cannot stand functionally alone—shopping malls, or residences, or places of public assembly, or centers of work—are severed from one another.[32]

As much as auto use is responsible for the decline of public space the problem is much broader. As Jacobs pointed out, "we blame automobiles for too much."[33] Rather, blame should fall on the general transport and social arrangements of urban space. Transport is related to housing, employment, recreational and shopping facilities. Thus, it is the systematic spatial arrangements of the various functions of city life that are the central issue. Jacobs, and more recent students of urban life like Peter Newman and Jeffrey Kenworthy, suggest such a holistic analysis, which is the basis for comprehensive solutions to urban transport problems.[34]

Auto use crystallizes an important connection between space and social life. A driver in an auto takes up about 100 times the space that is needed by a pedestrian.[35] In addition to its sheer consumption of space, the auto changes the ways in which humans interact spatially. The physical apparatus of the auto spreads humans out—it distances them. The auto is a fixed and enclosed container that speeds. This material configuration affects social intercourse. Auto drivers cannot rub shoulders with each other (only fenders!) as pedestrians can. Auto drivers cannot look at other people eye-to-eye because of the speed at which they travel and because of the concentration re-quired by other features of the environment. This amounts to a new level of separation among people. Social relations among car drivers and connections between car drivers and their surroundings allow for a limited exchange of information.

It is clear that separation or distance from others has its ad-vantages. Thus one can avoid persons and interactions as well as danger. One reason why many people who live in cities, especially the middle class and women, drive autos where public transit is avail-able, is because they feel safer in their cars. What may not be so ap-parent are the disadvantages or distortions of auto-centred separation. Consider the following, for example: "Behavior which is the social equivalent of slamming a door in your face is not uncom-mon on the road, although that driver would never consider doing such a thing if you were not separated by a mass of steel and glass."[36] Cutting someone off on the road can be the social equivalent of slam-ming a door in someone's face. Such rude behavior can reach dangerous and quite anti-social proportions, as it does in freeway shootings and similar incidents, which have been increasing. The California Highway Patrol recorded 6,000 incidents of freeway violence between 1987 and 1991.[37]

The transformation of urban space and social life through in-creased dominance of auto traffic has been a gradual process, one that has been characterized by a self-propelling momentum. Again, Jacobs offered an excellent description of this process:

> No step in this process is, in itself, crucial. But cumula-tively the effect is enormous. At each step, it not only adds its own bit to the total change, but actually ac-celerates the process. Erosion of cities by automobiles is thus an example of what is known as "positive feed-back." In cases of positive feedback, an action produces a reaction which, in turn, intensifies the condition responsible for the first action. This intensifies the need for repeating the first action, which, in turn, intensifies the reaction, and so on, *ad infinitum*. It is something like the grip of a habit forming addiction.[38]

Auto addiction creates a space in its own image which makes alter-nate forms of mobility difficult or impossible. What is operating here is a kind of self-fulfilling prophecy. What is missing in Jacobs' description is an analysis of the role that the political economy, especially corporate interests, play in enhancing the feedback (see Chapter 8). Such feedback is fuelled by continuous underfunding of mass transit and overfunding of highways.

Family Life

The auto and the structure of auto space have helped to shape the nature of the contemporary family in other than the positive ways that are generally ascribed to it—the increase in family mobility, for example. Perhaps the first sociological analysis of the impact of the auto on family life was that of Robert and Helen Lynd in their classic study, *Middletown*. The study had numerous comments about the growing importance of the auto, including a lengthy discussion of it being one of the inventions that was remaking leisure. The Lynds found evidence that the auto was helping to bring families together, at least husbands and wives, in their leisure pursuits, especially "in spreading the 'vacation' habit."[39] However, they also found evidence that the auto was encouraging developments in the opposite direction, particularly a growing generational separation between parents and children. Use of the auto was in the top one-third of disagreements that boys and girls had with their parents. Thus, while the auto was shared by the whole family for Sunday drives or for vacations, it was also used separately by family members and increased the mobility and autonomy of individual family members. For example, of thirty girls charged with "sex crimes" in juvenile court in Middletown in 1923-1924, nineteen had committed the offense in an auto.

The auto has continued to add to centrifugal pressures on the family.[40] The irony of increased mobility is that it contributes to the social and existential isolation experienced by modern family members—from other family members as well as from other families. In contemporary auto-dependent, decentralized and suburbanized residential patterns, regular access to an auto is necessary for social life within and between families. Those without this access, the very young and the elderly among others, are subject to isolation. The public life of auto-dependent society also suffers as communal neighbourhood and street activities—often casual—have to be planned around auto transport. Teenagers must get rides to school and to the mall, for example. The fragmenting over-consumption of the auto has produced "his" car, "her" car and often a third car for junior in many middle- and upper middle-class families in the U.S. It is not uncommon today for family members to travel to the same social occasion in separate autos.

Despite its advantages for family mobility in recreational activities, the auto is primarily used for getting to and from work, shopping, and running errands. The percentage of trips made in pursuit of recreation has declined in the past twenty years. According to Department of Transportation data, in the United States social and recreational trips declined from 22.2 percent of all vehicle trips in 1977 to 20.5 percent in 1990. The proportion of family or personal business trips has increased and the largest category of such trips is transport-generated, including picking up or dropping off someone or taking the car in for maintenance.[41] Thus, the transformation of social space has made the auto less a means of leisure than when it first appeared; a goodly number of auto-driving time and mileage now are devoted to new forms of "transport work" such as searching for a parking place, which are generated by auto-dependence.

The hegemony of the auto over space, particularly in cities, has meant that space once used for other functions, such as socializing and playing, has been appropriated. Children and families in poorer inner city neighbourhoods are particularly affected by this. For example, one woman recalled a play street that existed in the New York City neighbourhood of her childhood:

> When I was five years old I played in the street. There was no fear of being hit by a car because the street was a Play Street. This may be an unknown phenomenon to many children of today, but when I was growing up, the Play Street was the center of my universe!
>
> My block of Thompson Street, which ran between Canal and Grand Streets in what is now called SoHo, was guarded by a white sign with black lettering atop a pole anchored in cement. Its borders were a church, a basketball court, a luncheonette and the Grand Street Bus. The traffic thundered across Canal Street, yet our Play Street was a safe haven where we could romp, minimally supervised from dawn until dusk. And did we play!
>
> The neighborhood consisted of tenement buildings that surrounded the street so that our mothers could glance out of the window to check up on us from time to

time. If we were out of sight, one call would bring us running into view. This flexibility let us develop a sense of independence at an early age. And there was always some adult on the street—just in case. Everyone looked out for everyone else in those days, and kept an eye on the children.[42]

For the narrator the play street was an "extension of her apartment"—an urban "backyard," so to speak. It allowed her freedom of movement and provided for neighbourhood surveillance as well as community socializing. The growing scarcity of such spaces today has an adverse impact on family and community life in many inner city areas.

In conclusion, the structure of space that has been fostered by auto-centred transport has had a meaningful impact on the quality of our social lives, including our family lives. In order to extend our understanding of how auto-centred transport became and remains dominant, we now turn our attention to an analysis of the politics of transport policy.

NOTES

1. Manuel Castells, *The Urban Question: A Marxist Approach*, trans. Alan Sheridan (Cambridge, MA: The MIT Press, 1977); Manuel Castells, *City, Class and Power*, trans. Elizabeth Lebas (New York: St. Martin's Press, 1978); David Harvey, *Social Justice and the City* (London: Edward Arnold, 1973); Henri Lefebvre, *Le Droit à La Ville* (Paris: Anthropos, 1968); Henri Lefebvre, *Everyday Life in the Modern World*, trans. Sacha Rabinovitch (New York: Harper & Row, 1971).
2. Doreen Massey, "Politics and Space/Time," *New Left Review* 196 (1992):65-84.
3. Mark Gottdiener, *The Social Production of Urban Space* (Austin: University of Texas Press, 1985); David Harvey, *The Condition of Postmodernity: An Enquiry into the Origins of Cultural Change* (Oxford: Basil Blackwell, 1989); Fredric Jameson, *Postmodernism, or, The Cultural Logic of Late Capitalism* (Durham: Duke University Press, 1991); Henri Lefebvre, *The Production of Space*, trans. Donald Nicholson-Smith (Oxford: Basil Blackwell, 1991); Edward W. Soja, *Postmodern Geographies: The Reassertion of Space in Critical Social Theory* (London: Verso, 1989).
4. Robert A. Burco, "Urban Public Transport: Service Innovations in Operations, Planning, and Technology," in Ralph Gakenheimer, ed., *The Automobile and the Environment: An International Perspective* (Cambridge, MA: The MIT Press, 1978) p. 117.

5. Wolfgang Sachs, *Die Liebe Zum Automobil* (Reinbeck bei Hamburg: Rohwohlt, 1990).

6. Cited in: Marshall Berman, *All that is Solid Melts into Air: The Experience of Modernity* (New York: Penguin Books, 1988), pp. 165, 167.

7. Peter Calthorpe, "The Post-Suburban Metropolis," *Whole Earth Review*, No. 73, Winter, 1991, p. 45.

8. Joseph Interrante, "The Road to Autopia: The Automobile and the Spatial Transportation of American Culture," in David C. Lewis and Laurence Goldstein, eds., *The Automobile and American Culture* (Ann Arbor: University of Michigan Press, 1983), p. 100.

9. *Ibid.*, p. 93.

10. Sachs, *op. cit.*, p. 217.

11. David M. Gordon, "Capitalist Development and the History of American Cities," in William K. Tabb and Larry Sawers, eds., *Marxism and the Metropolis: New Perspectives in Urban Political Economy* (New York: Oxford University Press, 1984), pp. 21-53.

12. Robert M. Fogelson, *The Fragmented Metropolis* (Cambridge, MA: Harvard University Press, 1967).

13. June Manning Thomas, "Detroit: The Centrifugal City," in Gregory D. Squires, ed., *Unequal Partnerships: The Political Economy of Urban Redevelopment in Postwar America* (New Brunswick, NJ: Rutgers University Press, 1989), pp. 142-160.

14. K.H. Schaeffer and Elliott Sclar, *Access for All: Transportation and Urban Growth* (Baltimore: Penguin, 1975), p. 91.

15. Samuel E. Wallace, *The Urban Environment* (Homewood, IL: The Dorsey Press, 1980), p. 78.

16. Harvey, *op. cit.*

17. Roger Friedland, "Space, Place and Modernity: The Geographical Moment," *Contemporary Sociology* 21 (1992):11-15.

18. Fredric Jameson, "Postmodernism, or the cultural logic of Late Capitalism," *New Left Review* 146 (1984):83.

19. Philip Cooke, "The Postmodern Condition and the City," in Michael Peter Smith, ed., *Power, Community and the City* (New Brunswick, NJ: Transaction Books, 1988), p. 68.

20. John Lichtfield, "No Particular Place to Live," *The Independent*, November 15, 1992, p. 9.

21. Peter Hall, *Cities of Tomorrow: An Intellectual History of Urban Planning and Design in the Twentieth Century* (Oxford: Basil Blackwell, 1988), p. 315.

22. *Ibid.*, p. 277.

23. Michael Peter Smith, *City, State, and Market: The Political Economy of Urban Society* (New York: Basil Blackwell, 1988), pp. 6-7.

24. Berman, *op. cit.*

25. Joseph A. Schumpeter, *Capitalism, Socialism, and Democracy* (New York: Harper & Brothers, 1947).

26. Richard K. Untermann, "Why You Can't Walk There: Strategies for Improving the Pedestrian Environment in the United States," in Rodney Tolley, ed., *The Greening of Urban Transport: Planning for Walking and Cycling in Western Cities* (London: Belhaven Press, 1990), pp. 173-174.

27. Deborah Gordon, *Steering a New Course: Transportation, Energy and the Environment* (Cambridge, MA: Union of Concerned Scientists, 1991), p. 46.

28. Joseph Kupfer, "Architecture: Building the Body Politic," *Social Theory and Practice* 11 (1985):178.
29. Richard K. Untermann, "Can We Pedestrianize the Suburbs?" in Anne Vernez Moudon, ed., *Public Streets for Public Use* (New York: Van Nostrand Reinhold Company, 1987), pp. 123-132.
30. Simon Breines and William Dean, *The Pedestrian Revolution: Streets without Cars* (New York: Vintage Books, 1974), p. 8.
31. "Manhattan Walkers Need More Space," in *The Region's Agenda* (New York: Regional Plan Association, 1990).
32. Jane Jacobs, *The Death and Life of Great American Cities* (Baltimore: Penguin Books, 1965), p. 352.
33. *Ibid.*, p. 352.
34. Peter G. Newman and Jeffrey K. Kenworthy, *Cities and Automobile Dependence: A Source Book* (Brookfield, VT: Gower Technical, 1989).
35. Karen Christensen, *Home Ecology: Simple and Practical Ways to Green Your Home* (Golden, CO: Fulcrum Publishing, 1990), p. 115.
36. *Ibid.*, p. 115.
37. James T. Drummond, "A New Era in Road Policy," *Nation's Business* 79 (1991):20.
38. Jacobs, *op. cit.*, p. 363.
39. Robert S. Lynd and Helen Merrell Lynd, *Middletown: A Study in American Culture* (New York: Harcourt Brace Jovanovich, 1929), p. 261.
40. George T. Martin, Jr., "Family, Gender, and Social Policy," in Laura Kramer, ed., *The Sociology of Gender* (New York: St. Martin's Press, 1991), pp. 323-345.
41. David Morris, *Self-Reliant Cities: Energy and the Transformation of Urban America* (San Francisco: Sierra Club Books, 1982).
42. Livia Pantoliano, "Thompson Street, My Backyard," *Auto-Free Press* 2 (1991):5.

PART THREE

Politics and Alternatives

CHAPTER 8

The Politics of Transport Policy

Because of its taken-for-granted nature, transport is assumed to be apolitical. It is seen as just a way of getting somewhere. However, in modern societies the routine ways of getting somewhere are dominated by one mode—the auto. Consequently, the auto has profound political implications for the social uses and meanings of space, time, and motion. In the first place, the success of the auto-centred transport system as a global model has been made possible by certain political and economic forces. Furthermore, the system as it exists now has pervasive and meaningful political dimensions.

One of the clearer ways in which auto-centred transport has political implications is in its differential availability to groups of citizens (see Chapter 3). It is almost axiomatic by now that transport policy neglects the interests of the poor, the aged, women, children, and the physically and mentally impaired. Thus, central city subways that largely serve the urban poor are generally in woeful condition in the United States, while rapid rail service for suburban commuters is in considerably better shape. The newer light rail systems are being built to connect central business districts with suburbs, not to serve the needs of poorer inner city workers. For example, plans to build a branch of the Washington, DC, Metro in a central city area were abandoned as not being cost effective.[1] Members of the middle and upper classes as well as corporate interests dominate the agencies that make decisions about transport.

Furthermore, an auto-centred transport system's emphasis on geographic mobility can be understood in a political and economic context. On the most general level, high rates of rapid mobility stimulate and have an affinity with advanced capitalism's compression of time and space. Social needs (i.e., energy efficiency, reduced pollution, democratic transport) are decidedly inferior to private economic imperatives in the development of transport infrastructures. In the United States, government has played an important role in helping to subsidize such systems.

Government Subsidy of the Auto

Auto transport is conventionally seen as cheaper than it really is. This is because the costs of auto transport are not as readily perceived as those of mass transit. In the case of rail transport, for example, tracks, stations, bridges, and personnel are not organizationally separate, hence, their costs are apparent. In the case of auto-centred transport there is a separation between the physical (highways) and personnel (highway and police departments) infrastructures that are publicly maintained, and the private costs paid by individual drivers. Auto-centred transport systems combine private and public consumption in such a way as to mask the total cost of the systems. The fact that the real costs of automobility are more dispersed and obscured makes them harder to perceive. The way a transport system is organized therefore may affect our perception of its cost. When one uncovers the true costs of automobility by revealing its hidden subsidies—for instance, for roads and environmental costs—one deconstructs the myth of automobility: That it is an individual pay-as-you-go form of transport. As both the costs of auto production and consumption are unveiled so is the systemic quality of auto-centred transport.

One of the more subtle hidden costs of energy-resource intensive technologies such as the auto is that they rely on what Amory Lovins and Hunter Lovins have called brittle power.[2] Brittle power is a system of energy use that requires centralized sources and a continuity of flow, and that lacks diverse options in case of breakdowns. These and other characteristics of petroleum energy make it geopolitically vulnerable and encourage expensive military measures to defend sources and distribution. The recurrent crises in the oil-rich Middle East demonstrate this liability of brittle power.

The costs of automobility are also obscured on the level of individual use; consumers frequently underestimate its costs. A typical commuter will figure his or her variable costs of driving to work (gasoline, tolls, parking fees) with the cost of transit (the fare) and see little difference. For example, the authors commute from New York City to suburban New Jersey to work. We have heard fellow workers who drive say that the day's cost is about $5, while public transit costs twice as much—about $11 (for subway and bus). However, these drivers do not include the full costs of driving. In 1992 in the U.S. the average passenger car operating costs were 45.77 cents per mile. This figure included variable costs (gas and oil, maintenance, and tires) and fixed costs (insurance, license and registration, depreciation, and financing), but did not include parking fees and tolls.[3] Thus the real cost to our colleagues who drive is about $18 for the thirty-mile round trip (including toll but excluding parking charges), 60 percent more than the cost of transit. The cost of driving is even higher for those drivers who rent garage space. Even if one considers that the auto is used for other trips, it is no bargain at these costs.

The costs of the auto are hidden in yet another way—government subsidies to drivers. A critical reason why Americans drive so much more than do citizens of other nations is the existence of hidden government subsidies which are above and beyond the out-of-pocket costs for drivers. These subsidies are spent for the purchase of land, for road construction and maintenance, for policing and for other services. The total public expenditure for these services in the United States was estimated at $300 billion in 1990, or about 7 percent of the GNP. Only 62 percent of these costs were recovered from driver (user) fees such as gasoline taxes, leaving a subsidy of $114 billion in 1990.[4]

The final manner in which the costs of automobility are hidden is the least apparent—its societal costs, including the deleterious effects on public health created by auto pollution and auto accidents. Public and private insurance plans distribute much of these rising health costs of automobility throughout the population. One way in which to conceptualize the societal costs of auto-centred transport is in terms of its externality costs, or the costs external to actual purchase and operation: "The essential characteristic of an externality is that it escapes normal market transactions."[5] The leading external costs of motor vehicle operation include air and noise pollution, pavement wear and tear, vibration damage, congestion, and traffic accidents. The most expensive of these costs, congestion, amounted to over $150 billion in the United States in 1990. External costs of congestion in the U.S. are quantified by the Federal Highway Administration; they include excess travel time and additional vehicle operating costs. A number of external costs of motor vehicle operation are not yet even quantified, including the costs of environmental damage and clean-up resulting from oil spills and the costs of auto chassis and tire disposal.[6]

Direct and indirect subsidy of the auto is a public policy decision; in effect, it is a political decision. These and other government measures comprise transport policy, which can be seen as one aspect of overall domestic or social policy. Levels of auto use then are neither "natural" nor the simple outcome of individual choices. Government, especially in the U.S., has not been neutral with regard to the development and maintenance of transport modes. The government promotion of rail transport in the nineteenth century through right-of-way land grants and other subsidies is a historical reality. In the twentieth century, public policy has been dominated by the promotion of vehicular transport. The conventional wisdom among traffic engineers and other transport specialists is that their work is shaped exclusively by scientific and technical imperatives, which exist apart from political and economic contexts. Yet political considerations do shape the context of their work—its funding, planning priorities, and its impacts on various social groups.

Our argument here challenges the conventional wisdom. Contrary to the popular myth that auto-centred transport is the outcome of technical imperatives, consumer choice, and free enterprise, in fact it would not have become entrenched without the benefit of massive government subsidy. Technical imperatives, consumer choice, and the market have been shaped and constrained by policy decisions to promote automobility. The conventional wisdom is that it is mass transit that is supported by tax payers and lives at the public trough, while auto transport is funded only by private individuals. However, the reality is otherwise, as James Flink noted some twenty years ago:

> Reactionary defenders of the mythical free enterprise system ignore the reality that our highway system is already nationalized and that the irrational proliferation of the post World War II automobile culture occurred less because of consumer demands in a free market than because of the government's massive indirect subsidization of the automobile and oil industries, especially through the Interstate Highway Act of 1956.[7]

The U.S. Interstate Highway Act of 1956 initiated one of the largest construction projects in human history—about 41,000 miles of freeways. The public was not very informed about this system, and there was no public clamour for it.[8] Auto manufacturers, trucking companies, and construction firms, while not always agreeing on details, were the primary movers in creating this vast subsidy for the auto and the truck. The Act appealed to President Eisenhower because of his regard for the contribution that Germany's autobahn system had made to its war effort. The Act was also justified on national defense grounds and took advantage of the Cold War mentality that characterized the early 1950s. The auto industry seemed to be aware of the implications of the Act for land use patterns (e.g., urban sprawl), including the advantages that the Act provided for its own economic interests.[9]

Building freeways is not the only way that government subsidizes automobility; it has indirectly subsidized automobility by encouraging dispersed, less dense land use. In the early 1990s the U.S. Federal government provided about $70 billion annually to subsidize the private suburban home market, primarily through the tax deductibility of home mortgage interest. Renters, concentrated in central cities, receive no such housing subsidies.

Government has shown a consistent bias in favour of auto transport for the past half century, as well as in favour of promoting the utilization of fossil fuels such as oil.[10] One example is illustrative of the hidden costs of automobility. It is estimated that about 40 percent of the expenses for the Pasadena, California police department are auto related, including traffic control costs. If Pasadena could impose a gasoline tax to cover these auto related expenses, the amount would have to be 39 cents per gallon of gasoline sold within the city.[11]

Between 1956 and 1970 the U.S. government spent $70 billion for highways and $795 million, only 1 percent of its transport budget, for rail transit.[12] In the 1970s subsidies for mass transit increased somewhat but were cut back during the Reagan Administration years. Between 1980 and 1989 the proportion of all Federal transport infrastructure expenditures that went to highways rose from 45 percent to 54 percent, while the share that went to mass transit declined from 16 percent to 13 percent. Expenditure on rail, aviation, and waterway infrastructure declined from 39 percent to 33 percent.[13] The Bush Administration of 1988-1992 followed the lead of the Reagan policy; mass transit subsidies were cut further and Amtrak subsidies were almost eliminated.[14] State and local governments have also been reducing public transit budgets in response to fiscal crises.

Pro-auto public policies are not unique to the United States. In Canada there has also been a trend towards reducing support for mass transit.[15] In West Germany between 1960 and 1983, 210 billion deutschmarks were invested in highway construction, but only 23 billion DM were invested in the development of the rail network. The West German rail system has been eroding for years. Between 1950 and 1981, 7,000 kms of rail line were abandoned in West Germany.[16] A study found that government protection and promotion policies were one of the four factors accounting for the growth of Japan's motor vehicle industry.[17]

While pro-auto public policies are not unique to the United States, the high level of government support for the auto coupled with its low level of support for alternatives is unique. In European nations, transport policy is less shaped by corporate and market considerations than it is in the United States. Urban mass transit in Europe is viewed as an essential social service that should not be subjected to the vagaries of the market. After World War II, Japan and European nations rebuilt their mass transit systems; during the same time mass transit in the United States was allowed to decline. Currently, European and Japanese local governments are more apt to recognize the need to create a balance among various transport modes, to develop intermodal connections, and to link transport policy to land use.

Private economic interests often motivate government transport policy, especially in the United States. With regard to auto transport, these private economic interests can be seen as comprising a network of corporate and other players—a network that can be referred to collectively as the auto-industrial complex.

The Auto-Industrial Complex

In the United States three groups of interests dominate government transport policies. The first of these is the private-sector highway lobby, which includes oil companies, the auto industry, trucking companies, and road construction companies. The second consists of central city business interests, including the headquarters of transnational corporations, which seek to facilitate access to businesses and to increase property values in downtown areas.[18] The third interest group is composed of public-sector highway and transport departments, including professionals and bureaucrats whose jobs depend upon the building and maintenance of highways and other roadways. Taken together, these three interest groups can be said to comprise the auto-industrial complex, a potent player in U.S. politics—far more powerful than public interest groups which often oppose it.

The principal base of the political influence of the auto-industrial complex is the large role that it plays in modern economies. Autos comprise about one-fifth of the dollar value of retail sales in the

United States. Employment in motor vehicle and related industries in the United States was 13.1 million in 1989; this represented 14.3 percent of all employment, or about one in seven of all workers. These employees include chauffeurs and truck drivers, auto and refinery workers, sales and service workers, and road construction, safety, and maintenance workers, as well as workers in vehicle and vehicle parts' plants. In 1991, motor vehicle production alone represented 3.3 percent of the GNP of the United States.[19] The central role of the auto in economies is reflected in other ways. For example, data from the U.S. Census Bureau showed that the single largest category of expenditure for television network advertising in 1990 was automotive, representing 17.6 percent of the total expenditure of $1.8 billion. In Japan, which has been the world's largest motor vehicle producer since 1980, the industry demonstrates similar economic strength. In 1985, employment in Japan's motor vehicle and related industries totalled 5.3 million workers, or 10.2 percent of the labour force.

While the specific ways in which the political influence of a national auto-industrial complex operate vary because of institutional and historical differences, that influence is considerable in all major auto-producing nations. Glenn Yago's historical analysis has demonstrated the critical role played by what he calls the "corporate car complex" in the United States and in Germany in the twentieth century in the transition from a rail/electric to an auto/oil transport technology.[20] A major difference between the two national experiences was the earlier and more rapid decline of public transit in the U.S., due mainly to two factors: the longer tenure of competitive capitalism and the earlier rise of an auto-industrial complex.

The origins of the auto-industrial complex in the United States can be traced to the 1930s, when urban transport was still dominated by mass transit. A major impetus for the adoption of auto-centred transport was the dismantling of urban electric railways and their replacement by bus and auto transport, beginning in the 1930s.[21] General Motors played a leading role in this change, through the National City Bus Lines and other of its subsidiaries. The 1,100-mile Pacific Electric Red Car System in Los Angeles and Orange Counties was purchased and torn up by GM, Firestone Tire and Rubber Company, and Standard Oil Company of California; the system was gone by 1962. The Key System Lines connecting San Francisco and East Bay cities was similarly dismantled.[22] This so-called GM conspiracy was not the only contributor to the decline of light rail mass transit. The already growing rise of automobility was also a factor. Other causes included the rail transit companies themselves. They were mismanaged, they used their power to promote suburban real estate ventures, and they bribed elected officials to promote their financial interests at tax-payer expense.[23]

One contemporary example of how the auto-industrial complex operates is the Coalition for Vehicle Choice in the United States. This national lobbying organization works to convince politicians and the public that stricter fuel-efficiency rules would force drivers into cramped and unsafe cars. While the organization's spokesperson asserts that it is independent, it was reported that by 1991 the auto industry had poured more than $10 million into the organization and that its sole mission is "to defeat proposed legislation mandating much tougher fuel-efficiency standards."[24]

Despite the influence of the auto-industrial complex the government is not simply its agent. Within limits other interest groups and constituencies—even those antagonistic to corporate interests—can prevail. The more important point is that not all interest groups are equal in their command of money and political influence. Thus, between 1981 and 1988, the political action committees of the Big Three (General Motors, Ford, and Chrysler) gave U.S. Congressional candidates over $700,000. Additionally, all the PAC's opposed to clean air legislation gave political candidates $23 million during that period, according to the U.S. Public Interest Research Group. GM alone spent $1.8 million between 1981 and 1988 to oppose clean air legislation.[25] These sums dwarfed expenditures by supporters of clean air legislation. The auto-industrial complex is monied and quite influential; the interest groups that oppose it are considerably less monied and less influential. These conditions create contradictions. The government is often in the position of simultaneously supporting improved mass transit and other alternatives to the auto, while at the same time it supports the auto-industrial complex which mitigates strongly against mass transit use.

The effect of the auto-industrial complex is not one of mechanically determining outcomes but one of constraining the range of available options and of influencing discourses about them. Within certain parameters and under particular conditions public interest groups and critics of the auto do influence transport policy. The power of the auto-industrial complex is not monolithic but it is real. There are at least three examples in recent U.S. history of the auto-industrial complex giving way to the public will. The first was the anti-freeway revolt. In the 1950s and 1960s citizen groups effectively organized to stop the construction of freeways in Boston, Washington, DC, and San Francisco. These local citizen groups comprised a wide variety of ethnic and racial groups and different social classes.[26] The second example of defeat for the auto-industrial complex in the 1960s was made possible by a conjunction of favourable conditions that brought about a shift in the discourse about injuries resulting from auto accidents. Thereafter, considerably more emphasis was placed on the auto industry's responsibility to build safer cars. The third example of auto industry retreat was fuelled by the worldwide oil supply crisis of 1973. The U.S. government for the first time mandated fuel-efficiency standards.

These three setbacks show that the auto-industrial complex is not omnipotent. We now turn our attention to a more detailed analysis of previous and current challenges to the auto-industrial complex.

Challenges to Auto Hegemony

Criticism of the auto is not new. The first big dents in auto ideological hegemony in the U.S. were made in the late 1950s. The witty auto riposte by John Keats began with the following lines: "Once upon a time, the American met the automobile and fell in love. Unfortunately, this led him into matrimony, and so he did not live happily ever after."[27] The title of Keats' serio-humorous tract—*The Insolent Chariots*—was suggested in a speech given by Lewis Mumford in 1957. Although now it seems somewhat corny and sexist, Keats' book caught the popular fancy at the time and expressed the inchoate rumblings that were being heard about the escalating costs and declining quality of the auto.

The signal success of the German-made Volkswagens in the 1960s was dramatic evidence of a shift; the VW captured the attention of millions of U.S. autoists precisely because it countered Detroit's weaknesses—it was inexpensive to buy and to operate and it was durable. Another blow to the auto-industrial complex in the United States was struck in the 1960s around a new issue—safety. Ralph Nader's publication of *Unsafe at Any Speed* in 1965 was the single most instrumental factor in the passage of the Traffic and Motor Vehicle Safety Act of 1966.[28] Despite the recalcitrance of the auto-industrial complex there was a general shift in public policy towards emphasizing safety technology. This shift was partly the result of the general growth in regulation in the late 1960s and early 1970s, which also produced the Occupational Safety and Health Act of 1970. It was also a period in which profits were healthy and regulatory changes were not as financially burdensome for the auto industry. Furthermore, it has been argued that the leadership of the auto industry was not politically experienced at the time; it was somewhat taken by surprise by the growing criticism of the auto, notably that of consumer activist Nader.[29]

Air pollution was quickly added to the list of auto problems by the burgeoning environmental movement, which had been heralded by Rachel Carson's publication of *Silent Spring* in 1962.[30] After research demonstrated the auto's high air pollution quotient, the Motor Vehicle Air Pollution Act of 1965 was passed. The 1960s also witnessed the expansion of Lewis Mumford's critique (an earlier cry in the wilderness against automobility) among another generation of urbanologists, most notably Jane Jacobs. The variety and density of auto critiques reached a new level as they were tied to separate critiques of urban renewal ("urban removal"), which paved the way for the construction of auto infrastructures, and of urban sprawl.

By the early 1970s it had even become somewhat fashionable to be an auto critic and a spate of anti-auto books appeared.[31] However, news of the auto's demise was greatly exaggerated and the criticism receded. Although James Flink's analysis that the Automobile Age had ended by the early 1970s was overly optimistic, it is apparent that the new government initiatives directed to the safety, energy, and environmental costs of the auto did have an impact.[32] The auto had become by the 1970s a somewhat mitigated blessing.

The heightened criticism of the 1970s abated with only marginal effects on automobility. Perhaps the most important factor in the success of the auto-industrial complex to counter the increasing criticism was "the growing perception of the economic importance of a healthy auto industry," which "largely diffused the political forces that once threatened to constrain the automobile."[33] U.S. Census Bureau data illustrate the resurgence of automobility in the 1980s. Between 1980 and 1985 the proportion of all U.S. workers who drove alone to work rose from 64.4 percent to 72.6 percent, while the proportion who used public transit or who walked declined from 12.0 percent to 9.2 percent.

Another factor in the increasing concern about the economic health of the U.S. auto industry in the late 1970s and early 1980s was the growing strength of Japanese and European competition. Criticism and regulation of the auto began to shift and to emphasize the costs of regulation to the industry. For example, the auto industry successfully lobbied the U.S. government to delay the mandatory installation of air bags, on the grounds that they were not cost effective.[34] In the Reagan Administration years, 1980-1988, market ideology again took a decided precedence over safety. There was also a renewed focus on the individual such as the drunken driver as the primary cause of auto accidents, as opposed to unsafe cars and highways, lack of alternative transport, and increased traffic.

One barrier to mobilizing opposition to the auto-industrial complex is the perception that regulations to reduce energy use and to protect the environment cost jobs. Since about one-seventh of the U.S. labour force is employed in producing and marketing cars and in related industries, the perception carries significant potential. Thus, in addition to the fact that the everyday social lives of Americans are intricately auto-involved, the very livelihoods of many Americans are auto-dependent as well. Also, the limited range of discourse about the negative aspects of auto-centred transport illustrates the constraining market-oriented assumptions with which policy makers operate. For instance, public policy towards injury from accidents is constrained by the "culture of the regulatory process," which takes a market ideology as one of its basic assumptions.[35]

An example of the market ideology of regulation is the comprehensive plan—the Air Quality Management Plan—to clean up the environment in the Los Angeles basin, which has been approved by local and regional officials. In respect to those aspects of the plan pertaining to auto pollution, the burden of change is placed on individuals and on private cars. Furthermore, the plan does not provide for a flexible, neighbourhood-oriented transport system (possibly subsidized); instead it focuses on super projects such as a rail link between the Los Angeles airport and Las Vegas.[36] Additionally, the Air Quality Management District has limited legal powers; for example, it cannot intervene in land use decisions which are so crucial to long-range efforts to control pollution.[37]

Thus, the embeddedness of auto-centred transport is grounded in more than the auto-industrial complex. Automobility meshes well with the short-term economic rationality that is the strength of the market, which sets the price of everything but which does not reveal the value of anything. Additionally, automobility provides livelihoods for many people. In so far as any proposals to reduce auto use are advanced, the opposition of the working class cannot be considered irrational. It reflects well-grounded fears about the loss of jobs. It is another example of the contradiction between individual and collective interests in society. Any attempts to nurture alternatives to auto-centred transport, to regulate and to discourage auto use, have to be considered in light of economic realities. Such attempts must also address concerns about the loss of personal freedom, privacy, and travel flexibility that the auto can provide. We take up these issues in Chapter 9.

Conclusion

It is clear that transport policy in the United States, even more than in Europe, is constrained by market forces that favour auto-centred transport. A particularly central role in these constraints is played by the auto-industrial complex and its influence over public policy. These constraints prevent the development of an ecologically and socially healthy transport policy that would emphasize less energy- and resource-intensive modes in more diversified systems. However, it is also clear that any efforts at reform of auto-centred transport must deal effectively with the realistic concerns of many persons about the threat of such reforms to their jobs, firstly, and secondly, to their individual choice.

The 1990s may witness a renewed critique of automobility. There is evidence that vehicular traffic is viewed as a major problem by the American public. For example, a 1990 San Francisco poll found that transport problems were regarded as the top local issue—ahead of drugs, homelessness, pollution, and crime. This was the eighth consecutive year of the annual San Francisco Bay Area Poll in which transport was deemed the leading local problem. A few months later the same poll found that traffic and gridlock continued to be seen as the most important local problem, ranking ahead of (in order) drugs, drought, homelessness, and crime. In 1991, transport held its number one position as the most important problem facing the Bay Area; in 1992, it slipped to second place, behind the economy and jobs.[38]

Currently two general conditions provide a backdrop for successful challenges to auto-centred transport. These conditions are the energy and environmental crises. There are a number of specific objective reasons that now make autos an increasing social liability: (1) auto emissions are a growing problem as increased auto use outpaces technical gains in emission reduction; (2) congestion and its economic costs are an increasing problem in urban areas; (3) the Persian Gulf War of 1991 highlighted yet again the costs and vulnerability of petroleum supplies. However, these conditions alone will not produce more diversified transport systems. In order to challenge the embedded structures of auto-centred transport, varied constituencies have to be mobilized; in turn, these constituencies have to put pressure on their elected representatives and on officials. Finally, achievable reforms have to be developed so that we have viable alternatives to auto-centred transport. We now turn our attention to this subject.

NOTES

1. Larry Sawers, "The Political Economy of Urban Transportation: An Interpretative Essay," in William K. Tabb and Larry Sawers, eds., *Marxism and the Metropolis* (New York: Oxford University Press, Second Edition, 1984), p. 246.
2. Amory B. Lovins and L. Hunter Lovins, *Brittle Power: Energy for National Security* (Andover, MA: Brick House Publishing Co., 1982).
3. Motor Vehicle Manufacturers Association, *Facts & Figures '92*, Detroit, 1992, p. 51.
4. Gordon E. Hart, Claudia Elliott, and Judith Lamare, "Heading the Wrong Way: Redirecting California's Transportation Policies," in Robert L. Deen, ed., *The Alternatives to Gridlock: Perspectives on Meeting California's Transportation Needs* (Sacramento: California Institute of Public Affairs, 1990), p. 92; Gerald Meral, "Back on Track: Trains in California's Future," in Robert L. Deen, ed., *The Alternatives to Gridlock: Perspectives on Meeting California's Transportation Needs* (Sacramento: California Institute of Public Affairs, 1990), p. 95.
5. Carolyn S. Konheim and Brian Ketcham, "Toward a More Balanced Distribution of Transportation Funds" (Brooklyn NY: Konheim & Ketcham, 1991), p. 14.
6. Brian Ketcham, "Making Transportation Choices Based on Real Costs," *Auto-Free Press* 3 (1992):4.
7. James J. Flink, *The Car Culture* (Cambridge, MA: The MIT Press, 1975), p. 213.
8. David St. Clair, *The Motorization of American Cities* (New York: Praeger, 1986), p. 25.
9. *Ibid.*; James J. Flink, *The Automobile Age* (Cambridge, MA: The MIT Press, 1988).
10. Walter A. Rosenbaum, *Energy Politics and Public Policy* (Washington, DC: Congressional Quarterly Press, 1989).
11. Marcia D. Lowe, *Alternatives to the Automobile: Transport for Livable Cities* (Washington, DC: Worldwatch Institute, Paper No. 98, 1990), p. 34.
12. Bradford Snell, "American Ground Transport," in J.H. Skolnick and E. Currie, eds., *Crisis in American Institutions* (Boston: Little, Brown, 1983), pp. 316-338.
13. *Delivering the Goods: Public Works Technologies, Management, and Financing* (Washington, DC: U.S. Office of Technology Assessment, 1991), p. 3.
14. Robert Schaeffer, "Car Sick, Automobiles Ad Nauseam," *Greenpeace* 15 (1990):13-17.

15. *Ibid.*

16. Institut fur Angewandte Umweltforschung, *Der Auto Knigge* (Reinbeck bei Hamburg: Rowohlt Verlag, 1990).

17. Shujiro Urata, "The Development of the Motor Vehicle Industry in Post-Second-World-War Japan," in *Industry and Development*, No. 24 (Vienna: United Nations Industrial Development Organization, 1988), pp. 1-33.

18. Sawers, *op. cit.*

19. Motor Vehicle Manufacturers Association, *op. cit.*, pp. 59, 61.

20. Glenn Yago, *The Decline of Transit: Urban Transportation in German and U.S. Cities, 1900-1970* (Cambridge: Cambridge University Press, 1984).

21. See: Snell, *op. cit.*; St. Clair, *op. cit.*; Glenn Yago, "Corporate Power and Urban Transportation: A Comparison of Public Transit's Decline in the United States and Germany," in Maurice Zeitlin, ed., *Classes, Class Conflict and the State: Empirical Studies in Class Analysis* (Cambridge, MA: Winthrop, 1980), pp. 296-323.

22. Meral, *op. cit.*

23. St. Clair, *op. cit.*; Deborah Gordon, *Steering a New Course: Transportation, Energy and the Environment* (Cambridge, MA: Union of Concerned Scientists, 1991).

24. Kristen Bruno, "The Detroit Shuffle," *The San Francisco Bay Guardian*, March 31, 1993, p. 17.

25. Alexandra Allen, "The Auto's Assault on the Atmosphere," *Multinational Monitor* 11 (1990):25.

26. Sawers, *op. cit.*

27. John Keats, *The Insolent Chariots* (Philadelphia: J.B. Lippincott Co., 1958), p. 11.

28. Ralph Nader, *Unsafe at any Speed* (New York: Grossman, 1965).

29. Carol A. MacLennan, "From Accident to Crash: The Auto Industry and the Politics of Injury," *Medical Anthropology Quarterly* 2 (1988):233-250.

30. Rachel Carson, *Silent Spring* (New York: Fawcett Crest, 1962).

31. See: Ronald A. Buel, *Dead End: The Automobile in Mass Transportation* (Baltimore: Penguin Books, 1972); John Jerome, *The Death of the Automobile* (New York: W.W. Norton, 1972); Emma Rothschild, *Paradise Lost: The Decline of the Auto-Industrial Age* (New York: Random House, 1973); Kenneth R. Schneider, *Autokind vs. Mankind* (New York: W.W. Norton, 1971).

32. Flink 1988, *op. cit.*

33. Alan Altshuler *et. al.*, *The Future of the Automobile: The Report of MIT's International Automobile Program* (Cambridge, MA: The MIT Press, 1984), p. 60.

34. MacLennan, *op. cit.*, p. 244.

35. *Ibid.*, pp. 247-248.

36. Robin Bloch and Keil Bloch, "Planning for a Fragrant Future: Air Pollution Control, Restructuring and Popular Alternatives in Los Angeles," *Capitalism, Nature and Socialism* 2 (1991):44-65.

37. Eric Mann, *L.A.'s Lethal Air* (Los Angeles: Labor/Community Strategy Center, 1991), p. 50.

38. Suzanne Espinosa, "Jobs, Economy Lead Bay Worries," *San Francisco Chronicle*, December 12, 1992; Ramon G. McLeod, "Transportation Problems Again Top Bay Poll," *San Francisco Chronicle*, January 8, 1991; Tim Schreiner, "Traffic Remains Area's No. 1 Worry," *San Francisco Chronicle*, January 28, 1991.

CHAPTER 9

Modifying Auto-Centred Transport

No attempt at changing auto-centred transport can succeed if it takes the form of a grand vision for reconstructing space without any sensitivity to existing ecologies and human habits. Herbert Marcuse is reputed to have said that after the revolution, "we will tear down big cities and build new ones."[1] Such stances embody the same grandiosity that gave us massive highway construction and urban renewal projects. Grandiose plans tend to treat human arrangements and settlements as if they were things—objects to be manipulated. This results in visions that become ultimatums dispensed downward from elites and experts to citizens. Instead, we need to nurture realistic, achievable alternatives that can gradually transform social spaces and that respect the *present* needs of people. For example, auto disincentives can be effective only where there is substitutability. Current drivers need to have substitutes for their autos; indeed the substitutes should be realistic and attractive. This requires innovation.

Any measures to restrict auto use need to meet several conditions in order to accomplish their goals. Worldwide, the successful efforts to curtail auto traffic have been accompanied by greater investment in public transit and improved pedestrianization. To restrict the auto is a limited policy in and of itself; unless it is made part of a larger effort to balance, to diversify, and to integrate all modes of transport, it is likely to fail. Indeed, auto-dependence is a product of the existence of specialized spaces, lifestyles, and sensibilities. In order to reduce automobility, whole transport systems and related infrastructures need to be reconfigured. As Lewis Mumford noted, "No adequate rebuilding of the transportation system is possible without introducing many coordinate measures outside the field of transportation itself."[2] Successful restriction of automobility is not likely "unless it is reasonably possible for people to share in the normal life of the city without the aid of an automobile."[3]

There is support for change in the United States. A 1989 *New York Times*—CBS poll found that 80 percent of respondents agreed with the statement, "Protecting the environment is so important that requirements and standards cannot be too high and continuing environmental improvements must be made at all costs." This was much more agreement than in 1981. Gallup and Roper public opinion polls have shown similar results.[4] Also, public opinion, at least in some parts of the United States, supports specific measures that would control the auto in order to reduce pollution. A 1990 poll of San Francisco Bay Area residents found majority support for the following measures to improve air quality: Pay ten cents more per gallon for gas (84 percent agreed that they would), take public transit to work one day a week (80 percent), pay a smog fee (64 percent), have more frequent smog checks (58 percent), raise bridge tolls by $2 (53 percent). Almost half the respondents supported highway tolls while only one-fourth would be willing to drive their cars on odd or even days only.[5] In a subsequent 1991 poll, San Francisco Bay Area residents demonstrated strong support for public transit and opposition to more freeway construction. Of all respondents, 87 percent favoured spending more public funds for expanding public transit, while 55 percent opposed spending public funds for building more freeways.[6]

In addition to public support for change, there are throughout the world local models of the successful reform of transport systems. Some of these models are American. For example, in Davis, California, city government has developed building codes and ordinances to conserve energy and promote alternatives to auto transport.[7] Several alternatives to the auto have been put in place there, including the following: (1) an extensive system of bikeways; (2) convenient and cheap public transit; (3) cottage industries that should reduce commuting.

In this chapter we discuss examples of achievable alternatives to auto-centred transport. The alternatives are achievable because they have already been demonstrated to work, at least on the local level. Some of the alternatives build upon previous successes, for example, strengthening and widening regulation to improve auto safety and fuel efficiency and to reduce auto emissions. Some of the alternatives involve the elaboration of new approaches for planning and for urban development based on access by proximity rather than by transport, an approach that results in greater job and residential density. Throughout this discussion of achievable alternatives our focus is on the overall necessities to relate land use to transport needs and to integrate and diversify transport modes. The auto has an important place in transport but so do rail, bus, walking, and cycling.

Regulation

Regulation of the auto has been moderate in the U.S., as noted in a study by the Brookings Institute: "Although some may argue that regulatory policies have been designed to discourage automobile use, it is clear that Congress has opted to try to civilize this mode of transportation rather than to encourage wholesale substitution for it."[8] Some states, notably California, have been more advanced in regulating the auto than the Federal government has been. The increased initiative of state governments in transport issues is a way to spur further regulation at the Federal level.

There are three types of regulation in place in the U.S. with regard to the auto: air pollution, fuel economy, and safety standards. The major federal legislation for these regulatory areas are the National Traffic and Motor Vehicle Safety Act of 1966, the Motor Vehicle Information and Cost Savings Act of 1972, the Energy Policy and Conservation Act of 1975, and the Clean Air Act Amendments of 1970 and 1977. Air pollution standards are the responsibility of the Environmental Protection Agency; fuel economy of the Secretary of Transportation; and safety of the National Highway Traffic Safety Administration. These government regulatory bodies have not been aggressive enough in dealing with the problems of auto-dependence; they are consistently more sympathetic to the problems of auto producers than they are concerned with the problems of auto-dependence. To its credit, the State of California, in which the problems of auto-dependence may be most serious, has led the way in developing effective and strong air quality rules. In its 1990 standards, the California Air Resources Board promulgated a set of regulations meant to create a whole new generation of less-polluting fuels and vehicles, including electric cars.[9]

The major limitations of auto regulation have been their lack of strength and comprehensiveness. Regulation has been consistently and considerably weakened by the auto-industrial complex. Whether in air pollution, fuel economy, or safety, the influence of the auto-industrial lobbies has successfully diluted standards or delayed their implementation. Auto and gasoline manufacturers in California, for example, have been successful in softening even the tough approach taken to air pollution by that state. With the weak performance of the U.S. economy in recent years, the auto-industrial lobby has been successful in arguing that new regulations will be costly. Such economic concerns were a major factor in the defeat in 1990 of an initiative for a new batch of environmental restrictions in California. Voters were evidently concerned about the higher costs of goods and the loss of jobs that might result from the stricter regulations.

The lack of comprehensiveness of auto regulation is illustrated by two examples produced by empirical study. First, auto regulation concentrates on new cars. The added cost of standards for new technology has raised the price of new cars, "thereby postponing the replacement of dirty, unsafe, gas-guzzling older cars."[10] Although it is impractical to refit or remake older cars there are mechanisms by which their numbers could be reduced. For example, regulatory agencies can provide incentives or penalties to encourage owners of older cars to get rid of them. A second glaring limitation in the comprehensiveness of auto regulation concerns safety standards. While auto safety regulations have helped to decrease the fatality rate for auto passengers substantially, "they may have had some deleterious effects upon pedestrians, bicyclists, and motorcyclists due to offsetting behavior by passenger-car drivers."[11] Auto safety regulations have been shortsighted in not trying to protect pedestrians and cyclists as well as auto occupants.

Broader regulation of auto-centred transport is needed to ensure that traffic engineering considers the safety of vulnerable pedestrians and cyclists who are not protected by a metal box. Examples of traffic engineering measures that help include lower speed limits, larger sidewalks, more cycling lanes, crosswalks that are better marked, and traffic lights that are set for pedestrian, not auto, traffic. Regulation thus far has narrowly focused on incremental improvements in auto performance—what can be referred to as the technological fix to the problems of auto-centred transport.

The Technological Fix

The technological fix is widely touted and carries some promise for reducing auto pollution. This strategy includes the development of green cars or ecocars such as electric autos, cars with cleaner internal combustion engines that use cleaner fuels, and computerized "smart" autos and freeways that reduce congestion and idling. While these technologies offer only marginal reduction of the pollution created by auto traffic, they are the most prominent solutions to the problems of auto-centred transport put forth by the auto-industrial complex and the government. The reason is that these technologies do not challenge auto hegemony. They do not address the central social necessities to upgrade alternatives to the auto and to restrain auto use.

The most modest technological change in the works is cleaner-burning gasolines, which are presently offered in some form by most major oil companies. These reformulated gasolines, while improvements, serve to delay the introduction of more effective technological changes, such as entirely new fuels (e.g., electricity and hydrogen) and entirely new autos (e.g., small solar-powered vehicles). Thus, in California, "the auto and oil industries see the less-polluting gasolines as one way to meet pending clean-air regulations ... without reinventing the automobile or its fuel."[12]

The cleanest of green fuels are hydrogen and electricity. Hydrogen fuel emits virtually no pollutants and is a non-fossil fuel that is nearly limitless—it can be made from water and many other sources.[13] Mazda and Mercedes-Benz are the leaders among auto makers in hydrogen-engine research, and Mazda has built a prototype car. However, the hydrogen-fuelled auto will not be mass produced for decades. The technology is totally new for autos and it will take considerable time to perfect. Electricity is a fuel that has been used for a long time in autos. It is cleaner and cheaper than methanol, reformulated gasoline, or compressed natural gas. The four major players in the alternative fuel competition are reformulated gasoline, methanol (M85), compressed natural gas, and electricity. A comparison of these four alternatives with gasoline on twenty-three variables, including various environmental risks, costs, and convenience, showed electricity to be best, followed by CNG, M85 and RFG (tied), and gasoline.[14]

Because of pressure from consumers and governments many auto manufacturers are developing electric vehicles. EV technology has actually been around since the nineteenth century, when both electric and steam vied with oil as an auto energy source.[15] Of the 4,200 autos sold in the United States in 1900, only 22 percent were gasoline powered; 38 percent were electric-powered and 40 percent were steam powered. In fact there are already some 30,000 EV's currently registered in California and the 1990 California Air Resources Board ruling will require auto manufacturers to produce fleets that are 2 percent EV's by 1998, 10 percent by 2003. The California regulations are under consideration in other states, including New York. The potential is that EV's will be mandated to include about one-third of the new-car market in the U.S.[16]

EV's have been touted because they produce far less pollutants than gasoline-powered autos. At present, a state-of-the-art EV operating in the Los Angeles area would produce 79.0 percent less nitrogen oxides, 99.8 percent less carbon monoxide, and 99.0 percent less hydrocarbons than a comparable gasoline-powered vehicle.[17] Even modest electrification will yield tangible results. A New Jersey study found that a 10 percent reduction in auto-generated air pollutants would occur if the state's auto fleet were to change to 10 percent EV's, and that this would not produce an increase in electricity-generation emissions.[18] EV's have advantages other than pollution reduction. Their motors are nearly silent, which would help to quiet the current urban din. Also, because EV motors have so few moving parts, service and maintenance costs are drastically reduced—EV's don't require mufflers, oil, radiators, or emissions tests. Finally, when they are stalled in traffic they use *no* energy at all.[19]

One frequently heard reason for the lack of marketing success of green cars is that motorists will not drive smaller and less powerful autos. However, there are numerous examples of just this. The most famous case is of course the Volkswagen Beetle. Autos even smaller than the Beetle have been successful in the market place. The *voiturette*, which has been used in rural France for years, has recently become popular in Paris. The *voiturette* has a one-cylinder engine and reaches a maximum speed of 28 mph. Driving it is very simple—the transmission has only three positions (forward, reverse, park) and uses no clutch. One can drive the car without a license and registration if one is at least 14 years old. The car is excluded from parking regulations because it takes so little space. Thus far the market for the *voiturette* consists largely of motorists who have lost their licenses. However, after re-acquiring their licenses many who used the car end up buying it. One owner was quoted as saying, "It's the perfect answer for city and environmental problems; good on mileage, takes less space than regular cars, causes less pollution and reduces the aggression French drivers are famous for because you have to drive more carefully and rely less on power."[20]

In addition to more fuel-efficient and less polluting cars, other technological innovations are in the process of development. One is the smart car-smart roadway combination. These computer-based engineering innovations would reduce traffic congestion by providing drivers and automated roadways with instantaneous data about current traffic conditions over a wide area. The United States is one of several nations in which research is currently being conducted on such Intelligent Vehicle and Highway Systems. However, the application of these systems is many years away, and even when realizable, promises only some relief for congestion.[21]

The development and use of smart systems, alternative fuels, and green cars should be encouraged. Technical improvements are both possible and desirable. For example, lead emissions in the United States declined by over 90 percent in the decade after lead-free gasoline was introduced. However, there is some danger that the level of attention given to all these technological fixes will deflect needed attention away from the larger problems of auto-centred transport. Improving auto technology is certainly necessary but in addition we must develop alternatives to the auto; the success of alternatives depends on their convenience and attractiveness among other factors. One way to improve the convenience of non-auto transport modes is to reduce the distances over which people must travel.

Access by Proximity

The mythology of auto culture views more widespread car use as the solution to present transport problems, but as William Leiss observed almost two decades ago:

> ... even if it were possible for every individual to own a private vehicle, this would not in itself assure any of them of the requisite mobility. The reason is that the demand for mobility is determined by the social arrangements as a whole, for example, the physical separation of work-place and dwelling-place. The overall arrangements may make personal mobility progressively more difficult (i.e., more scarce) in proportion to, or even more rapidly than, the expanding aggregate supply of private and public power-driven vehicles. The complexity of the overall structure deprives individuals of the ability to rely upon directly accessible means (such as their own physical capacity for mobility) for the effective discharge of their required functions.[22]

Obviously, more widespread auto use will not solve the problems of mobility in an urban sprawl structure. Moreover, present structures of deconcentrated urbanization make the simple substitution of a transit system with enough flexibility most difficult. To make mass transit more viable ultimately requires a restructuring of auto space.

Of course it is not merely the dispersal of functions that inhibits mobility on foot or by bicycle in the exurbs and suburbs. Aerial photos of suburbs show that residences actually are not that far from stores, parks, and schools.[23] In a high percentage of suburbs, the distance between residences and community services is just a half mile to three miles. The lack of safe passage via pedestrian or bicycle paths and the presence of uncrossable freeways are barriers to walkers and cyclists. Therefore, the problem is not merely one of distance (and travel time).

In the final analysis, the key to restructuring auto space is to re-concentrate it. In their analysis of data from thirty-two major European, North American, Australian, and Asian cities, Peter Newman and Jeffrey Kenworthy concluded that there is an empirical correlation between urban density and auto-dependence:

> In other words, higher population and job densities in all parts of the city are significantly associated with more public transport passenger kms per person, a higher proportion of total passenger kms on public transport, greater public transport provision per person, more annual trips per person, and a higher proportion of workers using public transport. Similarly, higher densities are in each case associated with a greater proportion of people using foot and bicycle to get to work.[24]

Urban areas wishing to reduce auto-dependence thus need to increase land use density. It is higher density that provides the basis for further changes: Improved options for non-motorized modes of travel, improved mass transit and restrained high speed traffic flow.

It is this last measure—restraining high speed traffic flow—that seems to fly in the face of assumptions made by many transport planners, who argue that more roads and wider roads will facilitate higher speed and reduce congestion. Yet "planned congestion," as Newman and Kenworthy suggest, can reduce auto-dependence, increase energy efficiency and help to diversify and balance transport modes. Free flowing traffic encourages urban dispersal and less dense land use patterns. Research which shows that free flowing traffic saves fuel and lowers emissions does not consider traffic flow as part of a total urban *system*. Since in the long run free flowing traffic decreases density in land use it eventually increases auto-dependence. In cities like Chicago, New York, and Detroit, extensive freeway systems dispersed land use, generated more traffic, and led to even greater congestion.[25]

Tailoring social space to high speed traffic erodes a historical and psychosocial sense of place (discussed in Chapter 6) as well as changing the unique character of a given place. Large roads with fast moving traffic often slice up local communities, interfere with other forms of mobility such as walking, and make movement within a small radius of neighbourhood activity more difficult. This approach reduces space to the status of something to move through rather than somewhere to *be*. The pressure to be underway—to be going somewhere—has altered city and country so that simply being in a place no longer provides real pleasure. With an emphasis on the "short way," trips would be made easier and the kind of travel that makes neighbourhoods become merely space to be driven through would be discouraged.[26] In urban areas the emphasis might be on dividing the city into self-contained areas that are hard to penetrate with through traffic but are easy for local traffic to traverse. The locations of work, residential, and play activities would be placed in proximity to each other. Rapid mobility over long distances would be de-emphasized, while local mobility would be improved by the better location of activities and by better local, non-motorized transport. This concept of transport space is quite different from that held by most planners. Most transport policy emphasizes super highways, elaborate by-pass arteries, and high speed rail commuter trains, all at the expense of expanding services that use short trips and would "thicken" local transport networks.

Many transport planners fail to see urban space as an organic whole, as an ecology that cannot be adapted to auto needs without considerable costs to the urban fabric. The planner, Robert Moses, an advocate of radial routes through cities, argued that when "you operate in an overbuilt metropolis you have to hack your way with a meat ax."[27] Moses' perspective is shared by many city and transport planners. Highway designers tend to see two points in space joined by a freeway as having little social significance.[28] Since the 1950s in particular, cities have been seen as sources of traffic obstruction and as places to escape from with the car. The meat axe that carved the way for freeways chopped up and destroyed thousands of neighbourhoods, leaving scars that still have not healed.[29] Freeways were routed through low-income neighbourhoods because of their proximity to the urban core, their lower property values, and less political resistance.[30]

Greater densities of population and social functions foster easier non-auto access to daily activities. Access can be grounded in the understanding that there is a hierarchy of ecologically healthy transport modes, with walking being the best, followed by (in order), bicycles, buses and ferries, trains and, last and worst, autos. This hierarchy of transport modes is generally the same for personal health as it is for the protection of the environment: Walking and cycling are better than the other transport modes.

Access by proximity depends on mixed land use patterns. One cannot easily access one's job or shopping on foot if they are far away. The separation of land uses into residential, commercial, and industrial zoning categories increases the need for transport. Given the auto-dependence of transport, this means more frequent and longer trips by auto. Suburbanization led to the rigid separation of residence from social activities, including shopping, schooling, and recreating. Research indicates that such nonwork trips are the major factor in the growth of congestion and that they were largely created by the separation of land uses.[31] Access by proximity based on mixed land use and increased housing density help to decrease auto use dramatically in the San Francisco Bay Area. In the Nob Hill neighbourhood of San Francisco, where there are 117 housing units per acre, residents travel 2,670 miles per year by auto. In the Danville/San Ramon suburbs, where there are only four housing units per acre, residents travel 10,000 miles per year by auto.[32]

Integrated land use patterns will promote the job and housing density that are the keys to access by proximity. In their study of thirty-two world cities, Newman and Kenworthy found strongly negative correlations between automobility (as measured by gasoline use per capita) on the one hand, and land use intensity (as measured by people and jobs per hectare) on the other hand.[33] For example, in Phoenix, land use intensity is just thirteen people and jobs per hectare and only 6 percent of workers take public transit, or walk or bike to work. In contrast, in Toronto land use intensity is fifty-nine people and jobs per hectare and 37 percent of workers get to their jobs by means other than an auto. It is important to note that it does not require *high* density to reduce automobility. Moderate density, typical of European cities, is sufficient. At six housing units per acre, transit surpasses an energy-efficiency threshold favouring it over autos.[34] The problem in the United States is its very *low* land use intensity, especially in suburbs. In order for access by proximity to succeed it requires public support and government action. For example, between 1965 and 1974, Toronto provided tax incentives for residential construction within 1,500 feet of subway stations. During that period more than 160,000 housing units were built near stations and mass transit ridership made a large gain.[35]

Access by proximity provides the structural basis for making alternatives to the auto viable. We now turn our attention to these alternatives.

Alternatives to the Auto

There are a number of strategies available for diversifying transport and reducing automobility. Upgrading mass transit by all the strategies available is achievable and desirable on both efficiency and equity grounds. Auto control and disincentive strategies are also necessary but care must be taken to prevent punishment of autoists and to ensure reasonable equity for various social groupings.

Stimulation is a key to the success of alternatives to the auto. The auto's present popularity is based in some measure on stimulation for its consumption and on the construction of a built environment that is dependent on auto transport. In order to change this situation we need to stimulate use of public transit and other alternatives, and we need to construct built environments that are not auto-dependent.

There are three principal alternatives to the auto for transport in urbanized areas—public transit, bicycle, and walking. All are quite underdeveloped in the United States. Only 3.4 percent of Americans use public transit for urban trips, while 26 percent of Italians and 20 percent of the Swiss do. Less than 1 percent of Americans bike for their urban trips, while 20 percent of Danes and 10 percent of Swedes do. Only 10.7 percent of Americans walk for their urban trips, while 39 percent of Swedes and 31 percent of Austrians do.[36]

The primary alternative to the auto is mass transit. There are four varieties of mass transit: Bus; heavy rail (underground, surface, and elevated); light rail (including trolleys); and commuter rail. The successful examples of urban mass transit (those that operate without deficits) emphasize the coordination of different transport modes within a framework of high density land uses.[37] Coordination of varieties of transport is necessary to ensure intermodal connections so that travellers can bike, walk, or drive to public transit facilities, and then can transfer easily between different transit modes.

Automobility is negatively correlated with public transit use. In their study, Newman and Kenworthy found that the cities with higher per capita gasoline use, vehicles, car ownership, and private car miles were also the cities with lower per capita public transport miles, percent of passenger kms on public transport, and public transport passenger trips.[38] Cities in the United States had the highest levels of automobility and the lowest levels of public transit use. The ten U.S. cities in the survey averaged only 4.4 percent of total passenger kms on public transport; the other twenty-two cities averaged 29.1 percent. In the U.S. cities the average proportion of workers using public transit, foot, or bicycle transport was only 17.1 percent; in the other cities 53.7 percent of workers used these alternatives to the auto.

The need for improved mass transit is essential but the deeply ingrained popularity of the individual passenger car in the United States makes it important that new forms of small group transport be considered. The great majority of commuters drive alone in their autos to and from work. In the San Francisco Bay Area, where mass transit is available and has considerable public support and where alternatives to auto transport have been widely encouraged, 68 percent of employed residents still drove alone to and from work in 1991.[39] Of the remainder, 13 percent used a car pool or van pool, 13 percent used public transit, and 6 percent walked or cycled. In order to deal with the popularity of the individual passenger car and its advantages of convenience within a physical context of urban sprawl, we have to develop new forms of individualized small-group transport. If done right, new approaches that provide the flexible door-to-door service of the auto can be successful because there is a need. For example, empirical research concluded that "dial-a-bus service for the elderly in Buffalo showed that either latent demand existed or new demand could be stimulated."[40]

The type of individualized small-group transport that is developed will depend on assumptions about the size of groups that will use them, the availability of fuel, the distances traveled, and the variability of destinations. Smaller vehicles using environmentally more benign energy sources are among the possibilities. Chicago is developing a demonstration model of a personal rapid transit. PRT is a fully automated system that travels on its own pathways; it takes passengers directly from their point of origin to their point of destination in vehicles with two to five passengers.[41]

In addition to public transit, cycling is another alternative to the auto. While in less developed countries like China bicycles are an ubiquitous part of the landscape, in most developed nations transport planners underestimate their potential. Transport professionals generally trivialize bicycle transport and there is a low level of funding for it. Until 1990, the U.S. Department of Transportation had no full-time person dealing with bicycles.[42] Despite the bike's potential for everyday transport in many cities of the United States, necessary facilities are lacking, with a few exceptions, notably the San Francisco Bay Area and Seattle. There is great potential for bicycle commuting. A Harris poll found that the number of bicycle commuters in the U.S. would increase from 3 to 35 million if better facilities were available.[43] While the rate of bike usage is quite low in the United States, it is increasing. One survey found that the number of Americans who biked to work more than doubled between 1983 and 1991.[44]

Bicycles are far more widely used in other motorized societies than they are in the United States. In Britain the rate of bicycle use and walking is still fairly high despite a decline over the years due to motorization. Yet, official statistics in Britain distort figures on bicycling by underestimating the extent of their use; public policy there does not take such forms of transport seriously.[45] Continental Europe is more progressive in this area. In parts of Europe bicycles are a vital mode of transport. Bike and ride transit stations, facilities for bikes on buses and rail, and a well-developed network of bike paths have supported biking in Denmark, Japan, West Germany, and the Netherlands.[46] Since 1975, the Netherlands has devoted 10 percent of its surface transport budget to bicycle facilities.[47]

In an auto-dominated culture bicycles tend to be viewed as second-class vehicles—used by poorer people, as toys by children, or for recreation. As a result, bicycle technology is underdeveloped. Bicycles that have some of the comforts, security, and multiple uses of the car have not yet fully evolved. Recumbent bicycles, light-weight folding bicycles, bicycles that can transport goods, and bicycles that are usable by those with impairments, are a few of the possibilities.[48] Conveyances that resemble bicycles, both motorized and not, offer great potential for development. "Amigos," small motorized mini-vehicles which can go over curbs are used by people with disabilities in Europe and increasingly in the United States. Non-motorized three-wheeled carriages used by parents to take their babies along when they jog are an example of how available technology can be reconfigured. Finally, the technology being developed to enable persons with impairments to be mobile may prove to have applications for the development of environmentally-friendly transport.

A third major alternative to the auto for transport in urbanized areas, after mass transit and bicycles, is walking. For ecological and health reasons, it is the preferred alternative to the auto.

Pedestrianization

There are three reasons why pedestrianization needs to be promoted in urban areas: It will improve the quality of social life and the physical health of individuals, and it will reduce auto-dependence. Mumford was one of the first in the auto age to argue for the values of pedestrianization: "If we took human lives seriously in recasting the whole transportation system, we should begin with the human body and make the fullest use of pedestrian movement not only for health, but for efficiency in moving large crowds over short distances."[49] More recently, architect Peter Calthorpe forcefully stated the case for pedestrianization:

> Pedestrians are the catalysts for healthy communities; they make these essential qualities of towns—centre, edge, diversity and public space—meaningful. They are the lost measure of community, setting the scale for centre and edge. They create the place and the time for the casual encounters that provide the connections and integration within diverse communities. Without pedestrians a city's common ground—its parks, plazas and sidewalks—become useless obstructions to the car.[50]

Pedestrian street life is the heart and soul of urban life, and its degradation in many contemporary cities is a prime sign of their decline. The pedestrian is a vanishing breed who is beset by a hostile urban environment. Battling motorized traffic and overloaded sidewalks or using deserted streets at night can frustrate or daunt even the most ardent walker.

Cities can make safe and humanized pedestrian routes through a number of eminently doable strategies, including the creation of natural walking paths connecting public facilities, and of promenades and arcades.[51] Greenways or greenbelts can be routes for pedestrians and cyclists and they add to the general quality of life for all urban residents. A greenway is a "natural or landscaped course for pedestrian or bicycle passage."[52] As a result of increasing interest in protecting the natural environment, in walking, hiking and cycling as physical exercise and recreation; and in appreciation of the natural landscape, greenways have enjoyed growth in recent years in the United States.[53]

The idea of greenways in urban areas is an old one—they go back at least to the work of Frederick Law Olmstead in the nineteenth century. They have been almost totally ignored by contemporary planners, in part because they are not for autos and may even impede them. Greenways do have potential for reducing auto-dependence although that has not been one of their rationales. If they were to be made more functional without abandoning their current leisure-time focus, they could help to revive urban pedestrianism. Consider, for example, the potential for the use of greenways to connect major intersections for pedestrian traffic in cities; connecting transportation hubs with municipal buildings might be a good place to start.

However, it is not enough to provide walking routes—they must be made appealing. Pedestrians also have to be supplied with public accommodations along routes, including comfortable, clean, safe and accessible toilets. These facilities are more than amenities, a word that tends to trivialize them.[54] They are vital for public health and for fostering pedestrianism and social interaction; indeed they are essential for making the city usable for all its citizens.

The street has always been the common meeting ground of all citizens and it long predated the auto age. Donald Appleyard noted at the beginning of his now classic study of streets:

> Nearly everyone in the world lives on a street. People have always lived on streets. They have been the places where children first learned about the world, where neighbors met, the social centers of towns and cities, the rallying points for revolts, the scenes of repression.[55]

Human domestication created the street; in turn the street is the basis for the second most important social relationship in traditional society—that of neighbours. The social status of neighbour becomes as important as that of kin when humans begin to live in permanent settlements.[56]

A more livable city for all its citizens can be achieved by respecting the more subtle and subjective dimensions of the urban environment—its ambience or pervading atmosphere. A city's ambience, though elusive, is rooted in quite concrete uses of space. A comparative study of transport in the U.S.S.R. and the U.S. concluded:

> The term urban ambience encompasses the cumulative effects of the environmental, visual, economic and intrusive impacts of the automobile .... It is this general enhancement of living conditions—through reduced pollution, fewer roads and parking areas, and better pedestrian conditions—which would result in a net gain to urban areas and which, though not quantifiable, would be larger than the sum of its separable parts.[57]

An important aspect of urban ambience is attractiveness. In their comparative study of world cities, Newman and Kenworthy rated thirty-one downtown areas on the availability of public facilities, the level of pedestrianization, and other appealing features.[58] The thirty-one city centres were then ranked on this cumulative scale of attractiveness. Of the ten cities in the United States, five ranked at the bottom and five in the middle of the order; none ranked at the top. Interestingly, the five U.S. cities (New York City, followed by Boston, San Francisco, Chicago, and Washington, DC) which were mid-ranked all have rapid transit systems. The five highest ranking city centres were all European cities, led by Paris. Newman and Kenworthy found a significant negative correlation between the attractiveness of city centres and gasoline use per capita. The most attractive city centres had the lowest per capita gasoline use and the least attractive city centres had the highest per capita gasoline use.

To conclude, there is a subtle but critical connection between the decline of the material environment for pedestrians and the deterioration of social interaction and civility in the city: "Built space provides a concrete, physical statement about how a society organizes itself at the scale of everyday life. And its design accounts for a good deal of pleasure or pain, social connectedness or social isolation."[59] Auto-centred transport is prominent among the features of our built environments contributing to the deterioration of urban street life.

Mass transit, cycling, and walking are alternatives to the auto that are practical for areas in which there is reasonably high job and residential density. What can be done about providing alternatives to the auto in suburbs and in situations characterized by high population growth?

Transport Diversity in a Context of Urban Growth

Sensible planning can decrease auto use and increase the use of alternatives, even in suburbs and in contexts of economic and population growth. Decreasing auto-dependence means, first, encouraging denser living patterns and more mixed land use. It is important for planners to produce models that will embody alternatives to single use, sprawling auto-dependent spaces. The urban sprawl/auto-dependent pattern of growth that is now so common is not foreordained for the future. A good example of a plan for non-auto-dependent development is the work of the Environmental Council of Sacramento, California, a coalition of community groups. ECOS uses achievable strategies to encourage the use of alternate transport in newly developed areas. One strategy is to develop neighbourhoods in suburban developments that foster walking by having the following: Central squares that include open space and services, housing of variable density, and pedestrian-friendly streets. One form of the walking neighbourhood is the pedestrian pocket developed by Calthorpe.[60] By balancing and clustering jobs, housing, shopping, recreation, and child care, pedestrian pockets use one-sixth the land of a typical suburban development. Also, unlike typical suburbs, pedestrian pockets preserve open space and agricultural land. Finally, they are capable of converting 60 percent or more of normal auto trips into pedestrian and transit trips.

Calthorpe's ideas for the post-suburban metropolis have been promoted by ECOS and are getting their first big test in a development south of Sacramento called Laguna West, which is being built as a dense, city-like community.[61] Laguna West, scheduled for completion in 1994, will contain apartments and single-family homes centred around acres of open space, shops and offices, a day care centre, a library, playing fields, and a community centre. Laguna West set the precedent for a new housing classification for Sacramento County's general plan: Transport Oriented Development. In TOD's, growth is channelled along transit routes. Laguna West will be connected to downtown Sacramento by a light rail stop that will be no farther than 2,000 feet from any of the higher density housing units and the shops. Additionally, in the detached house area the streets will be narrow in order to slow down auto traffic. Other less ambitious developments can also reduce auto-dependence. For example, some newer suburban condominium developments are being built within walking distance to train stations, shopping, places of worship, and libraries.[62]

In developing a variegated and integrated transport plan, ECOS advocates the creation of alternatives to the auto rather than its restraint. This is a reasonable approach because historically, residential development has tended to follow routes of transport. By putting in alternative transport *first*, development then follows in a format that is consonant with the transport. Such approaches have been promoted for the development of outlying Stockholm since the 1940s. The "finger development" in that city has served to locate high-density suburban housing along public transit routes and to preserve open space between the transit lines. The planning also provided the customers who made high-density rail transit realistic.[63] One of Stockholm's suburbs, Valingsly, epitomizes the possibilities of planning for transport diversity. A general plan begun in 1952 has promoted pedestrian access by clustering housing within close proximity to subway stations and retail outlets. In addition, auto parking access has been restricted and a sophisticated footpath network has been developed. As a result, of the total trips away from home in Valingsly, 37 percent are made by foot, 30 percent by auto, 27 percent by public transport, and 6 percent by bicycle.[64]

It is important to note that in Sacramento ECOS is working in an environment of high growth and is not opposing that growth. Between 1970 and 1987, the population of the Sacramento metropolitan area grew by 58 percent. Sacramento County's population of one million is projected to grow by more than 50 percent by the year 2010. The proactive stance that ECOS takes with regard to growth maximizes its credibility and influence across all sectors of the community, including city hall, organized labour, and business. Empirical study of the political economy of growth in Sacramento has demonstrated that the success of ECOS is based to a large degree on its ability to assemble a coalition composed of often-at-odds interests, groups, and social classes. This success will be challenged in the coming years by the addition of the new interests of Sacramento's burgeoning immigrant and low-income populations.[65]

In other communities where maturity or saturation already have been reached, opposition to growth may be a more environmentally sound and politically realistic choice than it is in Sacramento and similar locales. In mature communities retrofitting may be the necessary focus.

Retrofitting

ECOS is attempting to make diversified transport a feature of new development. What about already existing auto-dominated space in mature suburbs and congested central cities? Retrofitting is the process by which older structural arrangements are revisited and reconstructed to meet new needs. In fact, the older the settlement the better, for it is easier to pedestrianize environments that were built before the auto age. Old cities in Europe are a good example.

West Germany has been a leader in the creation of pedestrian-friendly areas in old city centres. One mode for creating more pedestrian friendly streets has been traffic-calming (*verkehrs-beruhigung*) or area-wide traffic restraint; it uses street changes to slow auto speed, alter driver behavior, and improve neighbourhood quality.[66] Specific measures include *cul-de-sac*, roadway humps, bottle-necking, sharp bends, and tree planting.

Approaches such as traffic-calming constitute the development of a new practice of environmental traffic management. ETM provides for positive discrimination on behalf of pedestrians, cyclists, and public transport in urban planning.[67] Examples include pedestrianization, as in the closing of streets to motorized traffic (except perhaps buses, taxis and service vehicles). This constructs what amounts to auto-free zones in central cities. Before and after research has demonstrated that traffic-calming reduces auto accidents and injuries, noise, and pollution, and that it is supported by *local* populations.[68]

The creation of *woonerven* ("living yards") in urban areas in the Netherlands is another example of how old residential neighbourhoods can be made safe for pedestrians and for children at play. Whole areas are rebuilt: Streets are narrowed, trees are planted, bollards are installed. This ensures that motorized traffic enters at slow speed and that it continues at low speed. Research has demonstrated the positive effects of the *woonerven* on driver behavior and on the reduction of traffic accidents.[69] This concept of *woonerven* is being extended from single streets to larger areas. Amsterdam may become the first major city that virtually eliminates the auto from its centre. In 1992 voters approved a plan for a car-free centre. The plan is being implemented in progressive steps involving a number of tactics: Widening sidewalks, adding bicycle lanes, reducing parking spaces, erecting "amsterdammers" (bollards) in streets, lowering speed limits, and increasing parking violation fines. Additionally, the city is expanding subway and tram lines and constructing auto garages near peripheral terminals. Eventually, only taxis, emergency vehicles, and small business vans will be allowed in the city's core. Disabled persons and some residents will be granted permits for auto access.[70]

In the United States attempts to create pedestrian streets sometimes have flourished and sometimes have failed. Those streets that have failed were not appealing areas to use, lacked access to wider mass transit, and did not provide people with a reason to be there, for instance, to shop.[71] Another problem is that while local residents are supportive of traffic-calming schemes, people who do not live in the local neighbourhood but who do drive through it are not supportive. For example, the use of blockades in Berkeley, California, to divert auto traffic has incurred the wrath of drivers who must go out of their way in order to avoid the obstacles. This represents another contradiction of auto use. It seems that on the one hand, people are in favour of auto obstacles in their own neighbourhood; on the other hand, they oppose them in other people's neighbourhoods. Overall, the Berkeley innovations have met with support and have produced positive outcomes: "The plan seems to be a success in terms of its support. A study made within a couple of years of its implementation showed the number of accidents to be down in the city."[72]

The policies of European cities are considerably ahead of those of American cities. William Whyte concluded in his comprehensive study of pedestrians that "almost every American city gives them the short end of the stick."[73] Examples of how walkers are disfavoured include the scarcity of pedestrian-friendly passageways, the fact that traffic lights are set for autos, not pedestrians, and the generally low quality of sidewalks. With regard to sidewalks, Whyte pointed to New York City's Lexington Avenue, especially between 57th and 61st Streets. Although one of the most used pedestrian ways in the world, the sidewalk is cracked and buckled and it slopes at precipitous angles in places. Because of dense commercial use and urban clutter such as subway stations, the effective sidewalk is only about 6 feet. Motorized traffic on the other hand gets 50 feet of roadway.

While efforts to retrofit city centres to make them more pedestrian-friendly have been going on for several decades in Europe, efforts to retrofit suburban sprawl are only now beginning to emerge. These efforts are taking place in the United States, where suburban sprawl reigns supreme. A prominent example of what can be achieved is the work of architect Elizabeth Plater-Zyberk in Mashpee, Massachusetts. Plater-Zyberk founded the first architectural degree program in the United States that treats auto-dominated suburban sprawl as a serious design *problem*: "Asphalt is a social problem: The more there is, the greater the distances between destinations and the grimmer the landscapes. Gradually, people stop walking. Neighbors even stop talking."[74] Plater-Zyberk's focus for retrofitting suburban sprawl is the ubiquitous mall. Her strategy is to remake malls into downtowns. In Mashpee, an older mall was transformed into a three-block downtown with streets, sidewalks, and pedestrians. Commons apartments for retired people were built near the downtown. New residential neighbourhoods with a variety of lot sizes to encourage heterogeneity will be built around the downtown. The key to the success of the Mashpee development is daily pedestrian use. To this end, the developers donated land for a library and will keep retail outlets open on summer evenings in order to facilitate an active street life.

Pedestrianization, retrofitting, and other strategies we have analyzed to modify auto-centred transport are effectively applicable only in urbanized areas. In rural areas, especially in the United States, residential densities are so low and travel distances so great that auto-centred transport will remain necessary, at least in the foreseeable future. Indeed, in the U.S., it was in rural areas in the early twentieth century that the auto first became a mode of everyday transport (as discussed in Chapter 4). According to data from the U.S. Census Bureau, in 1990 there were only 7.6 housing units per square mile in rural areas, while there were 876 housing units per square mile in urban areas. However, it is in urban areas where both the greater quantity and intensity of auto transport and its problems are located. In 1990, urban roadways accounted for 62.9 percent of all auto miles driven in the U.S.[75] Traffic congestion is not a serious problem in rural areas. Furthermore, the urban population continues to outgrow the rural population in the U.S. The 1990 U.S. population was 75.2 percent urban, up from 73.7 percent in 1980. Thus, the modification of auto-centred transport in urban areas offers great and growing leverage for significantly reducing the overall level of auto use. Additionally, all of the regulatory and technological advances that have the potential for substantially reducing auto pollution and energy use can be applied to auto transport in rural areas.

Whether it is retrofitting or some other achievable alternative, any substantial movement away from auto-centred transport and towards diversified transport will have costs—costs in the form of meaningful changes in human behaviour and financial resources. We now turn our attention to ways of addressing these costs. We make three basic assumptions about the costs: (1) That they be debated through a democratic process; (2) that they incur the least harm to those at the lower economic levels of society; and (3) that they be effective. Effective change in transport systems and in individual travel habits will not be an easy task, especially given the magnitude and the quality of the costs involved. However, there are ways to facilitate change for both societies and individuals.

The Cost of Change

The sensual, erotic, or irrational wellsprings of automobility cannot be ignored. The pleasure as well as the convenience that auto driving provides is a boon to many people. However, what is needed is a diversified transport system that allows people to find pleasure in many ways of travel. New policies must be as non-punitive as possible in discouraging auto use, and must develop seductive as well as affordable and efficient alternatives to the auto. How changes can be implemented without causing people hardship and inconvenience is an important consideration. It has been argued by some that any serious attempt to transform auto-centred transport systems must entail painful sacrifices for citizens.[76] It is our contention that if sacrifice is required, it can be mitigated in several ways, including making the sacrifice a shared one throughout society.

One direct way to discourage auto use across the board is to increase its cost by imposing higher gasoline taxes. The United States has unusually low gasoline prices and taxes. Adjusted for inflation, gasoline prices were at the same level in 1990 as they were in 1975, even though taxes were added during those years.[77] Additionally, because of improvement in miles per gallon (about 21 mpg today as compared to only 15 mpg ten years ago), drivers are actually driving more miles for the same cost. If the hidden or external costs of driving (discussed in Chapter 8) were added to the pump price in order to cover automobility's real costs, the pump price would just about triple. One estimate is that $2.57 per gallon would have to be added to the pump price of gasoline in the U.S. to cover its hidden costs.[78] In 1990, while an average gallon of gasoline was $1.22 in the United States, it ranged upward from that figure in comparable countries to a high of $4.74 a gallon in Italy. Taxes represented only 28 percent of the U.S. price, while they represented 77 percent of the Italian price. In the U.S., less than 1 percent of government revenue comes from gasoline taxes; in Italy, the figure is 5 percent and in Britain it is 17 percent.[79] Higher gasoline taxes are consistently correlated with lower consumption. Nations with the highest taxes, including Italy, Denmark, and Japan, have the lowest per capita gasoline consumption. The United States has the lowest taxes and the highest per capita gasoline consumption.[80]

Gasoline taxes are regressive; since every consumer, no matter what his or her ability to pay, must pay the same tax, they discriminate against lower-income persons. There are mitigating factors to this regressivity of gasoline taxes. Since miles driven rises with income, at least in the U.S., any extra cost for the rich will be considerably higher than the extra cost for the poor. However, because the *proportion* of income spent on gasoline rises as one moves *down* the income ladder, poor people face a greater burden from higher gasoline taxes. There are ways to compensate for this. For example, proceeds from higher gasoline taxes could be dedicated to providing lower cost alternatives to driving, especially mass transit, which is disproportionately used by persons of lower incomes. The basic thrust of reform should be that reduction of auto-dependence does not punish people unfairly and that it makes change attractive. As Jane Jacobs noted, "attrition [of auto use], too, must operate in positive terms."[81]

In addition to raising the price of gasoline, there are other ways to make auto drivers pay the true costs of their transport. Hong Kong and Singapore, for example, impose fees on drivers who use the centres of those cities. Fees are adjusted by time and location—the most expensive are for drivers who enter downtown during rush hours. Singapore also penalizes lone drivers, who pay a monthly fee for entering the city in rush hours. Although such measures may seem draconian by the standards of other cities, Hong Kong and Singapore have been forced to adopt them by their intensities of auto use. Hong Kong has the highest vehicle density in the world—about 280 vehicles per km of roadway.[82] Despite their somewhat idiosyncratic natures, Hong Kong and Singapore represent a likely future for many large cities with auto-centred transport systems. In New York City, city and regional officials are contemplating bans on private autos in the central business district during working hours in order to meet Federal clean air standards.

Any assessment of the potential costs of reducing auto-dependence needs to take into account the savings from curtailing the costly subsidies to auto drivers that currently exist. These subsidies amount to economic incentives that encourage automobility. A major example is the widespread availability of low-cost parking. The effect of this subsidy alone is illustrated in the case of one Los Angeles company that stopped paying for parking for its employees who drove to work alone. The proportion of employees commuting alone in their cars decreased from 42 percent to 8 percent, while the proportion of car poolers rose from 17 percent to 58 percent.[83]

There is a final point to make with regard to the cost of reconfiguring auto-centred transport systems. At a juncture when the world economy is suffering a major transition from the Cold War, reconfiguring transport presents opportunities as well as costs. Thus, there is the possibility that former arms manufacturers may be able to compensate partially for their lost role by converting to the production of transport equipment and technology. One economic analyst noted some of the advantages of converting from arms production to transport-related production: "Unlike some businesses that the defense contractors are considering entering, transportation is still an underdeveloped market, and a lot of the skills used in defense are applicable to mass transit."[84] For example, large military contractors are competing to build cars for the new Green Line light rail transit in Los Angeles.

Conclusion

Retrofitting older settlements and utilizing transport-sensitive planning in newer ones are the two principal ways through which to arrange the structure of social space so that alternatives to the auto are usable. Both are based on the idea that access to needed activities needs to be more and more based on proximity. This is a prerequisite to making the three principal alternatives to the auto—mass transit, cycling, and walking—feasible. It is also a prerequisite for making alternatives to single-occupancy autos, including van and car pools, workable. Additionally, any government regulations and any technological innovations that reduce auto pollution and increase auto efficiency are welcome. It is increasingly apparent that auto-centred transport can only be effectively modified by an approach that emphasizes the systemic nature of transport. We now turn to an analysis of the systemic nature of transport and of the ways in which it shapes the form and content of alternatives to auto-centred transport.

NOTES

1. Cited in: André Gorz, *Ecology as Politics* (Montreal: Black Rose Books, 1980), p. 76.
2. Lewis Mumford, "Transportation: Human Enrichment," *The New York Times*, March 17, 1971.
3. J. Michael Thomson, "Methods of Traffic Limitation in Urban Areas," in Ralph Gakenheimer, ed., *The Automobile and the Environment: An International Perspective* (Cambridge, MA: The MIT Press, 1978), p. 155.
4. Mark Sagoff, "The Greening of the Blue Collars," *Reports from the Institute for Philosophy and Public Policy* 10 (1990):1-5.
5. Ramon G. McLeod, "Top Bay Area Headache is Transportation," *San Francisco Chronicle*, January 7, 1991.
6. Frank Viviano, "Commuters Want More Mass Transit," *San Francisco Chronicle*, January 31, 1991.
7. Anne Whiston Spirn, *The Granite Garden: Urban Nature and Human Design* (New York: Basic Books, 1984), p. 85.
8. Robert W. Crandall *et.al.*, *Regulating the Automobile* (Washington, DC: The Brookings Institution, 1986), p. 2.
9. Richard W. Stevenson, "California to Get Tougher Air Rules," *The New York Times*, September 27, 1990.
10. Crandall *et.al.*, *op.cit.*, p. vii.
11. *Ibid.*, p. 84.
12. Donald Woutat, "GM Endorses Cleaner-Burning Reformulated Gas for Its Models," *The Los Angeles Times*, March 19, 1991.
13. John Vidal, "Hydrogen Car that Goes Like a Bomb," *The San Francisco Bay Guardian*, July 3, 1992.
14. S. McCrea and R. Minner, 1992. *Why Wait for Detroit?* (Fort Lauderdale: South Florida Electric Auto Association, 1992), p. 83.
15. Peter Tira, "Elec-trekking," *The San Francisco Bay Guardian*, October 10, 1990, p. 42.
16. Lesley Hazleton, "Really Cool Cars," *The New York Times Magazine*, March 29, 1992.
17. Lamont C. Hempel, "The Promise of Electric Vehicles," in Robert L. Deen, ed., *The Alternatives to Gridlock: Perspectives on Meeting California's Transportation Needs* (Sacramento: California Institute of Public Affairs, 1990), p. 123.
18. "Impact on Air Pollution in New Jersey: Electric Cars" (Upper Montclair, NJ: Department of Environmental, Urban and Geographic Studies, Montclair State, 1991).
19. Gordy Slack, "Sing the Auto Electric," *Pacific Discovery*, Summer, 1991, pp. 3-4.

20. Judson Gooding, "Le Un-Car Takes to the Streets of France," *San Francisco Chronicle*, March 3, 1991, p. 3.
21. *Bulletin* (Washington, DC: Surface Transportation Policy Project, October 18, 1991).
22. William Leiss, *The Limits to Satisfaction: An Essay on the Problem of Needs and Commodities* (Toronto: University of Toronto Press, 1976), p. 31.
23. Richard K. Untermann, "Can We Pedestrianize the Suburbs?" in Anne Vernez Moudon, ed., *Public Streets for Public Use* (New York: Van Nostrand Reinhold Company, 1987), pp. 123-132.
24. Peter G. Newman and Jeffrey K. Kenworthy, *Cities and Automobile Dependence: A Source Book* (Brookfield, VT: Gower Technical, 1989), p. 50.
25. *Ibid.*, pp. 106, 148, 164.
26. Gerd Hickmann und Klaus Dieter Kaser, *Trau keinem uber Tempo 30* (Stuttgart: Grunen im Landtag von Baden-Wurttemberg, 1988).
27. Cited in: David St. Clair, *The Motorization of American Cities* (New York: Praeger, 1986), p. 152.
28. Marvin G. Cline, "Urban Freeways and Social Structure—Some Problems and Proposals," in Enne de Boer, ed., *Transport Sociology: Some Aspects of Transport Planning* (Oxford: Pergamon Press, 1986), pp. 39-50.
29. Marshall Berman, *All that is Solid Melts into Air: The Experience of Modernity* (New York: Penguin Books, 1988), p. 307.
30. Robert L. Lineberry and Ira Sharkansky, *Urban Politics and Public Policy* (New York: Harper and Row, Second Edition, 1974), p. 282.
31. David C. Hodge, "Geography and the Political Economy of Urban Transportation," *Urban Geography* 11 (1990):92.
32. Tom Mattoff, John Holtzclaw, and Paul Downton, "Future of Urban Transportation," in Christopher Canfield, ed., *Report of the First International Ecocity Conference* (Berkeley, CA: Urban Ecology, 1990), pp.40-41.
33. Newman and Kenworthy *op.cit.*
34. Fred A. Reid, "Real Possibilities in the Transportation Myths," in Sim Van der Ryn and Peter Calthorpe, eds., *Sustainable Communities: A New Design Synthesis for Cities, Suburbs, and Towns* (San Francisco: Sierra Club Books, 1986), p. 176.
35. Frank Viviano, "Push for Homes Near Transportation," *San Francisco Chronicle*, March 19, 1991.
36. Deborah Gordon, *Steering a New Course: Transportation, Energy and the Environment* (Cambridge, MA: Union of Concerned Scientists, 1991), p. 48.
37. Marian Lief Palley and Howard A. Palley, *Urban America and Public Policies* (Lexington, MA: D.C. Heath, 1977), p. 225.
38. Newman and Kenworthy, *op.cit.*, p. 36.
39. Viviano January 31, 1991, *op.cit.*
40. Robert E. Paaswell and Wilfred W. Recker, *Problems of the Carless* (New York: Praeger, 1978), p. 173.
41. George Haikalis, "Planning Transportation Innovations for Livable Cities: Auto-Free Zones and Personal Rapid Transit," *Journal of Advanced Transportation* 24 (1990):3-7.
42. Gordon, *op.cit*, p. 15.
43. *Bulletin* (Washington, DC: Surface Transportation Policy Project, March 27, 1992).
44. Suzanne Alexander, "Riding a Bike to Work Gains in Popularity," *The Wall Street Journal*, December 26, 1991.

45. Mayer Hillman, "Planning for the Green Modes: A Critique of Public Policy and Practice," in Rodney Tolley, ed., *The Greening of Urban Transport: Planning for Walking and Cycling in Western Cities* (London: Belhaven Press, 1990), pp. 64-74.
46. Michael Renner, "Rethinking the Role of the Automobile," (Washington, DC: Worldwatch Institute, Paper No. 84, 1988), p. 51.
47. "Public Transit: The Vision for 2020," (Chicago: Center for Neighborhood Technology, 1990).
48. Michelle Herman, "A New Generation of Bicycle Offers More Comfort and Convenience," *Utne Reader*, No. 38, March-April, 1989, p. 92.
49. Lewis Mumford, "Transportation: 'A Failure of Mind'," *The New York Times*, March 15, 1971.
50. Peter Calthorpe, "The Post-Suburban Metropolis," *Whole Earth Review*, No. 73, Winter, 1991, p. 51.
51. Christopher Alexander, Sara Ishikawa, and Murray Silverstein, *A Pattern Language: Towns/Building/Construction* (New York: Oxford University Press, 1977), pp. 169-173; Manuel Castells, "Space and Society: Managing the New Historical Relationships," in Michael Peter Smith, ed., *Cities in Transformation: Class, Capital, and the State* (Beverly Hills: Sage Publications, 1984), p. 252; Kevin Lynch, *A Theory of Good City Form* (Cambridge, MA: The MIT Press, 1981), pp. 426-431.
52. Charles E. Little, *Greenways for America* (Baltimore: The Johns Hopkins University Press, 1990), p. 1.
53. Noel Grove, "Greenways: Paths to the Future," *National Geographic* 177 (1990):77.
54. George T. Martin, Jr., *Social Policy in the Welfare State* (Englewood Cliffs, NJ: Prentice Hall, 1990), p. 194.
55. Donald Appleyard, *Livable Streets* (Berkeley, CA: University of California Press, 1981), p. 1. Sadly and ironically, Appleyard was killed in Athens in 1982 when walking; he was hit by a car that went through a barrier at over 100 mph. He was 57 years old. See: Richard Jacobsen, "Berkeley Prof Dies in Athens," *The Daily Californian*, September 30, 1982.
56. Peter J. Wilson, *The Domestication of the Human Species* (New Haven: Yale University Press, 1988).
57. "Transportation and the Urban Environment: The Rational Relationship between Automobile and Public Transit Development," (Washington, DC: *Joint Report of the U.S./U.S.S.R. Urban Transportation Team*, October, 1978), p. 85.
58. Newman and Kenworthy, *op.cit.*, p. 84.
59. Dolores Hayden, "Capitalism, Socialism and the Built Environment," in Steven Rosskamm Shalom, ed., *Socialist Visions* (Boston: South End Press, 1983), p. 69.
60. Calthorpe, *op.cit.*; Peter Calthorpe, *Pedestrian Pockets: A New Suburban Design Strategy* (New York: Princeton Architectural Press, 1987).
61. John King, "Suburbia Without Sprawl," *San Francisco Focus*, January, 1991, pp. 26-32.
62. Diana Shaman, "No Need for Car at This Project," *The New York Times*, September 14, 1990.
63. Arnold J. Heidenheimer, Hugh Heclo, and Carolyn Teich Adams, *Comparative Public Policy: The Politics of Social Choice in Europe and America* (New York: St. Martin's Press, Second Edition, 1983), p. 254.

64. "Working Paper for a Better Sacramento" (Sacramento CA: Environmental Council of Sacramento), 1989, p. 4.
65. Michael Peter Smith, Gregory A. Guagnano, and Cath Posehn, "The Political Economy of Growth in Sacramento: Whose City?" in Gregory D. Squires, ed., *Unequal Partnerships: The Political Economy of Urban Redevelopment in Postwar America* (New Brunswick, NJ: Rutgers University Press, 1989), pp. 260-288.
66. Heiner Monheim, "Area-Wide Traffic Restraint: A Concept for Better Urban Transport," *Built Environment* 12 (1986):74-82.
67. Carmen Hass-Klau, "Environmental Traffic Management in Britain—Does It Exist?" *Built Environment* 12 (1986):7-19.
68. Carmen Hass-Klau, *The Pedestrian and City Traffic* (London: Belhaven Press, 1990), pp. 214-219.
69. Joop H. Kraay, "Woonerven and Other Experiments in the Netherlands," *Built Environment* 12 (1986):20-29.
70. Marlise Simons, "Amsterdam Plans Wide Limit on Cars," *The New York Times*, January 28, 1993.
71. Marcia Lowe, "Taming New York's Mean Streets," *Worldwatch* 4 (1991):5-6.
72. Reid, *op.cit.*, p. 181.
73. William H. Whyte, *City: Rediscovering the Center* (New York: Doubleday, 1988), p. 68.
74. Barbara Flanagan, "A Massachusetts Mall is Just Disappeared," *The New York Times*, March 14, 1991.
75. Motor Vehicle Manufacturers Association, *Facts & Figures '92*, Detroit, 1992, p. 79.
76. Hass-Klau 1990, *op.cit.*, p. 5; Robert Schaeffer, "Car Sick, Automobiles Ad Nauseam," *Greenpeace* 15 (1990):17.
77. Jeff Pelline, "Why Higher Gas Taxes Could Be Good Policy," *San Francisco Chronicle*, February 26, 1991.
78. Carolyn S. Konheim and Brian Ketcham, "Toward a More Balanced Distribution of Transportation Funds," (Brooklyn, NY: Konheim & Ketcham, 1991), p. 1.
79. Frank Viviano, "High Gas Tax a Way of Life in Europe," *San Francisco Chronicle*, January 22, 1993.
80. James J. MacKenzie and Michael P. Walsh, "Driving Forces: Motor Vehicle Trends and their Implications for Global Warming, Energy Strategies, and Transportation Planning" (Washington, DC: World Resources Institute, December, 1990).
81. Jane Jacobs, *The Death and Life of Great American Cities* (Baltimore: Penguin Books, 1965), p. 384.
82. "Make Drivers Pay," *New Internationalist*, No. 195, May, 1989, p. 23.
83. Gordon E. Hart, Claudia Elliott, and Judith Lamare, "Heading the Wrong Way: Redirecting California's Transportation Policies," in Robert L. Deen, ed., *The Alternatives to Gridlock: Perspectives on Meeting California's Transportation Needs* (Sacramento: California Institute of Public Affairs, 1990), p. 93.
84. Calvin Sims, "Five Big Arms Makers Vie to Build Rail Cars," *The New York Times*, May 8, 1993, p. 17.

CHAPTER 10

Social Change

The systemic nature of auto-centred transport has repeatedly surfaced as a theme in these chapters. It is not enough to simply look at the role of individual components of auto-centred transport because they do form an integrated totality. In order to effectively deal with transport, one must also think about housing, as well as about the location of work and other social activities. A holistic approach would not only improve mass transit but it would also nurture multi-functional public spaces and develop jobs at sites that do reduce auto commutes.

There is a demonstrated need for a comprehensive policy that would pursue sociopolitical changes simultaneously on a number of different fronts and levels. On the infrastructural level the goal of a holistic policy might be the social transformation of space to emphasize the communalization of transport and other collective resources. Denser and more heterogeneous land use patterns can be more ecologically sound, as well as being more transport efficient. A diverse system is potentially more democratic and more resilient than a homogeneous system. Social change means change on a societal level: Simultaneous attempts to alter cultural beliefs and time-space constraints, including the organization of work schedules and home-to-work journeys. Thus, flextime arrangements and child care facilities near workplaces need to be part of any overall attempt to reduce auto-centredness in transport.

Ultimately, social change must be global, as most auto-related ecological issues have global dimensions. It is important to recognize the North-South component of resource energy-intensive technologies such as auto-centred transport. In order to grasp the problem in its systemic and multi-levelled aspects, social change must include basic political and economic reforms as well. The power of elites and the marketplace to shape transport and social space must be modified so that societies can have more equitable and humane transport systems.

All social-ecological systems are sustained partly through ideological factors; these must also be addressed. We need a new vision that looks at transport in an ecologically and socially sound fashion. What is needed is a holistic vision of transport systems. Such a holistic vision would be sensitive to the following: (1) the political and economic contexts of transport, (2) the issues of individual empowerment and social status *vis-à-vis* transport policy, (3) the use of transport technology in its sociocultural context, (4) the structural properties of auto-centred social ecology.

The Political Economy of Transport

The political economic system of global capitalism influences the social ecology of transport on a number of levels. First of all the dynamic of contemporary capitalism accelerates a tendency found throughout the history of capitalism—time and space compression. As Marx noted about 130 years ago, time-space compression was a central feature of industrial capitalism.[1] Such compression is fed by new transport and communication technologies that reduce the constraints of time and space on production and consumption. Furthermore, time-space compression is reproduced in the subjective experiences of everyday life. Accelerated movement and speeded-up time are archetypical features of both industrial and post-industrial landscapes. Speeded-up time schedules and widely dispersed sites of human activity are some of the objective correlates of experiences such as placelessness, community deterioration, and ecological degradation.

As Glenn Yago has shown, transport systems are shaped by the imperatives of capital, such as the need to move labour and products.[2] Capitalist systems do not have ecological or social equity considerations as a top priority. In general, auto-truck transport systems have provided capitalist enterprises with a new flexibility to reach markets and to decentralize production. Autos and trucks provide greater flexibility than rail alone, but they do so at greater social and environmental costs.

The growth and entrenchment of auto-centred transport has itself provided a market for the expansion of capitalism. Auto-centred transport has an affinity with global capitalism not only because it is part of its infrastructure, but because it requires resource and energy-intensive consumption. Time-space compression speeds up consumption. Furthermore, the social and material conditions of everyday life become so transformed by widespread auto use as to eventually make the patterns of auto consumption necessities (for example, autos-suburbs-malls), not options. In the process of entrenching such patterns, a lifestyle and accompanying cultural formation emerge. The auto-industrial complex, through advertising, lobbying, and other influences on public discourse, helps to sustain an auto culture. One critical feature of auto ideology is the masking of its problematic and costly features. The belief in the individualized surface appearance of automobility and the masking of its social nature are central features of auto—and capitalist—culture.

The hegemony of the auto is sustained by cultural-ideological factors that make it a taken-for-granted part of our subjective lives. Mass marketing, deep appeals to our psyche—particularly gendered appeals—and an ideology that convinces us that the auto provides unlimited personal freedom and geographic mobility, are all part of the automobility ethos that penetrates our inner subjective worlds. The auto-centred transport system is welded to the political economy. The auto-industrial complex is a major source of jobs and it exerts considerable influence on the political sphere. The auto-industrial complex has been effective, particularly in the United States, in furthering the development of a government-subsidized auto infrastructure, for example, the interstate highway system. Relatively affordable sources of non-renewable energy further encourage the auto and its intensive use as a mode of transport. Any efforts at reducing auto-dependence must ultimately consider such political realities.

In this way, a complex of factors has embedded automobility in our lives, our environments and our consciousness. Its destructive features occasionally surface in our discourse but generally they remain denied or invisible—hidden behind ideological appearances of efficiency, freedom and mobility. A critical analysis of auto-centred transport can highlight its collectively irrational use of resources and energy and its undemocratic features. Such a critical analysis also enables us to see the dangers of allowing the logic of capitalist expansion to shape transport policy. Capitalist logic is predicated on growth; it drives the rapid consumption of resources and energy through the saturation of world markets with commodities such as the auto. This logic is now truly global; it has become dominant in the former centrally-planned economies as well as in the Third World. However, the globalization of auto-centred transport ultimately is not economically feasible, and it is not in the best interests of the earth's ecology and human transport needs.

One may ask about the extent to which the logic of capital accumulation, the power of the auto-industrial complex, and other systemic sources of support for auto-centred transport, limit the possibilities for social change. The issue of auto-centred transport ultimately raises the question of whether or not capitalism—at least in its present form—is compatible with ecologically sensitive production and consumption. For instance, shifting to a less auto-dependent society raises serious questions for workers, who:

> ... do not have a sense of options, except the option to choose between a job that is determined by some corporation or unemployment and even homelessness. That is not to say that workers should not or cannot be challenged to examine what they produce and the processes by which they're produced—merely to point out that any organizing work that does not begin with an appreciation of the psychology and material reality of worker's identification with their companies, their job and their "product" and that does not resonate to the deep insecurity and vulnerability of most workers in our society, cannot help workers move past that consciousness to play a role in shaping new economic alternatives.[3]

Mainstream environmentalism has not effectively linked its concerns with those of social justice.[4] Green oriented groups need to demonstrate the labour-intensive potential of greener modes of production, including green transport systems. Environmental, transport, and employment issues framed in a context of economic alternatives to capitalism could become centrepieces in a more general or holistic agenda, which would benefit the broadest of constituencies.

Developed nations need a new post-industrial policy that emphasizes less resource-energy intensive and ecologically destructive modes of production; transport could be a key component of such a policy. It is a lever by which to move on three fronts: Creating jobs by rebuilding transport infrastructures in order to be more ecologically and socially sound.

Individual Empowerment and Social Status

As we have argued, one's social position influences the quality of one's geographic mobility and one's ecological spaces. The contingencies of an individual's class, gender, age, and physical ability affect her or his degree of empowerment in auto-centred transport systems. German Greens advocate a "right to mobility" in which all citizens—old and young, rich and poor—are guaranteed at least a minimum level of mobility and access to shopping, educational, and other facilities.[5] This right to mobility can be conceptualized as similar to the medieval "right to the city" (*le droit à la ville*) that has been eroded in industrial capitalist society.[6]

Any vision of alternative transport has to confront the power arrangements of society. Green and feminist insights about masculine notions of power over others and over nature, and about the humanization of social space, need to be integrated into transport policies. Auto-centred transport creates groups of transport-disadvantaged persons. The very young and the old, people with disabilities, people with low income, and women may be included among those groups whose perspectives are often ignored in transport policy. The transport planners, politicians, and officials who shape policy generally experience the world from behind the windshield. Their view is filtered through the ideology of automobility and through gender (masculine) and class (*bourgeois*) biases—a professional ideology that is auto-centred, so to speak. The ideology of automobility, in turn, informs discourses about transport needs, and veils the systemic effects of auto-centred transport (for example, congestion and pollution).

Those who shape auto-centred transport systems only dimly perceive the perspectives of children forced to avoid streets, of elderly people and people with disabilities confronted by the demands and barriers of auto-centred space, of general experiences of placelessness and aesthetic impoverishment engendered by auto structures, and the experience of managing housework and transport work in dispersed communities. The subtle interplay among subjective experience, mobility, and social space are essential considerations in the configuration of transport technology. Chapter 6 and other parts of this book have highlighted the politics of subjectivity in human-auto interactions.

Transport ecologies need to be shaped by the ideas and needs of more representative constituencies. Feminist groups bring to the forefront particular problems faced by women in the social organization of space and transport; so do disability rights groups and groups representing the elderly, workers, and the poor. Feminist analyses address ancient, pre-capitalist and patriarchal systems of inequality.

The claim of some feminists that the industrial-technical ethos is a male-gendered view of the human relationship to nature may be relevant to our discussion of contemporary transport.[7] To what extent is the existing bias towards "hard" forms of mobility influenced by gender? How much power and mass are needed to drive ten miles to work? Once certain styles of transport come to prevail—autos of high horsepower and heavy mass, they create a traffic context in which alternative, softer means of automobility are less feasible and less safe. Feminism and other "outsider" perspectives provide a means of developing more humanized versions of transport, because they uncover and highlight the voices and needs of groups that auto-centred transport systems largely ignore.

Technology and Its Sociocultural Contexts

Technology considered in the abstract can be viewed as neutral but once utilized it automatically has social consequences and, hence, is not neutral. The idea that technology is morally neutral is based on an artificial separation between technology and its use.[8] Therefore, every use of technology brings with it some system of social control and some demands on human behaviour. The application of technology to solve problems of transport and energy use requires social organization and controls. Traffic regulations, licensing, and other controls constrain the use of autos. The supposed neutrality of technology and the notion that nature is a mere social construction lead even some Marxist analysts to ignore issues such as limits to the use of technology and to the exploitation of nature.[9] Auto-centred transport represents a *system of technology in use*, which is characterized by ecologically harmful factors like its resource and energy intensity. The technical form that auto transport takes, such as the size and power of cars, is not simply determined by functional criteria but also by consumerist, status-conscious and gendered social criteria.

The problem is not that the auto is an inherently bad technology. The moment any technology is put into use it has social consequences; for example, the auto has implications for the social organization of space, the division of labour, and the natural environment. As such, technology-in-use inevitably generates and influences moral issues. The uses to which a given technology is put and the form that it takes are shaped by the physical and social conditions under which its production takes place, by the ways in which the ability to produce the technology are socially developed, and by the social aspects of its use. To argue that the auto is intrinsically bad is nonsense, but to ignore that its intensive and extensive use has moral consequences, or that its very form of development may be influenced by social meanings, is self-deceptive.

An alternative vision of transport technology seeks to encourage more ecologically-friendly modes of production and consumption. Rather than simply retrofitting existing technology to eliminate pollution (for example, catalytic converters), we need to develop structures and processes that minimize auto-dependence. Priority should be given to developing less energy-resource intensive means of transport and to providing improved forms of collective transport. New non-auto transport technology would stress efficiency, security, and comfort but also provide a sensual and aesthetic dimension.

Aesthetic considerations are important in restoring the natural environment—by making the earth "'beautiful' we make it whole."[10] Indeed, the aesthetic impact of the use of technology is crucial to an evaluation of transport ecology. Space-time compression facilitates faster and more machine-mediated movements through natural landscapes. In the process, details like textures and smells are lost. These details are a part of the sensory experience that allows for an aesthetic appreciation of natural environments. Furthermore, auto-centred transport encourages the paving over of nature and the consignment of natural spaces to restricted areas such as parks. The experience for the driver is of moving from place to place and experiencing what is between places as if it were on a television screen. It is this flatness (not unlike that experienced in "virtual realities") that characterizes more and more our contacts with natural landscapes. As auto technology progressed, the more natural activities of driving were further attenuated, through power steering, air conditioning, etc.

The visual flatness of the driving experience is, of course, also a feature of travelling in trains and buses. Such travel actually can heighten aesthetic experiences by offering panoramas not available to those who travel on foot, and by providing the sensory experience of travelling at high speeds. However, it is the ubiquitous, everyday use of autos that erodes a sensual and aesthetic engagement of the natural environment. Flat and fast-changing visual experiences become the rule.[11] Auto travel becomes, in a sense, disembodied. We are *not* suggesting any technological determinism of social and aesthetic experiences, but rather the possibility of a more subtle influence on our sensibilities. The ubiquitous use of autos and other technologies that separate us from an immediate connection with the natural and socially constructed world has real consequences for our sensitivity to the environment. Aesthetics can help to sensitize us to our connections with nature. Principles of aesthetics and a thorough recognition of the importance of our need to enjoy and to take pleasure in our environments need to become central parts of any transport policy reform. Indeed, improved aesthetics and more engaged sensibilities can be incentives to encourage people to move away from auto-centred transport to pleasurable and gratifying alternatives.

In considering transport policy, the aesthetic and political dimensions of time also need to be addressed. The love affair with the auto both expresses and nurtures a compression of time. The metaphysical underpinnings of auto hegemony (and, earlier, the train) lie in a technological assault on time and its passage.[12] Cultural attitudes are a part of this assault, as are structural realities such as tightly scheduled work days. German Greens argue for the need to change attitudes towards time—the attitudes that are the basis for making it a scarce commodity. Such changes are an integral part of modifying general sensibilities about transport.[13] The long-term image here is one of a more relaxed society. The time lost in production can be more than offset by the greater productivity of workers who enjoy their work and their lives.

Speed can remain part of a more easy-going society. The "quest for excitement" is a part of our sociocultural make-up.[14] However, the contemporary masculine world view about speed is part and parcel of the industrial capitalist stance towards nature.[15] Auto racing and similar facets of auto culture are deeply embedded in the social psyche. Any alternatives to auto use need to provide adequate spaces for the expression of such needs. Perhaps spatial enclaves and technological options providing expanded opportunities for speed and excitement can be considered in urban planning. Also, the "softer" forms of mobility such as the bicycle can be vehicles for expressing sensual physical needs for pleasure, excitement, and speed. In any event the sensual, erotic and other irrational appeals of auto technology cannot be ignored.

A naive optimism about technology is a hallmark of twentieth century modernism. The images of technical utopians from the 1920s to the 1960s who wrote about the cities of the future showed one-person helicopters and other individualized transport options, but not the energy- and resource-intensity involved in the widespread use of such devices. Such utopians did not entertain the possibility that such technologically sophisticated mobility could not benefit everyone.[16] These images did not show an awareness of the full range of social consequences of technology. Despite a growing public awareness of the limits of technology since the mid-twentieth century (at least since the use of weapons of mass destruction), people in influential places continue to be optimistic about the role that technology alone can play in resolving environmental problems—environmental problems that the use of technology created. For example, German Chancellor Helmut Kohl has stated: "Only with the newest technology can the environment be better protected. Who is against technical progress cannot preserve the environment."[17] Transport officials who shape transport policy also favour technological solutions (i.e., more roads, cleaner cars). These measures only temporarily manage problems while ignoring the social contexts of technology.

The Structure of Auto-Centred Social Ecology

Auto-centred transport leads us to confront the conflict between individual and social needs. The pursuit of unlimited individual consumption can result in collectively destructive patterns, with their own mechanisms of social reproduction. Ecological critiques of consumption remind us of these patterns and their untenability. The logic of capitalism and the technological ethos with which it has an affinity posit that there are no limits to the consumption of resources. Energy- and resource-intensive production and consumption under capitalism encourage development in the fast lane. The problem with such development is that it is difficult to control and to slow down, even when it clearly has a negative impact on the quality of life and on the environment.

As with many other commodities in a market economy, it is not so much the auto that is the problem but its over-production and over-consumption. The auto has so dominated transport in countries like the United States that there is an almost exclusive social emphasis on developing and maintaining auto technology and infrastructures. Auto-centred transport arrangements have become socially embedded to the point that they inhibit us from utilizing extant technologies in order to develop alternate forms of transport.

Like rail, auto-centred transport favours a particularly rationalized and geometrical space. The infrastructure of the auto, with its ribbons and plots of asphalt and concrete, covers a more extensive area than that of rail. The flexible movements and incursions of the auto through the landscape are followed by ever-growing inflexible infrastructures which appropriate space in a way that is at odds with social ecology and social needs. The compression of time and space facilitated by automobility tends to produce a false sense of expanded horizons and efficiency of movement. Furthermore, time and space compression require transformations that homogenize—near and far become more and more indistinguishable, not only because of compressed time and distance but because they become more alike in appearance.

An auto-centred transport ecology is not sufficiently diversified. Despite its appearance of complexity and flexibility, it is a remarkably homogeneous system of transport, as Lewis Mumford noted over a quarter century ago:

> The fatal mistake we have been making is to sacrifice every other form of transportation to the private motorcar—and to offer, as the only long-distance alternative, the airplane. But the fact is that each type of transportation has its special use; and a good transportation policy must seek to improve each type and make the most of it .... There is not one ideal mode or speed: human purpose should govern the choice of the means of transportation. That is why we need a better transportation *system*, not just more highways. The projectors of our national highway program plainly had little interest in transportation. In their fanatical zeal to expand our highways, the very allocation of funds indicates that they are ready to liquidate all other forms of land and water transportation. The result is a crudely over-simplified and inefficient method of mono-transportation: a regression from the complex many-sided transportation system we once boasted.[18]

A diverse transport system is less vulnerable to failure and to disruption. For instance, had there not been alternatives to driving available in the San Francisco Bay Area after the 1989 Loma Prieta earthquake, the disruption of travel and all that depends on it, including economic activity, would have been far greater. As it was, the costs of the disruption were still greater than necessary because the density of available alternatives was lacking. Mass transit and ferries do not serve all areas in the region. A fully diversified transport system is characterized by a ready availability of alternative means of mobility; this enhances access for all in an urban population and at the same time decreases its vulnerability to disruption.

What might be a longer-term vision for an ecologically sound and economically efficient transport system for cities? An effort to create such a vision has been mounted by ecologists in the San Francisco Bay Area.[19] Richard Register's ecocity plan for Berkeley's downtown area imagines, among other changes, walkways in the sky that attract pedestrian traffic:

> But perhaps the most exhilarating, just plain fun new transportation feature would be the one with the highest visibility, literally: the bridges linking public spaces three and six stories above ground level .... With soaring views in all directions, we'd have the first inklings of a kind of grounded flight to be experienced in larger ecocities of the future, a mix of relatively high-tech construction with rich biological systems supported by sun, wind, and water energy, nurtured organically and maintained largely with recycled materials—a new world connected by stairs, escalators, elevators, bridges, and good old walking.[20]

In addition to reducing auto-dependence, the denser social spaces such as those Register describes provide the basis for a generally more efficient use of energy and resources. The genius of Register's vision is the arrangement of social space that provides for, even demands, playfulness—that invites us to take pleasure in *being* in our built environments.

At the heart of resolving general ecological problems is the question of how to reconfigure present patterns of consumption, particularly those in much of the developed world. These patterns include a highly energy-resource intensive use of space, in which urban sprawl and autos are two major culprits. This use of resources is one expression of the individualized mode of consumption fostered by capitalism. The reconstruction of such consumption patterns need not be based on an ascetic vision, which is often imputed to those who advocate sustainable development. It is important to recognize that auto-centred transport and the spatial patterns that accompany it are not synonymous with the good life and with freedom of choice—much less with social equity.

Visions that embrace asceticism and ask individuals to limit their choices and freedoms will not motivate change but will arouse resistance and fear. Ecologically sound and socially equitable transport and living do not mean lessening but improving the quality of life. The exhilaration that Register describes exemplifies the pleasurable visions that empower individuals and offer them a more joyful way of life.

There is evidence that the designers of the modern, auto-centred urban landscape are themselves questioning the quality of life it affords. The theme of the 1993 World Congress of Architects was sustainable development—design that provides shelter without environmental or human exploitation. The Congress was held in Chicago, the birthplace of the skyscraper and other foundations of modernist urban design, at the city's massive lakefront convention centre, McCormick Place. Located in a spot of grand vistas of Chicago's downtown (the Loop) along Lake Michigan, McCormick Place is virtually inaccessible by foot:

> You can walk to McCormick Place, but not without dodging cars. Though it is just minutes away by foot from the Loop, the cavernous convention center is so isolated from the rest of Chicago by the traffic streaming past that most visitors arrive and depart by taxi or bus. Intentionally or not, the building is a perfect example of the problem addressed ... by the more than 6,000 architects who gathered ... The extent to which architecture has contributed to the global environmental crisis.[21]

The architects focused on several strategies that can help curtail the gross consumption of resources involved in the modern built environment: More use of renewable resources like natural light and ventilation, and control of suburban growth. The closing remarks at the Congress were delivered by Jaime Lerner, an architect and former mayor of Curitiba, Brazil (see Chapter 4). He addressed the issue of what individual people can do to deal with global environmental problems: "Just do two simple things. Drive less the car. Separate the garbage."[22]

Conclusion

There are achievable strategies for reducing auto-centred transport. Short-term strategies include local transformations of space, such as by traffic-calming and greening of urban areas, as well as upgrading provision of alternate transport, especially walking. In the interim term, more energy-efficient, less polluting autos need to be made widely available and mass transit needs to be both improved and expanded. In the longer term, the focus needs to be placed on changing land use patterns, revitalizing inner city areas through in-fill, and developing new technologies for a variety of environmentally friendly transport modes. Other longer term projects include public education campaigns that encourage mass transit use and other options to autos.

Ultimately, if these strategies are to succeed, the political and economic context of transport has to be expanded from a focus on market considerations to include much more focus on the common good. Transport, like education and other vital societal activities, is far too critical to be left to the vagaries of the profit-driven market place. Additionally, modification of auto-centred transport will have to be accompanied by a recasting of psychopolitical ideologies that are linked to class and gender; for example, ways need to be found to curtail macho attitudes toward speed and power. Thus, it is clear that reconfiguring transport requires a systematic analysis and a comprehensive political programme.

Examples of alternative, systemic approaches to transport reform include the work of some contemporary green groups. The programmes and analyses of the German Greens, for example, generally demonstrate a holistic and ecological orientation towards transport. Transport is viewed as an organic *system*, with ideological, subjective, infrastructural, political, and economic levels. Land use patterns, gender-differentiated issues, social and political forces that shape technology—all these require consideration in thinking critically about transport. Ultimately, critical analysis of auto-centred transport forces us to address broader issues of political economy, ecology, and social inequality.

At present, even ecologically oriented activists, especially in the United States, treat transport as one more (and usually lower ranking) item in a laundry list of sensible changes. We believe that transport is more important than this, that it is inextricably bound up with the most basic parameters of human existence, including time,

space, and consciousness. Transport is organically linked to all the
significant realms of human social activity, including the workplace
and the home. Transport is a vital indication of the quality of our individual lives, as well as the quality of our relationships with each
other and with the earth.

NOTES

1. See: Marshall Berman, *All That is Solid Melts into Air: The Experience of Modernity* (New York: Penguin Books, 1988).
2. Glenn Yago, *The Decline of Transit: Urban Transportation in German and U.S.
Cities, 1900-1970* (Cambridge: Cambridge University Press, 1984).
3. Eric Mann, "Public Transit, Air Quality and Issues on Equity," in *Public Transit: The Vision of 2020* (Chicago: Center for Neighborhood Technology, 1990),
p. 15.
4. Eric Mann, "Auto Free: Reaction or Revolution?" *Transmission* (Toronto:
Transportation Options, Spring, 1993), pp. 18-20.
5. Gerd Hickmann und Klaus Dieter Kaser, *Trau keinem uber Tempo 30* (Stuttgart:
Grunen im Landtag von Baden-Wurttemberg, 1988).
6. Henri Lefebvre, *Le Droit à La Ville* (Paris: Anthropos, 1968).
7. See: Carolyn Merchant, *The Death of Nature: Women, Ecology and the Scientific
Revolution* (New York: Harper & Row, 1980).
8. Gregory H. Davis, *Technology—Humanism or Nihilism: A Critical Analysis of the
Philosophical Bias and Practice of Modern Technology* (New York: University
Press of America, 1981), pp. 46-47.
9. Stanley Aronowitz, *Science as Power: Discourse and Ideology in Modern Society*
(Minneapolis: University of Minnesota Press, 1988).
10. Jane Holtz Kay, "Applying the Brakes," *The Nation* 251 (1990):284.
11. Karl Otto Schallabock, "Grundsatze einer democratischen und umweltfreundlichen Verkehrsphilosophie," pp. 57-74 in Tom Koenigs und
Roland Schaeffer, eds., *Fortschritt vom Auto* (Munchen: Raben Verlag, 1991),
pp. 57-74.
12. Wolfgang Sachs, *Die Liebe Zum Automobil* (Reinbeck bei Hamburg: Rohwohlt,
1990).
13. Paul Beekmans *et.al.*, eds., *Welche Freiheit Brauchen Wir? Zum Psychologie der
AutoMobilen Gesellschaft* (Berlin: VAS in der Elefanten Press, 1989).
14. Norbert Elias and E. Dunning, *Quest for Excitement: Sport and Leisure in the
Civilizing Process* (New York: Basil Blackwell, 1986).
15. Merchant, *op.cit.*
16. Dirk Oblong, "Dromomane Rasergesellschaft oder Postmobile?" in Paul
Beekmans *et.al.*, eds., *Welche Freiheit Brauchen Wir? Zum Psychologie der Auto-
Mobilen Gesellschaft* (Berlin: VAS in der Elefanten Press, 1989), p. 166.
17. Cited in: *Umweltpolitik—Chancen fur unsere Zukunft* (Bonn: Reich Politik Informationen, 1990).
18. Lewis Mumford, *The Highway and the City* (New York: Mentor Books/New
American Library, 1964), pp. 247-248.

19. Peter Berg, Beryl Magilavy, and Seth Zuckerman, *A Green City Program for San Francisco Bay Area Cities and Towns* (San Francisco: Planet Drum Books, 1989).
20. Richard Register, *Ecocity Berkeley: Building Cities for a Healthy Future* (Berkeley, CA: North Atlantic Books, 1987), p. 104.
21. Herbert Muschamp, "Design vs. Environment: Architects Debate," *The New York Times*, June 23, 1993.
22. *Ibid.*

Bibliography

Adams, John. 1981. *Transport Planning: Vision and Practice*. London: Routledge and Kegan Paul.

— . 1992. "Towards a Sustainable Policy," pp. 320-333 in John Roberts *et. al.*, eds., *Travel Sickness: The Need for a Sustainable Transport Policy for Britain*. London: Lawrence and Wishart.

Ad Hoc Group to the Environment Committee of OECD. 1978. "Automotive Air Pollution and Noise: Implications for Public Policy," pp. 367-467 in Ralph Gakenheimer, ed., *The Automobile and the Environment: An International Perspective*. Prepared by the Organisation for Economic Co-operation and Development. Cambridge, MA: The MIT Press.

Advisory Commission on Cost Control in State Government. 1990. "Getting the Most Out of California's Transportation Tax Dollar." Sacramento, CA: Joint Publications.

Alexander, Christopher, Sara Ishikawa, and Murray Silverstein. 1977. *A Pattern Language: Towns/Building/Construction*. New York: Oxford University Press.

Alexander, Suzanne. 1991. "Riding a Bike to Work Gains in Popularity." *The Wall Street Journal*, December 26.

Allen, Alexandra. 1990. "The Auto's Assault on the Atmosphere." *Multinational Monitor* 11:22-26.

Altshuler, Alan *et. al.* 1984. *The Future of the Automobile: The Report of MIT's International Automobile Program*. Cambridge, MA: The MIT Press.

American Automobile Association. 1990. "Your Driving Costs." Heathrow, FL.

American Public Transit Association. 1990. *Transit Fact Book*. Washington, DC.

Appleyard, Donald. 1981. *Livable Streets*. Berkeley, CA: University of California Press.

Appleyard, Donald, Kevin Lynch, and John R. Myer. 1964. *The View from the Road*. Cambridge, MA: The MIT Press.

Aronowitz, Stanley. 1988. *Science as Power: Discourse and Ideology in Modern Society*. Minneapolis: University of Minnesota Press.

Baker, Susan B., Stephen Teret and Eric M. Daub. 1987. "Injuries," pp. 177-206 in S. R. Levine and A. Lilienfeld, eds., *Epidemiology and Health Policy*. New York: Tavistock.

Baldwin, J. 1990. "Eco-cars." *Whole Earth Review*, No. 68, Fall, pp. 32-33.

Barber, Gerald. 1986. "Aggregate Characteristics of Urban Travel," pp. 73-90 in Susan Hanson, ed., *The Geography of Urban Transportation*. New York: The Guilford Press.

Barde, Jean-Philippe and Kenneth Button. 1990. "Introduction," pp. 1-18 in Jean-Philippe Barde and Kenneth Button, eds., *Transport Policy and the Environment*. London: Earthscan Publications.

Bastian, Till. 1991. "Auto-Mobilitat." *Universitas* 46:515-516.

Bastian, Till und Harold Theml. 1990. *Unsere wahnsinnige Liebe zum Auto*. Beltz: Psychologie Heute/Taschenbuch.

Bayley, Stephen. 1986. *Sex, Drink and Fast Cars: The Creation and Consumption of Images*. London: Faber and Faber.

Beck, Ernst Gerhard und Pavel Schmidt. 1991. "Verkehr und gesundheit in Frankfurt," pp. 57-74 in Tom Koenigs und Roland Schaeffer, eds., *Fortschritt vom Auto*. Munchen: Raben Verlag.

Beckenbach, Frank. 1989. "Social Costs in Modern Capitalism." *Capitalism, Nature, Socialism* 3:72-91.

Berg, Peter, Beryl Magilavy, and Seth Zuckerman. 1989. *A Green City Program for San Francisco Bay Area Cities and Towns*. San Francisco: Planet Drum Books.

Berman, Marshall. 1988. *All that is Solid Melts into Air: The Experience of Modernity*. New York: Penguin Books.

Bloch, Robin and Keil Bloch. 1991. "Planning for a Fragrant Future: Air Pollution Control, Restructuring and Popular Alternatives in Los Angeles." *Capitalism, Nature, Socialism* 2:44-65.

Bogart, Leo. 1977. "The Automobile as Social Cohesion." *Society*, 14:10-15.

Boudreau, Thomas J. 1978. "Physical Activity, Health and Social Policies," pp. 239-250 in Ferdinand Landry and William Orban, eds., *Physical Activity and Human Well-Being*. Miami: Symposium Specialists.

Breines, Simon and William Dean. 1974. *The Pedestrian Revolution: Streets without Cars*. New York: Vintage Books.

Brodsly, D. 1981. *L.A. Freeway: An Appreciative Essay*. Berkeley, CA: University of California Press.

Brody, Jane E. 1993. "Personal Health." *The New York Times*, February 3.

Brog, Werner. 1991. "Verhalten beginnt im Kopf: Public awareness des offentlichen Personenverkehrs," pp. 291-306 in Tom Koenigs und Roland Schaeffer, eds., *Fortschritt vom Auto*. Munchen: Raben Verlag.

Brown, Lester. 1984. "The Future of Automobiles." *Society* 21:60-67.

Bruno, Kenny. 1991. "Not getting the Lead Out." *Greenpeace*, October-December, pp. 18-19.

Bruno, Kristen. 1993. "The Detroit Shuffle." *The San Francisco Bay Guardian*, March 31.

Buel, Ronald A. 1972. *Dead End: The Automobile in Mass Transportation*. Baltimore: Penguin Books.

Bulletin. 1991. Washington, DC: Surface Transportation Policy Project, October 18.

— . 1992. Washington, DC: Surface Transportation Policy Project, March 27.

Burco, Robert A. 1978. "Urban Public Transport: Service Innovations in Operations, Planning, and Technology," pp. 17-129 in Ralph Gakenheimer, ed., *The Automobile and the Environment: An International Perspective*. Prepared by the Organisation for Economic Co-operation and Development. Cambridge, MA: The MIT Press.

Bush, Donald J. 1989. "Emotive Power." *Design Quarterly* 146:21-31.

Calthorpe, Peter. 1987. *Pedestrian Pockets: A New Suburban Design Strategy*. New York: Princeton Architectural Press.

— . 1991. "The Post-Suburban Metropolis." *Whole Earth Review,* No. 73, Winter, pp. 44-51.

Campbell, Timothy. 1981. "Resource Flows in the Urban Ecosystem—Fuel, Water, and Food in Mexico City." Berkeley, CA: Working Paper No. 360, Institute of Urban and Regional Development, University of California.

Carp, Frances M. 1979. "Improving the Functional Quality of Housing and Environments for the Elderly through Transportation," pp. 127-146 in Thomas O. Byerts, Sandra C. Howell, and Leon A. Pastalan, eds., *Environmental Context of Aging.* New York: Garland Press.

— . 1988. "Significance of Mobility for the Well-Being of the Elderly," pp. 1-20 in *Transportation in an Aging Society.* Volume 2. Washington, DC. Committee for the Study on Improving Mobility and Safety for Older Persons, Transportation Research Board, National Research Council, Special Report 218.

Carson, Rachel. 1962. *Silent Spring.* New York: Fawcett Crest.

Carter, Everett C., Himmat S. Chadda, and Paul M. Schonfeld. 1984. "A Comparison of Transportation Planning in Developed and Developing Countries." *Transportation Quarterly* 38:69-86.

Castells, Manuel. 1977 [1972]. *The Urban Question: A Marxist Approach,* trans. Alan Sheridan. Cambridge, MA: The MIT Press.

— . 1978. *City, Class and Power,* trans. Elizabeth Lebas. New York: St. Martin's Press.

— . 1984. "Space and Society: Managing the New Historical Relationships," pp. 235-260 in Michael Peter Smith, ed., *Cities in Transformation: Class, Capital, and the State.* Beverly Hills: Sage Publications.

Christensen, Karen. 1990. *Home Ecology: Simple and Practical Ways to Green Your Home.* Golden, CO: Fulcrum Publishing.

Citizens Against Route Twenty. 1989. "The Solution to Route 20 and a New Vision for Brisbane." CART: Ashgrove, Australia.

Clark, Chris. 1989. "Driving Ourselves Crazy: The Real Costs of Bay Area Commutes." *Ecology Center Newsletter* 19:1-4.

Claybrook, Joan. 1984. *Retreat from Safety.* New York: Pantheon.

Cline, Marvin G. 1986. "Urban Freeways and Social Structure—Some Problems and Proposals," pp. 39-50 in Enne de Boer, ed., *Transport Sociology: Some Aspects of Transport Planning.* Oxford: Pergamon Press.

Commoner, Barry. 1990. *Making Peace with the Planet.* New York: Pantheon Books.

Conservation Law Foundation. 1990. "The Automobile: An Environmental Threat." Boston: CLF Newsletter, Summer.

Cooke, Philip. 1988. "The Postmodern Condition and the City," pp. 65-80 in Michael Peter Smith, ed., *Power, Community and the City.* Comparative Urban and Community Research. Volume 1. New Brunswick, NJ: Transaction Books.

Cowan, Ruth Schwartz. 1983. *More Work for Mother: The Ironies of Household Technology from the Open Hearth to the Microwave.* New York: Basic Books, Inc.

— . 1985. "More Work for Mother: Technology and Housework in the U.S.A.," pp. 88-128 in Les Levidow and Bob Young, eds., *Science, Technology and the Labour Process: Marxist Studies.* Volume 2. Atlantic Highlands, NJ: Humanities Press.

Crandall, Robert W. *et. al.* 1986. *Regulating the Automobile.* Washington, DC: The Brookings Institution.

Davis, Gregory H. 1981. *Technology—Humanism or Nihilism: A Critical Analysis of the Philosophical Bias and Practice of Modern Technology.* New York: University Press of America.

Davis, Mike. 1990. *City of Quartz: Social Struggles in Postmodern Los Angeles.* London: Verso.

de Boer, E. 1986. "Transport Sociology," pp. 7-15 in Enne de Boer, ed., *Transport Sociology: Social Aspects of Transport Planning.* Oxford: Pergamon Press.

Deleage, Jean-Paul. 1989. "Eco-Marxist Critique of Political Economy." *Capitalism, Nature, Socialism* 3:15-31.

De Lorenzo, Matt. 1993. "Viper Brings Wide Grins." *San Francisco Chronicle,* February 5.

Dickens, Peter. 1992. *Society and Nature: Towards A Green Social Theory.* London: Harvester Wheatsheaf.

Didion, Joan. 1970. *Play It As It Lays.* New York: Farrar, Straus & Giroux.

Die Grunen im Bundestag. 1989. Paul Beekmans *et. al.,* eds. *Welche Freiheit brauchen Wir? Zum Psychologie der AutoMobilen Gesellschaft.* Berlin: VAS in der Elefanten Press.

Dobson, Andrew. 1990. *Green Political Thought.* London: Unwin Hyman.

Dombois, Rainer. 1987. "Autos and Autoindustrie in der Dritten Welt," pp. 137-140 in Jobst Kraus, Horst Sackstetter und Willi Wentsch, eds., *Auto, Auto Uber Alles?* Freiburg: Dreisam Verlag.

Drummond, James T. 1991. "A New Era in Road Policy." *Nation's Business* 79:20-26.

Durning, Alan. 1992. *Who Much is Enough?* New York: W.W. Norton.

Eaton, Michael R. 1990. "What Climate Change Means for Transportation Policy in California," pp. 100-108 in Robert L. Deen, ed., *The Alternatives to Gridlock: Perspectives on Meeting California's Transportation Needs.* Sacramento, CA: California Institute of Public Affairs.

The Economist. 1986. "The Unfinished Revolution." January 25.

ECOS. 1989. "Working Paper for a Better Sacramento." Sacramento, CA: Environmental Council of Sacramento.

Eder, Margret. 1987. "Man kann doch nicht das Atmen verbieten," pp. 43-46 in Jobst Kraus, Horst Sackstetter, und Willi Wentsch, eds., *Auto, Auto Uber Alles?* Freiburg: Dreisam Verlag.

Ehrenburg, Ilya. 1976 [1929]. *The Life of the Automobile.* New York: Urizen Books.

Elias, Norbert. 1982. *Power and Civility.* New York: Pantheon Books.

Elias, Norbert and E. Dunning. 1986. *Quest for Excitement: Sport and Leisure in the Civilizing Process.* New York: Basil Blackwell.

Ellwood, Wayne. 1989. "Car Chaos." *New Internationalist.* No. 195, May, pp. 4-6.

Espinosa, Suzanne. 1992. "Jobs, Economy Lead Bay Worries." *San Francisco Chronicle,* December 12.

Faiz, Asif. 1992. "Motor Vehicle Emissions in Developing Countries: Relative Implications for Urban Air Quality," pp. 175-186 in Alcira Kreimer and Mohan Munasinghe, eds., *Discussion Papers #168.* Washington, DC: World Bank.

Faiz, Asif *et. al.* 1990. "Automotive Air Pollution—Issues and Options for Developing Countries." Washington, DC: World Bank.

Ferguson, Malcolm. 1991. "Factors Influencing Atmosphere Emissions from Road Traffic in Central and East Europe." Paper presented at conference,

"Tomorrow's Clean and Fuel-Efficient Automobile: Opportunities for East-West Cooperation." Berlin, March 25-27.

Fielding, Gordon J. 1986. "Transit in American Cities," pp. 229-246 in Susan Hanson, ed., *The Geography of Urban Transportation*. New York: The Guilford Press.

Flanagan, Barbara. 1991. "A Massachusetts Mall is Just Disappeared." *The New York Times*, March 14.

Fleming, Bruce E. 1990. "Another Way of Dying." *The Nation* 250:446.

Flink, James J. 1970. *America Adopts the Automobile, 1985-1910*. Cambridge, MA: The MIT Press.

— . 1972. "Three Stages of American Automobile Consciousness." *American Quarterly* 24:451-473.

— . 1975. *The Car Culture*. Cambridge, MA: The MIT Press.

— . 1988. *The Automobile Age*. Cambridge, MA: The MIT Press.

Fogelson, Robert M. 1967. *The Fragmented Metropolis*. Cambridge, MA: Harvard University Press.

Frank, Helmut. 1986. "Mass Transport and Class Struggle," pp. 211-222 in Enne de Boer, ed., *Transport Sociology: Social Aspects of Transport Planning*. Oxford: Pergamon Press.

Freund, Peter E.S. and Meredith B. McGuire. 1991. *Health, Illness, and the Social Body: A Critical Sociology*. Englewood Cliffs, NJ: Prentice Hall.

Friedland, Roger. 1992. "Space, Place and Modernity: The Geographical Moment." *Contemporary Sociology* 21:11-15.

Friedman, Stephen. 1989. *City Moves: A User's Guide to the Way Cities Work*. New York: McGraw Hill.

Gallagher, Margaret *et. al.* 1989. "Effects of the 60 MPH Speed Limit on Rural Interstate Fatalities in New Mexico." *Journal of the American Medical Association* 262:2243-2245.

Gallup, Jr., George and Frank Newport. 1991. "Americans Do Love Their Cars." *San Francisco Chronicle*, May 6.

Gartman, David. 1986. *Auto Slavery: The Labor Process in the American Automobile Industry, 1897-1950*. New Brunswick, NJ: Rutgers University Press.

Gianturco, Adrienna. 1989. "Die Verkehrspolitik der USA unter Feministichen Aspecten," pp. 130-134 in Paul Beekmans *et. al.*, eds., *Welche Freiheit Brauchen Wir? Zum Psychologie der AutoMobilen Gesellschaft*. Die Grunen im Bundestag. Berlin: VAS in der Elefanten Press.

Giddens, Anthony. 1984. *The Constitution of Society*. Oxford: Polity Press.

Gitlin, Todd. 1986. "We Build Excitement," pp. 136-101 in Todd Gitlin, ed., *Watching Television*. New York: Pantheon Books.

Glickman, Norman J. 1987. "Cities and the International Division of Labor," pp. 66-86 in Michael Peter Smith and Joe R. Feagin, eds., *The Capitalist City: Global Restructuring and Community Politics*. Oxford: Basil Blackwell.

Gooding, Judson. 1991. "Le Un-Car Takes to the Streets of France." *San Francisco Chronicle*, March 3.

Gordon, David M. 1984. "Capitalist Development and the History of American Cities," pp. 21-53 in William K. Tabb and Larry Sawers, eds., *Marxism and the Metropolis: New Perspectives in Urban Political Economy*. New York: Oxford University Press.

Gordon, Deborah. 1991. *Steering a New Course: Transportation, Energy and the Environment.* Cambridge, MA: Union of Concerned Scientists.

Gorman, Christine. 1991. "Mexico City's Menacing Air." *Time* Magazine, April 1, p. 61.

Gorz, André. 1980. *Ecology as Politics.* Boston: South End Press.

Gottdiener, Mark. 1985. *The Social Production of Urban Space.* Austin: University of Texas Press.

— . 1989. "Neo-Fordism, the Restructuring of Capital and the New Form of Settlement Space." Paper presented at Annual Meeting, American Sociological Association, San Francisco.

Greenpeace International. 1991. *The Environmental Impact of the Car.* Amsterdam: Greenpeace International.

Grove, Noel. 1990. "Greenways: Paths to the Future." *National Geographic* 177:77-99.

Gusfield, Joseph R. 1981. *The Culture of Public Problems: Drinking—Driving and the Symbolic Order.* Chicago: University of Chicago Press.

— . 1991. "Risky Roads." *Society* 28:10-16.

Haikalis, George. 1990. "Planning Transportation Innovations for Livable Cities: Auto-Free Zones and Personal Rapid Transit." *Journal of Advanced Transportation,* 24:3-7.

Hall, Peter. 1988. *Cities of Tomorrow: An Intellectual History of Urban Planning and Design in the Twentieth Century.* Oxford: Basil Blackwell.

Hamer, Mike. 1989. "Splitting the City." *New Internationalist.* No. 195, May, p. 11.

Hamlett, Patrick W. 1992. *Understanding Technological Politics: A Decision Making Approach.* Englewood Cliffs, NJ: Prentice Hall.

Hanson, Susan and Margo Schwab. 1986. "Describing Disaggregate Flows: Individual and Household Activity Patterns," pp. 154-178 in Susan Hanson, ed., *The Geography of Urban Transportation.* New York: The Guilford Press.

Hart, Gordon E., Claudia Elliott, and Judith Lamare. 1990. "Heading the Wrong Way: Redirecting California's Transportation Policies," pp. 81-94 in Robert L. Deen, ed., *The Alternatives to Gridlock: Perspectives on Meeting California's Transportation Needs.* Sacramento, CA: California Institute of Public Affairs.

Harvey, David. 1973. *Social Justice and the City.* London: Edward Arnold.

— . 1989. *The Condition of Postmodernity: An Enquiry into the Origins of Cultural Change.* Oxford: Basil Blackwell.

Hass-Klau, Carmen. 1986. "Environmental Traffic Management in Britain—Does It Exist?" *Built Environment* 12:7-19.

— . 1990. *The Pedestrian and City Traffic.* London: Belhaven Press.

Hayden, Dolores. 1983. "Capitalism, Socialism and the Built Environment," pp. 59-81 in Steven Rosskamm Shalom, ed., *Socialist Visions.* Boston: South End Press.

Hayes, Dennis. 1990. *Behind the Silicon Curtain: The Seductions of Work in a Lonely Era.* Montreal: Black Rose Books.

Hazleton, Lesley. 1992. "Really Cool Cars." *The New York Times Magazine,* March 29.

Health on the Move. 1991. "The Policy Statement of the Transport and Health Study Group." Birmingham: Public Health Alliance.

Heidenheimer, Arnold J., Hugh Heclo, and Carolyn Teich Adams. 1983. *Comparative Public Policy: The Politics of Social Choice in Europe and America.* Second Edition. New York: St. Martin's Press.

Hell, P. 1987. "Automobil production fur ein Volk ohne Schuhe." P. 95 in Jobst Kraus, Horst Sackstetter und Willi Wentsch, eds., *Auto, Auto Uber Alles?* Freiburg: Dreisam Verlag.

Hempel, Lamont C. 1990. "The Promise of Electric Vehicles," pp. 117-127 in Robert L. Deen, ed., *The Alternatives to Gridlock: Perspectives on Meeting California's Transportation Needs.* Sacramento, CA: California Institute of Public Affairs.

Herman, Michelle. 1989. "A New Generation of Bicycle Offers More Comfort and Convenience." *Utne Reader,* No. 38, March-April, p. 92.

Hewings, Geoffrey J.D. 1986. "Transportation and Energy," pp. 280-300 in Susan Hanson, ed., *The Geography of Urban Transportation.* New York: The Guilford Press.

Hickmann, Gerd und Klaus Dieter Kaser. 1988. *Trau keinem uber Tempo 30.* Stuttgart: Grunen im Landtag von Baden-Wurttemberg.

Hilgers, Micha. 1991. "Auto-Mobil oder das Selbst im Strassenverkehr: Zur Psychoanalyze des Automobilmissbrauchs." *Universitas* 46:541-556.

Hillman, Mayer. 1990. "Planning for the Green Modes: A Critique of Public Policy and Practice," pp. 64-74 in Rodney Tolley, ed., *The Greening of Urban Transport: Planning for Walking and Cycling in Western Cities.* London: Belhaven Press.

— . 1991. "Healthy Transport Policy," pp. 82-91 in Peter Draper, ed., *Health Through Public Policy.* London: Merlin Press.

Hillman, Mayer, John Adams, and John Whitelegg. 1990. *One False Move—A Study of Children's Independent Mobility.* London: Policy Studies Institute.

Hilts, Philip. 1991. "California to Test Children for Lead Poisoning." *The New York Times,* October 12.

Hodge, David C. 1986. "Social Impacts of Urban Transportation Decisions: Equity Issues," pp. 301-327 in Susan Hanson, ed., *The Geography of Urban Transportation.* New York: The Guilford Press.

— . 1990. "Geography and the Political Economy of Urban Transportation." *Urban Geography* 11:87-100.

Holzapfel, Helmut. 1987. "Steigende Mobilitat—Raum gewinn oder Raum ver-nichtung?," pp. 111-119 in Jobst Kraus, Horst Sackstetter, und Willi Wentsch, eds., *Auto, Auto Uber Alles?* Freiburg: Dreisam Verlag.

Homola, Samuel. 1968. *Backache: Home Treatment and Prevention.* West Nyack, NY: Parker Publishing Co.

Horton, Elizabeth. 1985. "Why Don't We Buckle Up?" *Science Digest* 93:22.

Hunt, Sonja M. 1989. "The Public Health Implications of Private Cars," pp. 100-115 in Claudia Martin and David V. McQueen, eds., *Readings for a New Public Health.* Edinburgh: Edinburgh University Press.

Institut fur Angewandte Umweltforschung. 1990. *Der Auto Knigge.* Reinbeck bei Hamburg: Rowohlt Verlag.

Interrante, Joseph. 1983. "The Road to Autopia: The Automobile and the Spatial Transportation of American Culture," pp. 89-104 in David C. Lewis and Laurence Goldstein, eds., *The Automobile and American Culture.* Ann Arbor: University of Michigan Press.

Jacobs, Jane. 1965. *The Death and Life of Great American Cities.* Baltimore: Penguin Books.

Jacobsen, Richard. 1982. "Berkeley Prof Dies in Athens." *The Daily Californian,* September 30.

Jaggi, Max. 1977. "Traffic Policy: 'Free Fares were Only the Beginning'," pp. 62-76 in Max Jaggi, Roger Muller, and Sil Schmid, eds., *Bologna*. London: Writers and Readers Publishing Cooperative Society.

Jameson, Fredric. 1984. "Postmodernism, or the cultural logic of Late Capitalism." *New Left Review* 146:53-92.

——. 1991. *Postmodernism, or, The Cultural Logic of Late Capitalism*. Durham: Duke University Press.

Jerome, John. 1972. *The Death of the Automobile*. New York: W.W. Norton.

Joint Report of the U.S./U.S.S.R. Urban Transportation Team. 1978. "Transportation and the Urban Environment: The Rational Relationship between Automobile and Public Transit Development." Washington, DC: October.

Kain, John F. 1970. "The Distribution and Movement of Jobs and Industry," pp. 1-43 in James Q. Wilson, ed., *The Metropolitan Enigma: Inquiries into the Nature and Dimensions of America's "Urban Crisis."* Garden City, NY: Doubleday/Anchor.

Kain, John F. and John R. Myer. 1976. "Transportation and Poverty," pp. 180-194 in Harold Hochman, ed., *The Urban Economy*. New York: W.W. Norton.

Kay, Jane Holtz. 1990. "Applying the Brakes." *The Nation* 251:280-284.

Keats, John. 1958. *The Insolent Chariots*. Philadelphia: J.B. Lippincott Co.

Ketcham, Brian. 1992. "Making Transportation Choices Based on Real Costs." *Auto-Free Press* 3:4.

King, John. 1991. "Suburbia Without Sprawl." *San Francisco Focus*, January, pp. 26-32.

Kinzer, Stephen. 1992. "Long-Stifled Dresden Debates Highway to Prague." *The New York Times*, January 2.

Knapp, Gudrun-Axeli. 1987. "Auto-Erotik: Sexualisierung und Sexismus," pp. 106-108 in Jobst Kraus, Horst Sackstetter, und Willi Wentsch, eds., *Auto, Auto Uber Alles?* Freiburg: Dreisam Verlag.

——. 1989. "Auto-Erotik: Sexualisierung und Sexismus," pp. 61-74 in Paul Beekmans et. al., eds., *Welche Freiheit Brauchen Wir? Zum Psychologie der AutoMobilen Gesellschaft*. Die Grunen im Bundestag. Berlin: VAS in der Elefanten Press.

Kolata, Gina. 1990. "What If They Closed 42nd Street and Nobody Noticed?" *The New York Times*, December 25.

Konheim, Carolyn S. and Brian Ketcham. 1991. "Toward a More Balanced Distribution of Transportation Funds." Appendix A. Brooklyn, NY: Konheim & Ketcham.

Kraay, Joop H. 1986. "Woonerven and Other Experiments in the Netherlands." *Built Environment*, 12:20-29.

Kremsmayer, Ulla. 1990. "Mit Autos Keine Zukunft." *Profil* 24:78-79.

Kunz, Jerry. 1985. "The Car—the Driver: Their Relationship in America." Unpublished.

Kupfer, Joseph. 1985. "Architecture: Building the Body Politic." *Social Theory and Practice* 11:265-283.

Lazare, Daniel. 1990. "Planes, Trains and Automobiles." *The Village Voice*, October 23, pp. 39-40.

——. 1991. "Urbacide: America Kills Cities Nine Ways." *The Village Voice*, December 10, p. 36.

Lefebvre, Henri. 1968. *Le Droit à La Ville*. Paris: Anthropos.

——. 1971. *Everyday Life in the Modern World*. New York: Harper & Row.

— . 1991. *The Production of Space*, trans. Donald Nicholson-Smith. Oxford: Basil Blackwell.

Leiss, William. 1976. *The Limits to Satisfaction: An Essay on the Problem of Needs and Commodities*. Toronto: University of Toronto Press.

Levin, Doron P. 1991a. "Detroit's Assault on Mileage Bill." *The New York Times*, May 11.

— . 1991b. "Experts Doubt Cutbacks Will Save G.M." *The New York Times*, December 23.

Lewis, Sinclair. 1929. *Dodsworth*. New York: Harcourt, Brace and Co.

Lichtenthaler/Reutter, Ulrike und Ute Preis. 1989. "Frauen Unterwegs-Wege fur eine weibliche stadt," pp. 114-128 in Paul Beekmans *et. al*, eds., *Welche Freiheit Brauchen Wir? Zum Psychologie der AutoMobilen Gesellschaft*. Die Grunen im Bundestag. Berlin: VAS in der Elefanten Press.

Lichtfield, John. 1992. "No Particular Place to Live." *The Independent*, November 15, pp. 8-11.

Lineberry, Robert L. and Ira Sharkansky. 1974. *Urban Politics and Public Policy*. 2nd Edition. New York: Harper and Row.

Little, Charles E. 1990. *Greenways for America*. Baltimore: The Johns Hopkins University Press.

Lovins, Amory B. and L. Hunter Lovins. 1982. *Brittle Power: Energy for National Security*. Andover, MA: Brick House Publishing Co.

Lowe, Marcia D. 1990. *Alternatives to the Automobile: Transport for Livable Cities*. Washington, DC: Worldwatch Institute, Paper No. 98.

— . 1991. "Taming New York's Mean Streets." *Worldwatch* 4:5-6.

— . 1992. "Shaping Cities," pp. 119-137 in Lester Brown, ed., *State of the World*. New York: W.W. Norton.

— . 1993. "Rediscovering Rail," pp. 120-138 in Linda Starke, ed., *State of the World*. New York: W.W. Norton.

Ludvigsen, Karl and David Burgess Wise. 1982. *The Encyclopedia of the American Automobile*. New York: Exter Books.

Lynch, Kevin. 1960. *The Image of the City*. Cambridge, MA: The MIT Press.

— . 1981. *A Theory of Good City Form*. Cambridge, MA: The MIT Press.

Lynd, Robert S. and Helen Merrell Lynd. 1929. *Middletown: A Study in American Culture*. New York: Harcourt Brace Jovanovich.

MacCannell, Dean. 1976. *The Tourist: A New Theory of the Leisure Class*. New York: Schocken Books.

MacEachern, Diane. 1991. "Tips for Planet Earth." *San Francisco Examiner*, January 20.

MacKenzie, James J. and Michael P. Walsh. 1990. "Driving Forces: Motor Vehicle Trends and their Implications for Global Warming, Energy Strategies, and Transportation Planning." Washington, DC: World Resources Institute, December.

Mackey, Heather. 1991. "Home on the Range." *The San Francisco Bay Guardian*, February 6.

MacLennan, Carol A. 1988. "From Accident to Crash: The Auto Industry and the Politics of Injury." *Medical Anthropology Quarterly* 2:233-250.

MacMillan, Neale. 1993. "Index on Cars." *Canadian Forum*, April.

"Make Drivers Pay." 1989. *New Internationalist*. No. 195, May, p. 23.

Mann, Eric. 1990a. "L.A.'s Smogbusters." *The Nation* 251:257, 268.

— . 1990b. "Public Transit, Air Quality and Issues on Equity." P. 15 in *Public Transit: The Vision of 2020.* Proceedings of a Colloquium on Public Transport, November 15. Chicago: Center of Neighborhood Technology.

— . 1991. *L.A.'s Lethal Air.* Los Angeles: Labor/Community Strategy Center.

— . 1993. "Auto Free: Reaction or Revolution?" *Transmission.* Toronto: Transportation Options:18-20.

Margolis, Mac. 1992. "A Third-World City that Works." *World Monitor* 5:42-50.

Marling, Karal Ann. 1989. "America's Love Affair with the Automobile in the Television Age." *Design Quarterly* 146:5-20.

Marsh, Peter and Peter Collett. 1986. *Driving Passion: The Psychology of the Car.* London: Faber and Faber.

Martin, George T., Jr. 1990. *Social Policy in the Welfare State.* Englewood Cliffs, NJ: Prentice Hall.

— . 1991. "Family, Gender, and Social Policy," pp. 323-345 in Laura Kramer, ed., *The Sociology of Gender.* New York: St. Martin's Press.

Marx, Karl. 1967 [1867]. *Capital,* ed. Frederick Engels, trans. Samuel Moore and Edward Aveling. Volume I: A Critical Analysis of Capitalist Production. New York: International Publishers.

Massey, Doreen. 1992. "Politics and Space/Time." *New Left Review* 196:65-84.

Mattoff, Tom, John Holtzclaw, and Paul Downton. 1990. "Future of Urban Transportation," pp. 40-41 in Christopher Canfield, ed., *Report of the First International Ecocity Conference.* Berkeley, CA: Urban Ecology.

Maxcy, George. 1981. *The Multinational Automobile Industry.* New York: St. Martin's Press.

Mayer, Harold M. and Richard C. Wade. 1969. *Chicago: Growth of a Metropolis.* Chicago: University of Chicago Press.

McCrea, S. and R. Minner. 1992. *Why Wait for Detroit?* Ft. Lauderdale: South Florida Electric Auto Association.

McLeod, Ramon G. 1991a. "Transportation Problems Again Top Bay Poll." *San Francisco Chronicle,* January 8.

— . 1991b. "Top Bay Area Headache is Transportation." *San Francisco Chronicle,* January 7.

McLuhan, Marshall. 1964. *Understanding Media: The Extensions of Man.* New York: New American Library/Signet.

Meral, Gerald H. 1990. "Back on Track: Trains in California's Future," pp. 94-100 in Robert L. Deen, ed., *The Alternatives to Gridlock: Perspectives on Meeting California's Transportation Needs.* Sacramento, CA: California Institute of Public Affairs.

Merchant, Carolyn. 1980. *The Death of Nature: Women, Ecology and the Scientific Revolution.* New York: Harper & Row.

Merck Manual. 1982. "Lead Poisoning." Rahway, NJ: Merck, Sharp and Dohme Research Laboratories, p. 1879.

Miller, Krystal. 1991. "On the Road Again and Again and Again: Auto Makers Try to Build Recyclable Car." *The Wall Street Journal,* April 30.

Monheim, Heiner. 1986. "Area-Wide Traffic Restraint: A Concept for Better Urban Transport." *Built Environment* 12:74-82.

Monheim, Rolf. 1986. "Pedestrianization in German Towns: A Process of Continual Development." *Built Environment* 12:30-43.

— . 1991. "Policy Issues in Promoting the Green Modes," pp. 134-158 in Rodney Tolley, ed., *The Greening of Urban Transport: Planning for Walking and Cycling in Western Cities.* London: Belhaven Press.

Montclair State. 1991. "Impact on Air Pollution in New Jersey: Electric Cars." Upper Montclair, NJ: Department of Environmental, Urban and Geographic Studies.

Moorhouse, M.D. 1983. "American Automobiles and Worker's Dreams." *Sociological Review* 31:403-426.

Morris, David. 1982. *Self-Reliant Cities: Energy and the Transformation of Urban America.* San Francisco: Sierra Club Books.

Morse, Mary. 1990. "Autocracy is Being Exported to Third World." *Utne Reader,* July-August, pp. 15-16.

Motor Vehicle Manufacturers Association. 1990. *Facts & Figures '90.* Detroit.

— . 1992. *Facts & Figures '92.* Detroit.

Mumford, Lewis. 1964. *The Highway and the City.* New York: Mentor Books/New American Library.

— . 1971a. "Transportation: 'A Failure of Mind'." *The New York Times,* March 15.

— . 1971b. "Transportation: Human Enrichment." *The New York Times,* March 17.

Muschamp, Herbert. 1993. "Design vs. Environment: Architects Debate." *The New York Times,* June 23.

Nader, Ralph. 1965. *Unsafe at Any Speed.* New York: Grossman.

Nasar, Sylvia. 1992. "Cooling the Globe Would be Nice, but Saving Lives Now May Cost Less." *The New York Times,* May 31.

National Institute on Disability and Rehabilitation Research. 1987. "Low Back Pain." *Rehab Brief* 9:9. Washington, DC.

Newman, Peter G. and Jeffrey K. Kenworthy. 1989. *Cities and Automobile Dependence: A Source Book.* Brookfield, VT: Gower Technical.

New York Times. 1991. "Threats: A Comparison." June 18.

Nielsen, Ole. 1990. "Safe Routes to School in Odense, Denmark," pp. 255-265 in Rodney Tolley, ed., *The Greening of Urban Transport: Planning for Walking and Cycling in Western Cities.* London: Belhaven Press.

Oblong, Dirk. 1989. "Dromomane Rasergesellschaft oder Postmobile?" pp. 158-160 in Paul Beekmans *et. al,* eds., *Welche Freiheit Brauchen Wir? Zum Psychologie der AutoMobilen Gesellschaft.* Die Grunen im Bundestag. Berlin: VAS in der Elefanten Press.

Ogunseitan, O'seun. 1989. "Tanked Up on Sugar." *New Internationalist.* No. 195, May, pp. 20-21.

O'Neill, John. 1985. *Five Bodies: The Human Shape of Modern Society.* Ithaca, NY: Cornell University Press.

O'Rourke, Peter. 1990. "Changing Driver Behavior: The Safety Dimension," pp. 40-44 in Robert L. Deen, ed., *The Alternatives to Gridlock: Perspectives on Meeting California's Transportation Needs.* Sacramento, CA: California Institute of Public Affairs.

Ossing, Franz *et. al.* 1991. "Innere Widerspruche und Aussere Grenzen der Lebensweise-Aspekte der Okologische Entwicklung," pp. 321-385 in Klaus Voy, Werner Polster, und Claus Thomasberger, eds., *Gesellschaftliche Transformationsprozesse und Materielle Lebensweise.* Marburg: Metropolis-Verlag.

Paaswell, Robert E. and Wilfred W. Recker. 1978. *Problems of the Carless.* New York: Praeger.

Padfield, Harland and Roy Williams. 1973. *Stay Where You Were: A Study of Unemployables in Industry.* Philadelphia: J.B. Lippincott Co.

Palley, Marian Lief and Howard A. Palley. 1977. *Urban America and Public Policies.* Lexington, MA: D.C. Heath.

Pantoliano, Livia. 1991. "Thompson Street, My Backyard." *Auto-Free Press* 2:5.

Peitschmann, Manfred. 1991. "Eine Stadt Macht Mobil." *GEO Wissen: Verkehr-Mobilitat* 2:31-41.

Pelline, Jeff. 1993. "Dodge Viper to Have Its Own TV Show." *San Francisco Chronicle,* May 3.

Perlez, Jane. 1993. "Toyota and Honda Create Global Production System." *The New York Times,* March 26.

Plane, David A. 1986. "Urban Transportation: Policy Alternatives," pp. 386-414 in Susan Hanson, ed., *The Geography of Urban Transportation.* New York: The Guilford Press.

Polster, Werner und Klaus Voy. 1990. "Freie Fahrt fur FreieBurger Auto-Mobilisierung der Nation," pp. 114-131 in Arthur Heinrich und Klaus Naumann, eds., *Alles Banane-Ausblicke auf das endgultige Deutschland.* Koln: Papy Rossa Verlag.

— . 1991. "Eigenheim und Automobil-Materielle Fundamente der Lebensweise," pp. 263-320 in Klaus Voy, Werner Polster, und Claus Thomasberger, eds., *Gesellschaftliche Transformationsprozesse und Materielle Lebensweise.* Marburg: Metropolis-Verlag.

Portney, Paul R. *et. al.* 1989. "To Live and Breathe in L.A." *Issues in Science and Technology* 4:68-73.

Preiss, Dietlind. 1989. "Frauen—Kinder—Auto—Traume," pp. 101-103 in *Welche Freiheit Brauchen Wir? Zur Psychologie der Automobilien Gesellschaft.* Die Grunen im Bundestag. Berlin: VAS in der Elefanten Press.

President's Council on Physical Fitness and Sport. 1987. *Transportation Energy Data Book.* Oak Ridge, TN: National Laboratory.

Presse und Informationsamt Bundesregierung. 1990. *Umweltpolitik— Chancen fur unsere Zukunft.* Bonn: Reich Politik Informationen.

Proceedings of a Colloquium on Public Transit. 1990. "Public Transit: The Vision for 2020." November 15. Chicago: Center for Neighborhood Technology.

Protzman, Ferdinand. 1991. "The Greening of the Auto Makers." *The New York Times,* September 16.

— . 1993. "Germany's Push to Expand the Scope of Recycling." *The New York Times,* July 4.

Queenan, Joe. 1991. "Drive, She Said." *The New York Times Book Review.* March 17.

Quick, Alison. 1991. *Unequal Risks: Accidents and Social Policy.* London: Socialist Health Association.

Raban, Jonathan. 1974. *Soft City: The Art of Cosmopolitan Living.* New York: E.P. Dutton & Co., Inc.

Rae, John B. 1965. *The American Automobile: A Brief History.* Chicago: The University of Chicago Press.

Rapoport, Amos. 1987. "Pedestrian Street Use: Culture and Perception," pp. 80-92 in Anne Vernez Moudon, ed., *Public Streets for Public Use*. New York: Van Nostrand Reinhold Company.

Regional Plan Association. 1990. "Manhattan Walkers Need More Space." *The Region's Agenda*. New York: Regional Plan Association.

Register, Richard. 1987. *Ecocity Berkeley: Building Cities for a Healthy Future*. Berkeley, CA: North Atlantic Books.

Reid, Fred A. 1986. "Real Possibilities in the Transportation Myths," pp. 167-188 in Sim Van der Ryn and Peter Calthorpe, eds., *Sustainable Communities: A New Design Synthesis for Cities, Suburbs, and Towns*. San Francisco: Sierra Club Books.

Reinarman, Craig. 1988. "The Social Construction of an Alcohol Problem." *Theory and Society* 17:91-120.

Reinecke, Siegfried. 1989. "Der Maas aller Dinge: Autoculture und Medienkurse," pp. 46-60 in Paul Beekmans *et. al.*, eds., *Welche Freiheit Brauchen Wir? Zum Psychologie der AutoMobilen Gesellschaft*. Die Grunen im Bundestag. Berlin: VAS in der Elefanten Press.

Relph, Edward. 1976. *Place and Placelessness*. London: Pion Ltd.

—— . 1981. *Rational Landscapes and Humanistic Geography*. London: Croom Helm.

—— . 1987. *The Modern Urban Landscape*. Baltimore: The Johns Hopkins University Press.

Renner, Michael. 1988. "Rethinking the Role of the Automobile." Washington, DC: Worldwatch Institute, Paper No. 84.

Richards, Larry G. and Ira D. Jacobson. 1978. "Perceived Safety and Security in Transportation Systems as Determined by the Gender of the Traveler," pp. 441-478 in *Women's Travel Issues: Research Needs and Priorities*. Washington, DC: U.S. Department of Transportation, Research and Special Programs Administration.

Rifkin, Glenn. 1991. "'Smart' Plans for Clogged Roads." *The New York Times*, November 20.

Rimer, Sara. 1992. "L.A.'s Phantom Toll Bus." *International Herald Tribune*, July 8.

Road Information Program. 1990a. "The Effects of Traffic Congestion in California on the Environment and on Human Stress." Washington, DC: May.

—— . 1990b. "California Congestion Now and in the Future: The Costs to Motorists." Washington, DC: January.

Roberts, John. 1990. "The Economic Base for Green Modes," pp. 34-46 in Rodney Walker, ed., *The Greening of Urban Transport: Planning for Walking and Cycling in Western Cities*. London: Belhaven Press.

Robertson, Leon S. 1989. "Motor Vehicle Injuries: The Law and the Profits." *Law, Medicine and Health Care* 17:69-72.

Robinson, A.A. 1988. "The Motor Vehicle, Stress and Circulation System." *Stress Medicine* 4:173-176.

Rose, Dan. 1987. *Black American Street Life: South Philadelphia, 1969-1971*. Philadelphia: University of Pennsylvania Press.

Rosenbaum, Walter A. 1989. *Energy Politics and Public Policy*. Washington, DC: Congressional Quarterly Press.

Rosenbloom, Sandra. 1978. "Women's Travel Issues: The Research and Policy Environment," pp. 3-40 in *Women's Travel Issues: Research Needs and Priorities*. Washington, DC: U.S. Department of Transportation, Research and Special Programs Administration.

— . 1988. "The Mobility Needs of the Elderly," pp. 21-71 in *Transportation in an Aging Society: Improving Mobility and Safety for Older Persons*. Volume 2. Washington, DC: Transportation Research Board, National Research Council, Special Report 218.

Ross, H. Laurence and Graham Hughes. 1986. "Drunk Driving: What Not to Do." *The Nation* 243:663-664.

Rothe, J. Peter. 1987. "Erlebnis of Young Drivers Involved in Injury Producing Crashes," pp. 49-130 in J. Peter Rothe, ed., *Rethinking Young Drivers*. British Columbia: Insurance Corporation of British Columbia.

— . 1991. *The Trucker's World: Risk, Safety and Mobility*. New Brunswick, NJ: Transaction Publishers.

Rothschild, Emma. 1973. *Paradise Lost: The Decline of the Auto-Industrial Age*. New York: Random House.

Sachs, Wolfgang. 1990. *Die Liebe Zum Automobil*. Reinbeck bei Hamburg: Rohwohlt.

Sagoff, Mark. 1990. "The Greening of the Blue Collars." *Reports from the Institute for Philosophy and Public Policy* 10:1-5.

Sale, Kirkpatrick. 1985. *Dwellers in the Land: The Bioregional Vision*. San Francisco: Sierra Club Books.

Sawers, Larry. 1984. "The Political Economy of Urban Transportation: An Interpretative Essay," pp. 223-253 in William K. Tabb and Larry Sawers, eds., *Marxism and the Metropolis*. Second Edition. New York: Oxford University Press.

Schaeffer, K.H. and Elliott Sclar. 1975. *Access for All: Transportation and Urban Growth*. Baltimore: Penguin.

Schaeffer, Robert. 1990. "Car Sick, Automobiles Ad Nauseam." *Greenpeace* 15:13-17.

Schallabock, Karl Otto. 1991. "Grundsatze einer democratischen und umweltfreundlichen Verkehrsphilosophie," pp. 57-74 in Tom Koenigs und Roland Schaeffer, eds., *Fortschritt vom Auto*. Munchen: Raben Verlag.

Scharff, Virginia. 1991. *Taking the Wheel: Women and the Coming of the Motor Age*. New York: The Free Press.

Schiller, Preston. 1993. "Turn Off the Traffic Rap!" *Auto-Free Press* 4:6.

Schmidt, William E. 1991. "Britain Puzzles Over a Peril: Crossing the Street." *The New York Times*, November 25.

Schneider, Joseph W. and Peter Conrad. 1983. *Having Epilepsy: The Experience and Control of Illness*. Philadelphia: Temple University Press.

Schneider, Kenneth R. 1971. *Autokind vs. Mankind*. New York: W.W. Norton.

Schreiner, Tim. 1991. "Traffic Remains Area's No. 1 Worry." *San Francisco Chronicle*, January 28.

Schumpeter, Joseph A. 1947. *Capitalism, Socialism, and Democracy*. New York: Harper & Brothers.

Seamon, David. 1980. "Afterword," pp. 188-195 in Ann Buttimer and David Seamon, eds., *The Human Experience of Space and Place*. New York: St. Martin's Press.

Seifried, Dieter. 1991. *Gute Argumente: Verkehr*. Munich: C.H. Beck.

Sennett, Richard. 1978. *The Fall of Public Man*. New York: Vintage Books.

Shaman, Diana. 1990. "No Need for Car at This Project." *The New York Times*, September 14.

Short, John R. 1989. *The Humane City*. New York: Basil Blackwell.

Simons, Marlise. 1993. "Amsterdam Plans Wide Limit on Cars." *The New York Times*, January 28.

Sims, Calvin. 1993. "Five Big Arms Makers Vie to Build Rail Cars." *The New York Times*, May 8.

Slack, Gordy. 1991. "Sing the Auto Electric." *Pacific Discovery*, Summer, pp. 3-4.

Smith, Barbara Ellen. 1981. "Black Lung: The Social Production of Disease." *International Journal of Health Services* 11:343-359.

Smith, Michael Peter. 1988. *City, State, and Market: The Political Economy of Urban Society*. New York: Basil Blackwell.

Smith, Michael Peter, Gregory A. Guagnano, and Cath Posehn. 1989. "The Political Economy of Growth in Sacramento: Whose City?," pp. 260-288 in Gregory D. Squires, ed., *Unequal Partnerships: The Political Economy of Urban Redevelopment in Postwar America*. New Brunswick, NJ: Rutgers University Press.

Smithson, Alison. 1983. *AS in DS: An Eye on the Road*. Delft: Delft University Press.

Smothers, Ronald. 1991. "Employers Becoming Targets of Suits in the Fight to Halt Drunken Driving." *The New York Times*, December 24.

Snell, Bradford. 1983 [1974]. "American Ground Transport," pp. 316-338 in J.H. Skolnick and E. Currie, eds., *Crisis in American Institutions*. Boston: Little, Brown.

Soja, Edward W. 1989. *Postmodern Geographies: The Reassertion of Space in Critical Social Theory*. London: Verso.

Sonn, Jochen. 1987. "Automobilismus oder die Freiheit der Entfernung," pp. 120-130 in Jobst Kraus, Horst Sackstetter, und Willi Wentsch, eds., *Auto, Auto Uber Alles?* Freiburg: Dreisam Verlag.

Spirn, Anne Whiston. 1984. *The Granite Garden: Urban Nature and Human Design*. New York: Basic Books.

Staeck, Klaus. 1990. *ADAC ADE*. Gottingen: Steidl Verlag.

Stang, Hakon. 1977. *Materialized Ideology: On Liberal and Marxist Power Analysis, Westerness and the Car*. Oslo: University of Oslo, Trends in Western Civilization Program No. 12.

St. Clair, David. 1986. *The Motorization of American Cities*. New York: Praeger.

Stevens, Amy. 1991. "Bosses Fret They May Be Liable for Tired Workers on Road Home." *The Wall Street Journal*, April 16.

Stevenson, Richard W. 1990. "California to Get Tougher Air Rules." *The New York Times*, September 27.

Stoddart, R. 1987. "Erfahrung of Young Drivers," pp. 131-198 in J. Peter Rothe, ed., *Rethinking Young Drivers*. British Columbia: Insurance Corporation of British Columbia.

Stokols, Daniel and Raymond Novaco. 1981. "Transportation and Well-Being," pp. 85-125 in Irwin Altman, Joachim Wohlwill, and Peter Everett, eds., *Transportation and Behavior*. New York: Plenum Press.

Stutz, Frederick P. 1986. "Environmental Impacts," pp. 328-356 in Susan Hanson, ed., *The Geography of Urban Transportation*. New York: The Guilford Press.

Sullivan, James B. and Paula Montgomery. 1972. "Surveying Highway Impact." *Environment* 14:12-20.

Suro, Roberto. 1991. "Where America is Growing: The Suburban Cities." *The New York Times*, February 23.

Susman, Warren I. 1984. *Culture as History: The Transformation of American Society in the Twentieth Century*. New York: Pantheon.

Syme, Leonard S. and Jack M. Guralnik. 1987. "Epidemiology and Health Policy: Coronary Heart Disease," pp. 85-116 in S. Levine and A. Lilienfeld, eds., *Epidemiology and Health Policy.* London: Tavistock.

Tagliabue, John. 1991. "Klunkers Go Kaput." *San Francisco Examiner,* January 20.

Taylor, Frederick Winslow. 1911. *The Principles of Scientific Management.* New York: Harper.

Templin, Neal. 1991. "Fewer Sexy 'Accessories' at Car Shows." *San Francisco Examiner,* January 20.

This Week in Germany. 1991. "German Car Industry to Invest DM 10 Billion in East." May 24, p. 5. New York: German Information Center.

Thomas, June Manning. 1989. "Detroit: The Centrifugal City," pp. 142-160 in Gregory D. Squires, ed., *Unequal Partnerships: The Political Economy of Urban Redevelopment in Postwar America.* New Brunswick, NJ: Rutgers University Press.

Thompson, E.P. 1988. "Last Dispatches from the Border Country." *The Nation,* March 5, pp. 310-312.

Thompson, Tim. 1992. "Where Have All the Clouds Gone?" *Earth Island News* 7:40-42.

Thomson, J. Michael. 1978. "Methods of Traffic Limitation in Urban Areas," pp. 131-228 in Ralph Gakenheimer, ed., *The Automobile and the Environment: An International Perspective.* Prepared by the Organisation for Economic Co-operation and Development. Cambridge, MA: The MIT Press.

Tira, Peter. 1990. "Elec-trekking." *The San Francisco Bay Guardian,* October 10, p. 42.

Todd, Halinah. 1989. "The Proton Saga Saga." *New Internationalist.* No. 195, May, pp. 14-15.

Turner, Frederick Jackson. 1962 [1920]. *The Frontier in American History.* New York: Holt, Rinehart and Winston.

Ullrich, Otto. 1987. "Die Kontraproductivitat des Automobils," pp. 152-155 in Jobst Kraus, Horst Sackstetter, und Willi Wentsch, eds., *Auto, Auto Uber Alles?* Freiburg: Dreisam Verlag.

— . 1990. "The Pedestrian Town as an Environmentally Tolerable Alternative to Motorized Travel," pp. 97-109 in Rodney Tolley, ed., *The Greening of Urban Transport: Planning for Walking and Cycling in Western Cities.* London: Belhaven Press.

United Nations. 1989. *Urban Transportation Development with Particular Reference to Developing Countries.* New York: Department of International Economic and Social Affairs.

University of California Wellness Letter. 1988. "When Rush Hour Never Ends." 4:1-2. Berkeley.

Untermann, Richard K. 1987. "Can We Pedestrianize the Suburbs?," pp. 123-132 in Anne Vernez Moudon, ed., *Public Streets for Public Use.* New York: Van Nostrand Reinhold Company.

— . 1990. "Why You Can't Walk There: Strategies for Improving the Pedestrian Environment in the United States," pp. 173-185 in Rodney Tolley, ed., *The Greening of Urban Transport: Planning for Walking and Cycling in Western Cities.* London: Belhaven Press.

Urata, Shujiro. 1988. "The Development of the Motor Vehicle Industry in Post-Second-World-War Japan." *Industry and Development*, No. 24, pp. 1-33. Vienna: United Nations Industrial Development Organization.

U.S. Bureau of the Census. 1984. "Journey to Work: Characteristics of Workers in Metropolitan Areas." Washington, DC: July.

— . 1989. "American Housing Survey for the United States in 1987." Current Housing Reports H-150-87. Washington, DC: December.

— . 1990. "The Journey-to-Work Supplement to the National American Housing Survey." Washington, DC.

— . 1992. *Statistical Abstract of the United States.* Washington, DC.

U.S. Energy Information Administration. 1989. *Energy Facts.* Washington, DC: Department of Energy.

U.S. General Accounting Office. 1989. *Traffic Congestion: Trends, Measures and Effects.* Washington, DC.

U.S. Office of Technology Assessment. 1991. *Delivering the Goods: Public Works Technologies, Management, and Financing.* Washington, DC.

Venturi, Robert, D.S. Brown, and S. Izenour. 1972. *Learning from Las Vegas.* Cambridge, MA: The MIT Press.

Vidal, John. 1992. "Hydrogen Car that Goes Like a Bomb." *The San Francisco Bay Guardian,* July 3.

Viviano, Frank. 1991a. "Commuters Want More Mass Transit." *San Francisco Chronicle,* January 31.

— . 1991b. "Push for Homes Near Transportation." *San Francisco Chronicle,* March 19.

— . 1993. "High Gas Tax a Way of Life in Europe." *San Francisco Chronicle,* January 22.

Wachtel, Paul. 1989. *The Poverty of Affluence.* Philadelphia: New Society Publishers.

Wajcman, Judy. 1991. *Feminism Confronts Technology.* University Park: The Pennsylvania State University Press.

Wald, Matthew L. 1990a. "How Dreams of Clean Air Get Stuck in Traffic." *The New York Times,* March 11.

— . 1990b. "Where All that Gas Goes: Drivers Thirst for Power." *The New York Times,* November 21.

Wallace, Samuel E. 1980. *The Urban Environment.* Homewood, IL: The Dorsey Press.

Wallis, Allan D. 1991. *Wheel Estate: The Rise and Decline of Mobile Homes.* Oxford: Oxford University Press.

Weisman, Alan. 1989. "L.A. Fights for Breath." *The New York Times Magazine,* July 30.

Wetzel, Tom. 1990. "The Case Against the Auto." *Ideas and Action,* No. 14, Fall, p. 20.

Whitelegg, John. 1990. "The Principle of Environmental Traffic Management," pp. 75-87 in Rodney Tolley, ed., *The Greening of Urban Transport: Planning for Walking and Cycling in Western Cities.* London: Belhaven Press.

Whyte, William H. 1988. *City: Rediscovering the Center.* New York: Doubleday.

Wilson, Peter J. 1988. *The Domestication of the Human Species.* New Haven: Yale University Press.

Wolf, Winfried. 1990. *Neues Denken oder Neues Tanken? DDR Verkehr 2000.* Frankfurt am Main: ISP Verlag.

Wolff, Simon P. 1992a. "Correlation between car ownership and Leukaemia: Is non-occupational exposure to benzene from petrol and motor vehicle exhaust a causative factor in Leukaemia and lymphoma?" *Experientia* 48:301-304. Basel: Birkhauser Verlag.

——. 1992b. "Air Pollution and Cancer Risk?" Correspondence in *Nature* 356:471.

Wolff, Simon P. and C.J. Gillham. 1991. "Public Health versus Public Policy? An Appraisal of British Urban Transport Policy." *Public Health* 105:217-228.

Womack, James P., Daniel T. Jones, and Daniel Roos. 1990. *The Machine that Changed the World.* New York: Macmillan Publishing Co.

Women and Transport Forum. 1988. "Women on the Move: How Public is Public Transport?," pp. 116-134 in Cheris Kramarae, ed., *Technology and Women's Voices: Keeping in Touch.* New York: Routledge and Kegan Paul.

Wood, Dennis. 1993. *The Power of Maps.* New York: The Guilford Press.

World Bank. 1986. *Urban Transport: A World Bank Policy Study.* Washington, DC.

Woutat, Donald. 1991. "GM Endorses Cleaner-Burning Reformulated Gas for Its Models." *The Los Angeles Times*, March 19.

Wright, Charles L. 1992. *Fast Wheels, Slow Traffic: Urban Transport Choices.* Philadelphia: Temple University Press.

Yago, Glenn. 1980. "Corporate Power and Urban Transportation: A Comparison of Public Transit's Decline in the United States and Germany," pp. 296-323 in Maurice Zeitlin, ed., *Classes, Class Conflict and the State: Empirical Studies in Class Analysis.* Cambridge, MA: Winthrop.

——. 1983. "The Sociology of Transport." *Annual Review of Sociology* 9:171-190.

——. 1984. *The Decline of Transit: Urban Transportation in German and U.S. Cities, 1900-1970.* Cambridge: Cambridge University Press.

——. 1985. "U.S. Lacks Transportation Policy." *In These Times* 9:7.

Yih, Katherine. 1990. "The Red and the Green: Left Perspectives on Ecology." *Monthly Review* 42:16-28.

Young, Bob. 1985. "Is Nature a Labour Process?," pp. 206-232 in Les Levidow and Bob Young, eds., *Science, Technology and the Labour Process: Marxist Studies.* Volume 2. Atlantic Highlands, NJ: Humanities Press.

Zuckermann, Wolfgang. 1991. *The End of the Road.* Post Mills, VT: Chelsea Green Publishing Co.

Name Index

Ludvigsen, Karl, 75
Lynch, Kevin, 107, 109, 169
Lynd, Helen Merrell, 122, 126
Lynd, Robert S., 122, 126
MacCannell, Dean, 109
MacEachern, Diane, 24
MacKenzie, James J., 170
Mackey, Heather, 94
MacLennan, Carol A., 43, 142
MacMillan, Neale, 12
Magilavy, Beryl, 185
Mann, Eric, 41, 58, 142, 184
Marcuse, Herbert, 143
Margolis, Mac, 76
Marling, Karal Ann, 62, 75
Marsh, Peter, 94
Martin, Claudia, 42
Martin, George T., Jr., 126, 169
Marx, Karl, 5, 12, 172
Massey, Doreen, 124
Mattoff, John, 168
Maxcy, George, 75
Mayer, Harold M., 3, 12
McCrea, S., 167
McGuire, Meredith B., 59
McLeod, Ramon G., 142, 167
McLuhan, Marshall, 109
McQueen, David V., 42
Meral, Gerald, 141, 142
Merchant, Carolyn, 184
Minner, R., 167
Monheim, Heiner, 170
Monheim, Rolf, 58, 95
Montgomery, Paula, 24
Moore, Samuel, 12
Moorhouse, M.D., 90, 95
Morris, David, 126
Morse, Mary, 76
Moses, Robert, 117, 151
Moudon, Anne Vernez, 109, 126, 168
Mumford, Lewis, 137, 138, 143, 156, 167, 169, 180, 184
Munasinghe, Mohan, 76
Muschamp, Herbert, 185
Myer, John R., 57, 109
Nader, Ralph, 137, 138, 142
Nasar, Sylvia, 76
Naumann, Klaus, 76
Newman, Peter G., 120, 126, 150, 152, 154, 158, 168, 169
Newport, Frank, 58
Nicholson-Smith, Donald, 124

Nielsen, Ole, 59
Novaco, Raymond, 42
Oblong, Dirk, 184
Olmstead, Frederick Law, 157
Orban, William, 42
O'Rourke, Peter, 95
Ossing, Franz, 24, 94
Paaswell, Robert E., 57, 168
Padfield, Harland, 58
Palley, Howard A., 168
Palley, Marian Lief, 168
Pantoliano, Livia, 126
Pastalan, Leon A., 59
Peitschmann, Manfred, 12
Pelline, Jeff, 95, 170
Perlez, Jane, 75
Picabia, Francis, 92
Plater-Zyberk, Elizabeth, 163
Polster, Werner, 24, 56, 59, 76, 94
Posehn, Kath, 170
Preis, Ute, 59
Protzman, Ferdinand, 12, 24
Queenan, Joe, 58
Quick, Alison, 58
Raban, Jonathan, 86, 95, 105, 109
Rabinovitch, Sacha, 124
Rae, John B., 75
Rapoport, Amos, 109
Reagan, Ronald, 133, 139
Recker, Wilfred W., 57, 168
Register, Richard, 181, 182, 185
Reid, Fred A., 168, 170
Reinarman, Craig, 109
Reinecke, Seigfried, 95
Relph, Edward, 45, 57, 108, 109
Renner, Michael, 24, 41, 57, 76, 169
Richards, Larry G., 58
Rimer, Sara, 96
Robinson, A.A., 42
Roos, Daniel, 75
Rose, Dan, 109
Rosenbaum, Walter A., 141
Rosenbloom, Sandra, 58
Ross, H. Laurence, 43
Rothe, J. Peter, 43, 58, 96, 100, 109
Rothschild, Emma, 142
Sachs, Wolfgang, 18, 24, 58, 95, 112, 113, 125, 184
Sackstetter, Horst, 41, 57, 76, 96
Sagoff, Mark, 165
Sale, Kirkpatrick, 109
Sawers, Larry, 125, 141, 142

Subject Index

Access, 74; and mobility, 85; by proximity, 144, 149-153, 166
Accidents, 4, 36-41, 54, 100, 101, 131, 137, 139; costs of, 10, 131; reduction of, 161, 162; and social class, 49-50; and speed, 39; and young people, 93
Advertising, 3, 38, 62, 83-84, 88, 90-93, 135
Africa, 16, 65
African Americans, 46-49, 57, 82, 104. See also Race.
Aged, 3, 32, 99, 122; empowerment of, 174-175; and mass transit use, 46; mobility of, 54-55, 103; as pedestrians, 36; segregation of, 57; as transport-disadvantaged, 55, 56, 129, 175
Air transport, 37, 106, 115, 133, 180
Alienation, 6, 107, 116
Amsterdam, 161-162
Architecture, 105, 182
Asia, 16, 65, 150
Australia, 5, 150
Autobahns, 37, 73, 83, 89, 132-133
Auto fleets, 15, 19, 20, 28, 61, 65, 122-123, 165
Auto-free zones, 161, 162
Auto-industrial complex, 132, 134-137, 145-146, 173
Auto parking, 111, 113; cost of, 130; reduction of, 160, 162; subsidy for, 166; as transport work, 22, 123; and use of space, 20, 112
Auto safety, 37-39, 137, 139, 144-146
Auto saturation, 7, 8, 16
Berlin, 71, 73, 89
Bicycles, 69, 119, 152; as alternative to auto, 153, 159; attitudes toward, 155; and calorie use, 17; commuting by, 36, 155; paths for, 35, 52-54, 70, 144, 146, 150, 157, 162; safety of, 102, 146; as soft mobility, 178
BMW, 18-19
Boston, 114, 137, 158
Brazil, 64, 70, 71

Britain, 3, 64, 103, 155; accidents in, 30, 36, 40, 49-50; children's mobility in, 54; gasoline taxes in, 165; rail travel in, 63; transport-disadvantaged population in, 50
Built environment, 57, 107, 111-113, 130, 133, 153; and hyperspace, 115-116; and quality of life, 158, 181, 182
Buses, 2, 4-5, 17, 46, 68-69, 81-82, 114, 135, 144, 152-154
California, 5, 70, 106, 121, 133, 147; commuting in, 103; freeways in, 7; mass transit in, 47; pollution in, 29; reconfiguration of transport in, 144, 159; regulation of auto in, 145, 146; traffic congestion in, 22, 84
Canada, 40, 74, 83, 91; autos in, 15, 16, 61, 63, 64; cities in, 150; planners in, 4; transport policy in, 133
Capitalism, 5, 135, 174; and consumption, 1, 181; globalization of, 63, 172; and growth, 173; and nature, 178; and production, 6, 10; and space-time compression, 118, 129; and technology, 179; transformation of, 114; and uneven development, 116, 117
Car. See Auto.

"Carcooning," 103
Car pools, 9, 99, 119, 154, 166
Chicago, 3, 23, 151, 154, 158, 182
Childcare, 52, 159, 171
Children, health of, 30-32; and mass transit, 52; mobility of, 54, 103; as pedestrians, 36, 49-50, 52-53; play space of, 52, 85, 123, 161; safety of, 54, 89; and street life, 157; and suburbs, 122; as transport-disadvantaged, 54-55, 129, 175
China, 20, 71, 155
Chrysler Motor Company, 136

209

Also published by

BLACK ROSE BOOKS

POLITICAL ECOLOGY
Beyond Environmentalism
Dimitrios I. Roussopoulos

Examining the perspective offered by various components of political ecology, this book presents an overview of its origins as well as its social and cultural causes. It summarizes the differences, and similarities, between political ecology and social ecology, while revealing, quite candidly, that the resolution of the present planetary crisis hinges on the outcome and consequences of this new politics.

180 pages, index
Paperback ISBN: 1-895431-80-8 $15.95
Hardcover ISBN: 1-895431-81-6 $34.95

GREEN POLITICS
Agenda For a Free Society
Dimitrios Roussopoulos

An international survey of various Green political parties is presented, featuring their programmes and progress. The result is a stimulating book that challenges accepted ideas about how the world should be organized, and suggests the possibility of a safe and more satisfying future for all of us.

200 pages, index
Paperback ISBN: 0-921689-74-8 $19.95
Hardcover ISBN: 0-921689-75-6 $38.95

THE NATURE OF CO-OPERATION
John G. Craig

The practice of co-operation is full of dilemmas. This book explores these dilemmas between the logic of co-operation and co-operatives, and furnishes illustrations of organizations and movements that have found ways to balance the conflicting tensions. It provides an overview of how co-operative organizations function, how they have evolved, and why they have been very successful in some places and dismal failures in others.

220 pages, index
Paperback ISBN: 1-895431-68-9 $19.95
Hardcover ISBN: 1-895431-69-7 $38.95

ELECTRIC RIVERS
The Story of the James Bay Project
Sean McCutcheon

...a book about how and why the James Bay project is being built, how it works, the consequences its building will have for people and for the environment, and the struggle to stop it...it cuts through the rhetoric so frequently found in the debate.
Canadian Book Review Annual

Electric Rivers is a welcome contribution to the debate...a good fortune for readers who would like to better understand a story that is destined to dominate the environmental and political agenda in Quebec and Canada for many years to come.
Globe and Mail

194 pages, maps
Paperback ISBN: 1-895431-18-2 $18.95
Hardcover ISBN: 1-895431-19-0 $37.95

EUROPE'S GREEN ALTERNATIVE
An Ecology Manifesto
Penny Kemp, editor
To meet the challenges of rigorous definition of the nature of society's crisis and the ways that we can begin to emerge from this dangerous period in history, an international group of well-known authors gathered together to produce this exceptional guide through the labyrinth of ideas and social/political action.

200 pages, appendices
Paperback: 1-895431-30-1 $16.95
Hardcover: 1-895431-31-X $35.95

GREEN CITIES
Ecologically Sound Approaches to Urban Space
David Gordon, editor
2nd printing
This anthology presents visions from around the world of an ecological urban model.
...it carves a scholarly depth into the radical changes needed to diffuse our urban crisis.
Montreal Mirror

...the ideas it contains are so sane and sensible that you'll end up wondering why civic politicians and officials have been dragging their heels on green issues for so many years.
Books in Canada
240 pages
Paperback ISBN: 0-921689-54-3 $19.95
Hardcover ISBN: 0-921689-55-1 $39.95

THE NUCLEAR POWER GAME
Ronald Babin
Foreword by Gordon Edwards
A careful and lucid analysis of nuclear power and why it deserves the protest it gets.
Kingston Whig-Standard

A remarkable demonstration of the emergence of technocratic power.
Le Devoir, Montréal
236 pages, bibliography
Paperback ISBN: 0-920057-31-4 $14.95
Hardcover ISBN: 0-920057-30-6 $34.95

ECOLOGY AS POLITICS
André Gorz
translated by Patsy Vigderman and Jonathan Cloud
A fascinating study of the relationship between the ecology movement and political structures.

...rich in ways and means to reinvent the future. A very good book.
City Magazine
215 pages
Paperback ISBN: 0-919618-71-5 $18.95
Hardcover ISBN: 0-919618-72-3 $37.95

Books by
MURRAY BOOKCHIN

URBANIZATION WITHOUT CITIES
The Rise and Decline of Citizenship
revised edition
Bookchin argues for an ecological ethics and citizenry that will restore the balance between city and country.

To reverse the city's dehumanization, social thinker Bookchin here advocates an agenda for participatory democracy...It is significant...
Publisher's Weekly, New York
340 pages, index
Paperback ISBN: 1-895431-00-X $19.95
Hardcover ISBN: 1-895431-01-8 $38.95

THE LIMITS OF THE CITY
2nd revised edition
"City air makes people free." With this mediaeval adage, Bookchin begins a remarkable book on the evolution and dialectics of urbanism. Convincingly, he argues that there was once a human and progressive tradition to urban life which has now reached its "ultimate negation in the modern metropolis."

Valuable for its historical perspective and its discussion of the effects on the individual of the modern city.
The Humanist in Canada
194 pages, index
Paperback ISBN: 0-920057-64-0 $17.95
Hardcover ISBN: 0-920057-34-9 $36.95

THE PHILOSOPHY OF SOCIAL ECOLOGY
Essays On Dialectical Naturalism

Since well before Rachel Carson's early 1960's warning about pesticides, Bookchin's thoughtful critiques of environmental politics have contributed a unique dimension to discussions of society and ecology. In this collection of four essays, he concentrates on the extraordinarily rich and diverse philosophical and theoretical underpinnings of his views on "social ecology."
Canadian Book Review Annual
170 pages
Paperback ISBN: 0-921689-68-3 $18.95
Hardcover ISBN: 0-921689-69-1 $37.95

THE ECOLOGY OF FREEDOM
The Emergence and Dissolution of Hierarchy
revised edition
...a confirmation of his [Bookchin's] status as a penetrating critic not only of the ways in which humankind is destroying itself, but of the ethical imperative to live a better life.
Stanley Aronowitz, The Village Voice

Elegantly written, and recommended for a wide audience.
Library Journal
395 pages, index
Paperback ISBN: 0-921689-72-1 $19.95
Hardcover ISBN: 0-921689-73-X $38.95

REMAKING SOCIETY

Remaking Society provides a clear synthesis of Bookchon's ideas for his faithful readers, and serves as an excellent introduction to anyone new to his work.

...an intellectual tour de force...the first synthesis of the spirit, logics, and goals of the European "Green Movement" available in English.
Choice
208 pages
Paperback ISBN: 0-921689-02-0 $18.95
Hardcover ISBN: 0-921689-03-9 $37.95

DEFENDING THE EARTH
Debate between Murray Bookchin & Dave Foreman
Introduction by David Levine
This book is the outcome of the first public meeting between the 'social ecologists' and the 'deep ecologists'.

...contains eloquent passages by Bookchin, who has a clear and humane sense of human's obligation to fellow human and the natural world...worth reading.
Vermont Times
120 pages, index
Paperback ISBN: 0-921689-88-8 $15.95
Hardcover ISBN: 0-921689-89-6 $34.95

THE MODERN CRISIS
2nd revised edition
The social ecologist and philosopher Murray Bookchin exposes the underpinnings of the arket economy and contrasts its destructive reality with the potential for social and ecological sanity offered by a moral economy.

Bookchin is invigorated by the inadequacies of the old isms...He sketches here a new ism called..."ecological ethics"...which is not based on self-interest.
Kingston Whig-Standard
194 pages
Paperback ISBN: 0-920057-62-4 $18.95
Hardcover ISBN: 0-920057-61-6 $37.95

TOWARD AN ECOLOGICAL SOCIETY
3rd printing
Bookchin is capable of penetrating, finely indignant historical analysis. Here is another stimulating, wide-ranging collection.
In These Times
315 pages
Paperback ISBN: 0-919618-98-7 $18.95
Hardcover ISBN: 0-919618-99-5 $37.95

POST-SCARCITY ANARCHISM
with a new Introduction, 8th printing
This book has energy and command. Its ecological, organizational, and political concerns are ever with us...Bookchin's caustic comments are ever important, rarely finding an equal in the field of contemporary socio-political analysis.
Canadian Book Review Annual
265 pages
Paperback ISBN: 0-920057-39-X $18.95
Hardcover ISBN: 0-920057-41-1 $37.95